A DREADED CATCH

The conger eel is a dangerous fish on board a small boat. If it once gets a hold of a man's leg, it is impossible to make it disengage its teeth. Even when its head is cut off, its mouth must be prised open.

CURIOUS METHODS OF FISHING IN THE WORLD

CURIOUS METHODS OF FISHING IN THE WORLD

By

SIDNEY WRIGHT

WITH TWENTY-FOUR ILLUSTRATIONS

GYAN

Published by

Gyan Publishing House
5, Ansari Road
Daryaganj, New Delhi-110002
Phone: 011-47034999, 9811692060
E-mail: books@gyanbooks.com

Distribution Network
gyanbooks.com
India, USA, Canada, UK, Australia, France

ISBN : 978-81-212-6540-9 (PB)
First Published, 1908

2nd Impression 2022

Printed at: Gyan Press, Delhi.

CURIOUS METHODS OF FISHING IN THE WORLD
Author: SIDNEY WRIGHT

THE ROMANCE OF THE WORLD'S FISHERIES

INTERESTING DESCRIPTIONS OF THE MANY & CURIOUS METHODS OF FISHING IN ALL PARTS OF THE WORLD

BY

SIDNEY WRIGHT

WITH TWENTY-FOUR ILLUSTRATIONS

1908

PREFACE

IN an account of the world's fisheries it is impossible to use the word "fish" only in its strictly scientific meaning; for what are everywhere known as "fisheries" include the taking of many creatures which are not really fish. Whaling, sealing, turtle-catching, and pearl-diving must necessarily have a place in the following pages.

Little attempt has been made to treat the subject from the commercial or industrial point of view. The author has rather endeavoured to give an animated picture of the fisherman's life, of his methods, his hardships and adventures, his disappointments, and his hardly won successes. The best authorities have been consulted, but many of the details are drawn from the author's own experience.

CONTENTS

CONTENTS

CONTENTS

CHAPTER IX

THE OYSTER

CHAPTER X

UNITED STATES FISH AND FISHERMEN

CHAPTER XI

THE BRITISH HERRING-FISHERY

CHAPTER XII

FISHING IN THE MEDITERRANEAN

CHAPTER XIII

THE PILCHARD—THE STURGEON

CONTENTS

CONTENTS

CONTENTS

CHAPTER XXII

TURTLES AND TURTLE-CATCHING

CHAPTER XXIII

AFTER THE SEAL AND THE WALRUS

LIST OF ILLUSTRATIONS

LIST OF ILLUSTRATIONS

THE ROMANCE OF THE WORLD'S FISHERIES

CHAPTER I

INTRODUCTORY

Fishing an occupation to which uncivilised man would naturally turn —Seasons and preferences—Other products of the sea besides fish —A few words on fishing from an historical point of view.

THE catching of fish is an occupation which must have arisen at a very early stage in the history of the human race; for man's staple food is necessarily decided by his surroundings, and it was as natural for a maritime people to look to the sea as its provider, as it was for forest inhabitants to sustain life on the fruit of trees or the flesh of birds and beasts. Early man could not, or would not, cultivate the soil; therefore he must either content himself with food that cost him little or no trouble to obtain—vegetable products that did not call for cultivation, eggs, or shell-fish that lay on the shore—or else he must combine business with pleasure by obeying his instinct to hunt; by living on fish, flesh, or fowl, the procuring of which had a seasoning of chance, or excitement, or danger in it. Often the land monster or the sea monster seemed to threaten him with death whether he hunted it or no; therefore he felt driven to slay it in self-defence; and, when slain, what was more natural than that its flesh should be eaten and its non-edible parts utilised as clothing, ornament, tool, or weapon?

When our fathers had learned the art of making and managing rafts or boats, they found that many fish which could not be obtained in shallow water might easily be caught at some distance from the shore. The appliances r catching them—baited hooks, nets, and baskets made skin or fibre or twigs—would suggest themselves, necessity being the mother of invention.

Then, as agriculture and the mechanical arts developed, it became the business of those who still refused to follow a land trade, to sell or barter the fish which they did not need to people who had not the time or the inclination to procure such food for themselves. And it was in this way that an industry began which, to-day in many countries, ranks in importance with agriculture, and often with manufactures.

By observation the fisherman or the fish-eater gradually learned that at one time of the year certain fish were more palatable or more plentiful than at another; that during some months shell-fish, for example, were nutritious, during others poisonous; thus the "season" for any special fish became recognised and defined. As the consumer's palate grew more discriminating, one fish was found to be richer in taste than another; and so creatures like the turbot, the sole, and the oyster were ruthlessly and greedily pursued, to the partial neglect of, say, the humbler herring and skate, which continued to increase and multiply, commanding but a poor market-price in comparison with their scarcer and more succulent brethren. Thus to-day the fishmonger who can afford to sell a herring for a halfpenny must charge a shilling for a sole.

From the further cultivation of arts and crafts, the man of the coast realised at length that fish had other profitable uses than those of the table; from increased knowledge of navigation, from experiments in diving, and from watching the beach at low tide, he learned that the sea had other saleable commodities to offer besides fish in the strict sense. For ages he had adorned himself and his family with sealskin, sharks' teeth, shells, coral; had converted fish-bones into knives and war-hatchets and needles and hooks; had collected cowries for his currency, and amber to conjure with; and perhaps it was not such a very wide step thence to the preserving and utilising of fish skins and oil, or to a systematic search for—and regular trade in—pearls, whalebone, sponge, or the purple dye secreted within the shell of the Tyrian murex.

From the time that the fisheries became once firmly established as a recognised industry, there is not a great deal to be said as to the history of their development. Probably the reason for this is that, unlike most trades, fishing does not easily lend itself to improvements and new fashions. The fisherman thinks that what was good enough for his father is good enough for him. Companies may have taken the trade out of the hands of individuals; steam-vessels may have ousted some of the old smacks; but methods and implements generally have undergone but little alteration even in a couple of thousand years; a net or a dredge or a pot or an enclosure is now what it was then. The few important modifications or improvements in gear will be dealt with presently.

Nor has political history much to tell us about the fisheries that would be of general interest. Henry I of England is supposed to have regarded the sturgeon as his exclusive property; and we know that the salmon forms the subject of a clause in Magna Charta. It is generally believed that Biscayan whalers as far back as the fourteenth century fished off the coast of what is now called Newfoundland, and even off Greenland and Spitzbergen. The Portuguese instituted the Grand Banks cod-fishery in the year 1500. In the time of Charles II, the British fisheries had so declined that the King, in 1662, offered £200 to every man who would fit out a "brisse," or Dutch herring-smack, within six months from the date of his proclamation.

Fishing-grounds have, of course, formed the subject of disputes between countries. In 1839 a treaty was signed between England and France to settle the exact boundaries of the oyster, and other, grounds, to which both nations laid claim; and in 1854 a similar agreement was drawn up between our Government and that of the United States, relating to the Canadian fisheries.

INTRODUCTORY

It is only within comparatively recent years that any serious step has been taken by Government to fix a close season for fish. At the present time our fisheries are under the control of local committees appointed by the Board of Trade.

CHAPTER II

THE FISHERMAN'S TOOLS

Various means of obtaining fish—The push-net—Rod and line—Bait—Means of getting nearer to the fish—The raft—The open boat—The smack—Tackle used in boat-fishing—Long lines and hand lines—Trawls—drift-nets, seines, moored nets, and dredges—Pots—Another important item: experience—The fascination of the fisherman's calling.

BEFORE dealing with special fisheries it may be well to give a brief description in outline of the "plant," so to speak, which constitutes the fisherman's capital; the means most generally in use for transporting the fish from their home in the sea or river to the storehouse or the market. Less commonly used appliances will receive separate mention later.

Obviously the simplest method of procuring fish is by picking them off the beach at low water. It is in this way that millions of cockles, mussels, and periwinkles are obtained every year; in many parts of the world oysters are obtained in the same way. Such creatures as these offer no resistance; make no attempt to escape their captors; but as soon as we come to the more lively fish that may be caught at low tide or in very shallow water — shrimps, for instance — some mechanical contrivance for securing them at once becomes necessary.

In the case of shrimps, this takes the form of the push-net, with the sight of which we are all familiar—a simple net-bag, kept open by a wooden framework to which a long pole is fastened.

The ordinary vertebrate fish, whether of the sea or the river, may also be caught from the land; but, as everybody knows, he is too timid or too wary to allow himself to be beguiled by other than artificial means more or less elaborate. From the banks of rivers and lakes, or from jetties and pier-heads, opportunities for large catches are rare; wherefore it is better to try patiently to secure the fish singly. This is done by means of a hook, usually barbed, fastened to a line long enough to reach that part of the water—surface, middle, or bottom—where the fish angled for is likely to be found. In fishing at any appreciable distance from the bank, the line is suspended over the water from the tip of a long rod which scarcely calls for minute description. To entice the fish, some bait, natural or artificial, living or dead, which will appeal to his curiosity or greed, is fixed to the hook, generally in such a manner as partially to conceal it. This bait varies according to the fish sought and the depth at which he swims: broadly speaking, for angling at or near the surface, imitation flies are used; for mid-water angling, real or sham fish; for fishing near the bottom, dough, worms, or gentles (the larvæ obtained from fly-blown meat).

To these methods "land" fishing may be said to be mainly confined; and we pass on to the consideration of the more important branch, which presses into its service not only nets and lines, but also a means of getting at somewhat closer quarters with those fish which cannot be caught very near to the shore—boats and ships.

The raft, the rudest type of water conveyance, is now, except by some of the Japanese and Chinese fishermen, used only by savages and boys. It has no particular shape or construction, and often no means of steering. It is said that the Phœnicians, who colonised Corsica and other islands near Italy, had no better craft in which to reach their destination; if so, the journey must have been a work of time and patience.

The open boat, the shape of which varies only triflingly in different parts of the world, comes next. Being of such light build and not affording much storage accommodation, one often thinks of it as merely an accessory to larger fishing-boats; yet on most coasts it is to be found used independently; and, for certain kinds of work—line-fishing, crabbing, etc.—it has a world-wide popularity. It draws so little water that it can be safely used where larger boats would go aground or strike the rocks; often its very lightness is its strongest recommendation; for, where a larger vessel may have to struggle with the wind or get becalmed for want of it, the open boat, propelled by stout oarsmen, can force a passage with more or less ease. Fitted with a "lug," i.e. a square sail fixed to a yard that hangs obliquely to the mast, it is used along the east coast for fishing on a small scale. A long open boat provided with two lug-sails, known as a Scotch lugger, is still a great favourite with the North Sea herring-fishers.

Next comes the type of vessel most associated in our minds with the sea-fisheries—the decked boat or smack. More often than not she is "cutter-rigged," having a single mast with main-sail, top-sail, jib-sail, and fore-sail. Yawls, or yawl-rigged smacks, only differ from the other kind in having a second mast aft—the mizzen. The smack has a cabin furnished with a stove and three or four bunks, while, for storage purposes, the ample spaces below hatches in the fore part of the ship are used. Larger decked boats—schooners, brigs, and other square-rigged craft—are employed in the whaling and sponge trade, and also by the American cod-fishers; but as a rule these are not so much actual fishing-boats as storehouses, lodging-houses for the crew, and workshops. They are supplied with a number of small rowing-boats which do the catching work and unload their cargo into the larger vessel at night.

Now as to the gear or tackle necessary in fishing from boats. It may be classified under three heads: lines, nets, and pots. Lines may be of the simpler sort, whether with rod and winch, as used in tarpon-fishing, or only intended to be held in the hand ("hand lines"), such as are employed on the east coast for cod, and on the south for whiting; or they may be of the more complicated kind known as "long lines." The last named are used by the Scotch and North Country fishermen for haddocks, and by many of the American cod-crews; they are furnished with hooks which vary in size and number, and which—like hand and rod lines—are baited according to the class of fish sought;

the baits most commonly in use being mussels, whelks, hermit-crabs, and squid or cuttle-fish. Long lines, when joined up to form a series, often stretch for more than a mile, and carry as many as four or five thousand hooks.

Under the head of nets are included trawls, drift-nets, seines, moored nets, and dredges. The *trawl* (or *trail*) net, the most important and elaborate of these, is a huge meshed bag which runs down to a point, and the mouth of which is fastened to a pole or "beam," ordinarily about forty feet long. At either end of the beam, and at right angles to it, is a sort of triangular broad hoop of iron, measuring about three feet from base to apex. These hoops—"trawl-heads" as they are called—serve the threefold purpose of sinking the net; of supporting the beam, keeping it well off the bottom; and of gliding over the sand like the runners of a sledge, as the boat moves. The same net, on a somewhat smaller scale and with finer mesh-work, is used for shrimping.

A *drift-net* is a much less pretentious arrangement, being a long wall ("fleet") of small single nets fastened together in a line. Buoyed above with corks and bladders so that it may hang perpendicularly in the water, the series of nets drifts gently along at the tail of a boat, and a shoal of fish swimming straight at it, or driven towards it by the current, would soon be inextricably fixed in the meshes.

The *seine* (the *sagēnē* of the old Greek fishermen) is a plain net, corked above and leaded below; the top level, but the bottom slightly curved; it may be of any size, from the Cornish pilchard-seine, which is twelve hundred feet long and sixty feet deep, to the little net worked by the fisher-girls in Brittany, or the ground-seine commonly found in the Channel sprat-fishing. In a general way the seine is shot from a rowing-boat, and is dragged ashore in a semicircle by ropes fastened to its two ends. *Moored nets* are those, no matter of what shape, which are fixed in certain spots by means of anchors. They may be seen in great numbers across the mouths of Scotch, French, and Scandinavian rivers, where the tide, whether ebbing or flowing, soon drives the fish against them. The *dredge*, used principally for oysters, is a very small bag-like net, the under part of which is composed of wire rings and the upper of small string meshes. It is supported by a triangular heavy iron frame, to which a stout rope long enough to reach to the bottom is attached. The dredge is thrown overboard, allowed to scrape along the sand for a few minutes, hauled up, emptied, and thrown over again.

The third class of contrivance, *pots*, are used for the snaring of crabs, lobsters, etc. They are made of wicker, or of network stretched on an iron frame; are baited with fish or meat, and are sunk singly or in rows by means of heavy stones, their position being marked by cork buoys.

To this list of fishermen's requisites must be added another item—experience. Every amateur angler, whether it be the small boy who fishes for minnows with cotton and a bent pin, or the stalwart sportsman who whips the Scandinavian streams for salmon, is aware that, without a knowledge both of the habits and whereabouts of his fish, and also of the proper manipulation of his tackle, he will never catch anything except by sheer chance. And such knowledge, important as it is, constitutes only a portion of what is essential to the professional fishermen of civilised countries.

Before the sea-fisher is at liberty to bestow many thoughts upon either fish or tackle, he must learn to be a sailor; must understand the mystery of tides and currents and winds; be well acquainted with the nature of the ground on which he has to work; and be prepared to perform every conceivable duty on board, from swabbing the deck to steering the smack through a squall or a fog. Even then his education is by no means complete. Apart from the thousand and one minor repairs to boat and tackle for which he is responsible, apart even from the many tricks of the trade that he must know before he can secure and land his catch, almost every class of fisherman has special duties to perform in connection with the fish after they are caught: cleaning, sorting, packing, drying, salting—all of it work, that sounds and looks far easier than it is.

From this it will be seen that the fisherman's life is not a lazy one; neither is it a very safe one, especially where open-boat fishing is concerned. It is, moreover, precarious in the extreme; too much or too little wind may keep the boats ashore for days at a time; an overstocked market may render a whole day's catch valueless, except as manure; a sea-monster or passing ship may ruin fifty pounds' worth of gear in fifty seconds.

But there is a brighter side to the picture. There are strokes of luck to be considered—extraordinary catches, at a time when prices are high—a few of which will make the fisherman comparatively wealthy. Of the healthiness

Photo, Jenkins Lowestoft

A GREAT CATCH OF MACKEREL

The hold was full, and the fish were even piled up on the deck. The value of the boatload was well over £200. The boat is lying in Lowestoft harbour.

of the occupation there can be no two opinions; some of the finest imaginable specimens of manhood can easily be picked from among British, Scandinavian, or American fishermen; men of seventy years of age may be seen working with the speed and energy of lads of twenty.

There is a romance too, a fascination, about the calling that is seldom to be found in any other. The hard labour, the ever-present danger, and the decidedly unromantic smell of fish or tar or oil are, in the fisher's estimation, amply outweighed by the sense of freedom that his daily contact with the sea produces. The labour and the smells he takes for granted; the danger he seldom troubles about—to think about it is often to incur it. He is a sort of cheerful fatalist; if he is marked for drowning, drown he must, some day or another.

He would not, in one case out of a hundred, change his trade for any other; all other methods of life are to him cramping and enervating, and lacking in liberty. There is an old Kent-coast fisherman who worked regularly on board his smack, in foul weather and fair, till he was eighty years old. Then he at length yielded to the persuasions of a wealthy grandson, who took him to London, gave him rooms in his own house, and supplied him with all manner of luxuries. The dear old fellow tried town life and idleness for nearly a year; then one day he suddenly disappeared—he had gone back quietly to the work of his boyhood. He is now eighty-three, and prides himself on doing as good a day's fishing as the rest of his crew. Had he remained in London he would probably have been dead long ago.

CHAPTER III

TRAWLING

"Off" with the boats—The start—The fisherman's attitude towards strangers—An East Coast trawler—The net—The fisherman at sea—Shooting the trawl—Special "catches"—The net hauled up—Where the hard work comes in—The steam carrier—What is done with the catch—Steam-trawling—Little private ventures.

TO sea-loving people there is a peculiar charm attaching to the departure, whether by day or by night, of a fishing-fleet. When the boats go off by daylight there is the pleasing bustle and scurry attendant on the putting out to sea of two or three hundred men, all of them robust, healthy, and light-hearted. There is the vivid, continually changing panorama, made up of picturesque costumes, gaily painted boats which are being dragged down the shingle or tossed up and down on the waves in their effort to reach the smacks lying at moorings; the steady rise of the white or brown main-sail as it is hauled up by a couple of men; finishing with the graceful movement of the vessel herself as she slips her cable and sets off on her little voyage.

At night the charm is different. It is there all the same; to the taste of many people it is even intensified. Darkness has taken the place of daylight, and it remains for the ear to be entertained rather than the eye. The crunch of boat-keels over the pebbly beach, the hollow shouts of the men, the plash and rumble of the oars—noises that, in the daytime, pass unnoticed because they are drowned by others from the land—are now not only heard, but almost felt. The atmosphere of gaiety that is a feature of a daylight departure is wanting now, for the men have been called out of snug beds to catch the tide that must be taken, if not "at the flood," at least soon after the ebb has begun; some are sulky, others half asleep, and the rest are silent because even the most civil remark might beget a surly answer or be ignored altogether.

As each boat reaches the water's edge there is a splashing sound; the big, sea-booted men are scrambling into their places. Then comes the rhythmical knock-knock of the oars against the rowlocks as the boat hurries away into the gloom, her passage marked by the phosphorescent line left as she passes through the water, and by the pale gold drops that fall from the oar-blades. Presently the watcher on the shore hears a bump and a grating noise; the little boat has got alongside the smack; the men are clambering on board; the boat is made fast astern of the larger vessel, and work is about to begin. How the crew have distinguished their particular smack from the fifty, hundred, or two hundred lying at anchor is, to the landsman, a profound mystery; yet there has not been an instant of hesitation in the fishermen's minds; they have threaded their way as easily and naturally among the large fleet as a London policeman would cross the Strand, and have pulled unerringly up to their own ship.

Now there are fresh noises that again we should probably be unconscious of by day: the spasmodic rattle of the rings on the mast, as the gaff and main-sail are hauled into position; or the more rapid and regular click-click of the chain-cable as it is allowed to run through the hawse-hole or over the bow. The fore-sail and jib-sail are set; perhaps the top-sail as well, if wind be scarce; and the smack at last separates herself from the others which are in various stages of readiness, and, in ghostly fashion, slips away into the darkness.

This gradual disappearance of boat after boat—or of the whole fleet together—rather piques the watcher's curiosity. The fisher crews are going away for a day or two; perhaps a week; most likely a couple of months or more, if they are trawlers. What is going to happen during all that time? The inquisitive one must go and see for himself, for he can, in that way, learn more in a few hours than six months' hearsay would teach him. If he is known to the men, a good sailor, and is prepared to "rough it," nothing is easier; if he knows enough about seamanship to be able to bear a hand on board (without going out of his way to try to teach the skipper how to manage his own boat) he may even be received with open arms. I say "if he is known to the men." Fishermen vary in their attitude towards landsmen. A Yankee cod-skipper who is short of a hand would not hesitate to engage even a tram-conductor or a hairdresser; and would argue that, by the time the ground was reached, the new man would be either competent or dead. An Irish crew would be "hail-fellow" with any man who did not look like being sea-sick. The Scotch, North Country, and East Coast fishermen will take the stranger aboard if they are once persuaded that he is prepared to learn a very great deal from them. They do not seek to magnify the danger; rather the reverse, in fact; but they *do* like the landsman to feel that he is being initiated into a mystery that is far too deep for his intellect to grasp all in a hurry.

A cheery word or two, and a readiness to hand round one's tobacco, or possibly a hint as to a trifling donation at the end of the day, are the only passports necessary to make one shipmates with the South Country fisherman, save and except him of certain parts of Devonshire. To the Clovelly or Brixham fisherman, the man from the next village is a stranger and a foreigner; and, till recently, it were better for that man that he should keep out of the way. Even to-day, unless there is very strong influence at work, the visitor from a distance would stand quite as much chance of being invited aboard the royal yacht as of being allowed to sail with a Brixham trawler.

Let the reader imagine himself, then, on board one of the Lowestoft or Yarmouth or Hull boats. She is either cutter- or yawl-rigged; probably the latter, as being safer in the heavy winter seas off the Dogger Bank. Instead of making sail from her moorings, she has most likely been towed out to sea, with others, by a steam-tug.

As the sun shows signs of rising, the stranger has an opportunity of looking about him and taking in his new quarters. Along the port (or left-hand) side of the boat is the trawl-net—the heavy, iron-runnered beam lying along the deck; the "cod," or pointed bottom of the net, looped up to the rigging. On examination it is seen that one side of the net's mouth is fastened, all the way down, to the beam and the trawl-heads; the other is formed by an enormously thick rope—the "foot-rope" —much longer than the beam itself, to which the first row of meshes on that side is attached. Close by are huge coils of rope which look as though they too ought to belong to the trawl.

Swish! A bucket of water eddies round your ankles, and you speedily resolve to postpone your investigations till a more seasonable hour, as an energetic fisher-lad diligently scrubs at the deck with his short-handled broom. Not that it wants scrubbing; the only marks on it are a few smuts from the chimney of the cabin, where some one is lighting a fire to boil the breakfast kettle; but the seaman is the cleanest soul on earth, and washes his decks from habit, and his hands twenty times to any other working man's once.

Somebody calls out that the kettle boils, and the hitherto silent fishermen show signs of growing talkative. In warm weather, or at busy times, they take their meal on deck; at other times in the cabin, going down by twos and threes, or occasionally—with the exception of the man at the helm—*en masse*. The tea has been made in the kettle, and is now poured into iron mugs or gallipots, while a condensed-milk tin is solemnly scrubbed out to serve as a drinking-vessel for that courteous member of the crew who has placed his own mug at the guest's disposal.

Fish might be the greatest rarity at sea, if one judged from the fact that at least three of the men have brought kippers or red herrings to toast for their breakfast.

The cabin of one of these smacks is not the perfection of comfort; in many of them a man of medium height cannot even stand upright; the floor is wet, sometimes sloppy, and the intense heat makes every one anxious to escape to the fresh air as soon as possible. Coming up on deck again, you find that it is broad daylight; the land has disappeared, or else stands out only in dark outline; perhaps you have broken away from the main fleet and there is not a boat within hail; the wind is fresh, the smack slips swiftly and delicately over the waves, and you begin to understand why the fisherman looks with contempt on all occupations except his own.

At length signs of attention to business reappear; pipes are stowed away; the after-breakfast chatter dies down; the taciturn old fellow at the helm takes a fresh quid of tobacco and mutters some order about easing the fore-sail or lowering the top-sail; the younger men abandon their speculations as to whether the *Skylark* or the *John and Mary* or the *Minnie Brown* ships just as much water as she did before she went for repairs, and give themselves up to a close inspection of the gear. A few minutes, or hours—as the case may be—pass; then the main-sail is pulled round to leeward, other sails are lowered or eased, and you realise that at last the men are going to fish.

TRAWLING

The smack is in thirty, perhaps forty, fathoms of water, and down at or near the bottom are soles and plaice, halibut and brill, with, perhaps, a score of other kinds of fish: turbot, lemon-soles, skate, cod, haddock, whiting—to say nothing of the less-known megrims, witches, pouting, coal-fish, and pollack—all waiting to swim into, or be scooped up by, the great trawl-net. The size of this net naturally varies according to the size of the vessel carrying it; the beam is any length from five-and-thirty to fifty feet; the meshes increase in size towards the mouth, being about an inch and a half square at the bottom, and about four inches at the top.

Now comes the moment for throwing it overboard (a fisherman always speaks of "shooting" the net). To each trawl-head or runner a long rope—the "bridle"—is made fast, and a third rope is shackled to the bridle-ends.

"All right! Let go!" growls the skipper.

The heavy beam has disappeared; trawling has begun; and, for so many days, weeks, or months, the crew has settled down to a seemingly monotonous and endless task. The boat has slackened her speed; often she appears to make no progress at all. If the weather is not too rough she is left to go whither she will, for, with the ponderous trawl clogging her like a sea-anchor, she cannot run far away. There she lies, tossed lightly about by wave and breeze; patiently dragging her net from left or right, according to the tide and wind. What will the first haul be like?

At present our skipper is only feeling his way; he

wants to find smooth ground, for only there can the trawl work satisfactorily.

And what is going on all that distance below our feet? We talk airily about so many fathoms, without perhaps readily grasping what such a depth means. Imagine a distance nearly four times the length of a cricket-pitch; that is how deep down our net is lying. The beam, held three or four feet off the ground by its two runners, is riding slowly and easily along; the foot-rope is scraping over the bottom, disturbing and bewildering the fish, which are scooped up by it before they know where they are; and, finding that they cannot escape above, they never seem to dream of trying to get out the way they came in.

Although it is an everyday incident in their lives—or, rather, an incident which happens a great many times every day and night of their life at sea—the trawlers always seem to get up a semi-enthusiasm, a few moments of the breathless excitement of expectation, when the time comes for hauling in. The older hands no doubt affect a sort of indifference, but the little pleasurable thrill—the gambler's "eye to the off-chance"—is there for those who can see it. And no wonder; for buried treasure has been brought up on various occasions. Did not some Margate fishermen once pull up a metal pot crammed full of golden guineas? Moreover, the memory of another, and perhaps more likely, treasure is still green in the minds of the North Sea trawlers. There are men still living who once saw a trawl-net pulled up near the Dogger packed as full as it could be with one of the most expensive fish on the market—soles. The net had somehow stumbled across a hollow, where a complete colony of these creatures had taken up its abode; and, in a short time, seven tons of them were taken. The value of such a catch would be at least £400. I have heard this tale from fishermen in various quarters, and Mr. James Runciman, writing in 1886, speaks of it as an established fact, adding that the haul was described to him by an actual member of the fortunate crew.

The methods of raising the net differ. Our East Coast boat will, in all probability, have a kind of patent capstan, worked by steam power, which hoists the trawl amidships; the southern boats, however, like the shrimpers, have a large hand-winch or windlass which draws up the fore-bridle over the bows, while the after-bridle is pulled up by hand, or wound round a smaller winch astern. These South Coast trawlers, by the way, do not usually fish in fleets as the others do.

At last the beam shows itself above water, and strong hands lift it over the bulwarks. But how on earth, asks the neophyte, can those ropes bear the strain of such a weight? More, how can those paltry-looking bits of string, that form the meshes, hold together when weighed down by a burthen so tremendous? Such a question belongs to the realm of mechanics; the fact remains that not one rope in ten thousand does break, and it is the exception rather than the rule for a mesh to give way.

Now only the net lies in the water, and, by means of stout ropes, this is hoisted up and its contents shot out on to a space temporarily boarded off on deck.

GUTTING THE FISH ON BOARD A DANISH BANKS TRAWLER

The deck bands lose no time in setting about the arduous task of cleaning the catch. Wading knee-deep into the slippery mass, they ply their gory knives with amazing speed and dexterity. Cod, of which a fine specimen is seen in the picture, are beheaded and split open in readiness for salting. Haddock, plaice, and halibut are packed in ice, and so kept fresh until port is reached.

The men cast a swift, appraising eye over the catch—the more experienced can tell, within a very little, what it is worth to them—then lower the trawl again; unless the catch is entirely unsatisfactory, in which case they may make sail a little farther away before doing so.

"Is that all?" asks the landsman. "Then where does the hard work come in?"

The hard work is only beginning. All those hundreds or thousands of fish that lie feebly gasping there, interspersed with shrimps, crabs, shells, and seaweed, have to be cleaned, sorted out, and packed in boxes ready for the carrier; cramping, back-breaking work it is, too; and, by the time it is done, the trawl is probably ready to be pulled up again. Up it comes; then the same moment of expectancy; the same straining and dragging; the same groping and stooping and sorting—then another net-full ready to be hoisted in. Night comes on, and the men "turn in" one or two at a time, according to the number of the crew.

Till lately (in many instances the custom still exists), in winter, the boats going off for a long spell carried ice with them and stored the fish in it, bringing back the whole cargo themselves at the end of the trip. This is most largely done in the case of plaice, soles, and halibut. But more commonly now, whether in winter or summer, whether fishing off the Dogger or the Danish and Dutch Banks, steam carriers go out from Yarmouth or Grimsby or Hull almost daily, and their visit makes a break in the monotony to which every one looks forward.

The carrier is a boat of powerful build, very high in

the bows, and as low in the stern as a Thames barge. As soon as she comes in sight all is bustle and excitement on board the trawlers. The little boat that has been trailing behind each smack is hauled alongside; one or two men get in, and the boxes are handed over to them. In the calmest weather there is a certain amount of risk attaching to this work of transporting the fish to the carrier. Every one knows what the swell from a good-sized steamer is; a small boat getting into its wash must expect a good deal of buffeting. But when the sea is really rough—and the German Ocean can afford as fair a sample of roughness as most—it seems impossible that these little dinghies can live in it. Yet an accident rarely happens. Very patiently the tiny craft makes her way to the side of the carrier, and before the spectator has had time to make up his mind whether or no she will be smashed to splinters against the larger vessel, she is on her way back again with a cargo of empty cases, perhaps a few necessaries in the way of food or fresh water, and, by chance, a letter or a couple of newspapers.

Nowadays carriers and tugs, having a shrewd eye to business, have a trawl-net on board; and, in their spare time, the crews do a little fishing on their own account. This is especially the case with the Falmouth and Cardiff tugs.

The Scotch, less conservative than the South Britons, have almost abandoned sailing-vessels for trawling; and, except in the case of small private ventures, it is safe to say that at Leith, Aberdeen, and other Scotch ports, the trawling is all done by screw-steamers. This, of course, means larger and heavier tackle, a larger crew (including deck-hands, whose work is to see to the cleaning and storing of the fish, and to do odd jobs aboard), and larger catches. Boats of this description are provided not only with patent capstans, but also with blocks and ropes for hoisting the bag of the trawl on board.

The Irish fleets still cleave to the older sailing-boat method; in 1900 Dublin alone possessed a fleet of over fifty cutter-rigged smacks averaging forty tons.

It must not be supposed that trawling is confined to Leith, Grimsby, Ramsgate, Brixham, and a few such important centres. In almost every fishing-town there are men who, in spring and summer, go out short distances for a day or two at a time with a view to supplying just the local market. If an owner does not happen to possess trawling-gear he can soon hire it; at a pinch he can use his shrimp-net, which is practically the same thing.

Private ventures such as this are often exceedingly lucrative, for the expenses and wear and tear are inappreciable as compared with those of a regular trawler; and each man frequently finds that he has earned as much in those few hours or days as he could make at other fishing in as many weeks.

CHAPTER IV

SHRIMPING, MUSSELLING, AND LINE-FISHING

Shrimps—The push-net—On board a Dutch *visschers-boot*—Dutch fishermen—Preparations for boiling—Hauling up the shrimp-net—Emptying—The catch—Sorting—'Ware crabs!—And fox-fish—Boiling—Hot shrimps—Danger of the trade—Prawns and prawn-catching—Mussels—What becomes of them all—Transplanting—Mussels by the barge-load—Line-fishing—Hand lines—Long lines—Ready-baited hooks—Paying out the lines—"Bending-on"—Two or three miles of lines—Bringing in the catch—Longer lines—"Bulters."

SHRIMPS are never out of season; and prawns only during the last two months of the year. Prices vary simply because the fish are so much more plentiful at one time than another.

The push-net, to be seen at all seaside places in the summer months, is apt to mislead us into the belief that the shrimp is a shallow-water fish, which he is not. In shallows he is an accident; in deep water a feature. The men whom you see "ploughing the sand" with a hand net at low water are either out of work or making over-time, and we cannot allow their claim to the dignified title of "shrimper." Ask the Dutchmen or the Kent and Essex fishermen what they understand by shrimping. Push-netting, they will tell you, is children's amusement;

some will even sarcastically affect never to have heard of it.

Let us have a day off with a Dutch *visschers-boot* (which we may manage to do if our command of German, Dutch, or Flemish be of such a nature as to persuade the crew that we are anything but British), and we shall have a chance of seeing why shrimpers demand to be classed with trawlers and other workers at dangerous trades.

Those who laugh at the Dutch fishermen have not seen them at their work (except English fishermen; and these justify the proverb that two of a trade seldom agree). They may let their hair grow rather long; they may wear wooden shoes—nowadays they far more often invest in English-made sea-boots; they may require a very great deal of alcohol to enable them to face a gale; but their clever seamanship, their industry, and, when it comes to the pinch, their cool courage, demand that we shall speak of them with all respect. It is to these men that the London market is indebted for its winter supply of shrimps; in fact, from December to June, by far the greater quantity comes from Holland, the fish being vastly inferior to those taken from the Thames estuary.

Each smack, with an average crew of four, carries a net shorter than a trawl and of much smaller mesh, but not otherwise differing; and the men work almost a whole tide, going off with the ebb and not returning till nearly flood. Such boats will go from fifteen to thirty miles away, working every minute of daylight. The men know well enough, within a little, where they will find their fish, and, with a favourable wind, will soon be on the spot. Most boats carry a dredge, attached to a very long warp, which, as soon as they have shortened sail, they throw over once or twice to test the bottom. If the result of the trial be satisfactory, the net is lowered as described in Chapter III, and in the same manner is towed slowly along the sand.

As soon as the net has been shot, preparations are made for the shrimp-boiling, which almost invariably is done on board. When the fore-hatch is taken up we see, below, an ordinary washing-copper with a good-sized grate under it, and, in it, the water and the waste shrimps from yesterday's boiling. The water is baled out and flung overboard, but not the shrimps. It may be superstition or it may be scientific fact, but all shrimpers are of opinion that boiled shrimps are poisonous to their own kind, and that the living fish have no instinct to warn them of that fact. Therefore any that are left over (the "cleanings") are made into a small parcel to be thrown away when the men come ashore.

The copper being filled with sea-water to which several generous handfuls of salt have been added, the fire is lit, and, by the time the men are ready for it, the copper will be boiling. Next the "zeef" (*anglice*, "strainer") is handed out and laid slanting from the bulwarks to the deck, to leeward; it is an oblong wooden frame about six feet by three, with a wire bottom, just such as bricklayers' labourers use for screening sand.

The hauling up of a shrimp-net is a less arduous undertaking than the raising of a trawl, though it is quite heavy enough to keep four men well employed for several minutes. In the bows is a powerful windlass to which the fore-bridle, or else a tow-line connected with the two bridles, is fixed, and then the winding up begins—hard work even for a couple of strong men accustomed to such labour. If the net is being pulled up by the fore-bridle only, two other men are working in the stern, hauling in the aft-bridle; if by a tow-line, they stand by to haul on the after-bridle as soon as it comes in sight. At last the beam comes up, is hoisted in, and the full net hangs over the side, half in the water. Now a space must be made for the fish. From the main-hatch to the after-cabin a plank is laid on its edge on either side, thereby making, with the uprights of the hatchways, a rectangular case into which the net may be emptied.

As far as in them lies, these Dutch fishers evince the same momentary excitement over the contents of the net that we have seen among the trawlers. After looking at a full trawl-net this one seems curiously small and empty; and, as a hauling-line is thrown round the waist of the net, it looks as though we could pull it out of the water with one hand; nevertheless, there is four hundredweight or more in that bag-like contrivance, and the men find quite enough difficulty in hoisting it out of the water and over the bulwarks.

The mouth is laid inside the temporary enclosure, and then, with a good deal of lifting and shaking, the catch is emptied, the net examined in case of possible breakages among the meshes, and then thrown in again.

Now have a look at the catch; a most interesting sight when seen for the first time; a grey-green, glistening, and slightly palpitating mass, speckled with the dark green, pink, red, or white bodies of crabs of all sorts and sizes. Here and there is a something that brings a moment's pleasure to the eyes of the men: a good plump sole or two, for which a private buyer will probably give fifty cents apiece; perhaps even a turbot, the sale of which will keep the crew in tobacco for close on a week; perhaps a handful of prawns.

But looking at them will not sort the fish. Here begins the really hard work; shrimps, and nothing but shrimps, must go into the boiling-copper, and no genius has yet arisen to separate them from the rubbish by other means than going down on the hands and knees and picking out good from no good. In warm weather this part of the work is troublesome enough; but try it in winter with the rain or sleet beating in your face, and your hands aching with cold. *Aching* is a very mild term; I have seen stalwart fellows, who have experienced all the terrors of Antarctic and Iceland weather, almost cry with the cold in their fingers, while engaged in shrimp-sorting within thirty miles of the English coast.

But to work; and go gingerly, for there be crabs about; not one of them big enough to be eaten, but literally thousands that are prepared to eat as much of *you* as you feel disposed to let them. Here is one nasty little wretch—the "fliker" or fly-crab the men call it—no bigger than a five-shilling piece, that will make a dead set at you and bite to the bone. Smash him with your boot or a stone, for he devours the fish and is no good even as whelk-bait. Other kinds of crabs are allowed to depart in peace, but not this one if it can be helped.

Lightly flicking out the shrimps with the finger-tips, the men gradually raise them into heaps, which are soon scraped into a tub by the "boiler," and thrown into the copper. Now and then a few dabs, codling, or whiting are found; they are thrown into a bucket for subsequent sale or supper. Lightly veiled by a sparse covering of shrimps is another white body; "more fish," you say, and go to take hold of it; but it is a white-bellied crab, which fact you may not discover, if you are foolish enough to put your hand on it, till the crab himself informs you. Now here is a fox-fish; a thing something like a fat whiting, spotted with grey and black. Take him by the tail and throw him overboard behind you as quickly and carefully as if he were red-hot; hold him two seconds and you will regret it. His gill-cover is elongated into a sharp, stiff spike, and the moment he is touched he springs round salmon-like and digs this into you, or scratches you with it. Fishermen say that the sting is poisonous, but, *experto crede*, it is nothing of the kind. He is no good for eating, but if you find a relative of his, the weever, put him aside; skinned and fried it would be difficult to find a fish more delicate and satisfying. It has the same weapon—and the same handy way of using it—as the fox-fish.

At last the sorting is done; the waste is brushed through the port-holes and the crew are ready for the second hauling. The number of the hauls will depend on the light, the weather, and the plentifulness of the fish. If these are scarce, the sorting will be finished quickly, and the men all the sooner free for another haul; if there is little wind the net must stay down longer, for in such a case it is often being dragged over the same spot again and again instead of going on to fresh ground. Four hauls per day would be a fair average.

Now let us watch the man who is responsible for the boiling. There he is, down in the hold, giving the fish a stir round from time to time, or throwing them up by the dipper-full into the strainer. His water has nearly boiled away, and one of the crew dips him another couple of bucketfuls from over the side; and, as this comes to the boil, we have an opportunity of watching the cooking process right through. Into the copper goes a piled pailful of the grey-green, semi-transparent fish, and as the water closes over them, we hear a faint *cheep-cheep* sound; this is *not* the wailing of the shrimps; it is merely the water running into the air-passages, and you would hear the same noise were the fish given a cold bath instead of a hot.

In a minute or two the shrimps have changed their colour; they are "done," and the boiler dips them out and throws them on the top of the others that are draining in the sieve. Now try them; if you have once tasted newly caught shrimps hot, you will not give a *fico* for them eaten cold. You can eat as many as you like, for they are plentiful enough generally; many are destined never to come to the shop or the market at all, but to be thrown on the land as manure. Perhaps, when these poor fishermen get ashore, a telegram will be awaiting them to the effect that their dealer can take no more shrimps for another three days.

A shrimp-boiler has one trouble in life, for which the young skate and other small fry are responsible. Many dark-skinned fish, in their baby form, are the exact length and colour of shrimps, and, however carefully sorted the fish may have been, several of these are sure to appear among those set aside for boiling. Before these are thrown into the copper they are closely inspected again, and even then a score of trespassers will appear in the boiling water, time after time deluding the boiler into the belief that they are half-cooked shrimps.

As the sieve fills, the shrimps are taken out and put into bags; and so the day goes on till eighty or a hundred or more gallons are thus stowed away, and the boat heads for home with the returning tide. The shrimps will be taken ashore, measured into barrels, canvased down, and sent away by cart or train.

Is there much danger in shrimping? A certain amount, weather apart, even; because, when men are working a whole tide, it is often necessary to do some of the fishing in the half-light of morning or evening, and it is then that accidents take place. At such a time a man may be unwittingly standing in the way of a warp which he can scarcely see, while the net is being shot, and may find himself entangled in it suddenly and dragged overboard almost before he can cry out. In this way a certain number of lives are lost every year, for the bulk of the work being done by daylight, few boats ever trouble to carry a lamp.

SHRIMPING, MUSSELLING

Why are some shrimps pink and others brown? is a question that has puzzled many of us in childhood. The pink shrimps appear to be a sort of connecting link between the brown ones and prawns. The two are seldom found together in great numbers; in a neighbourhood where the shrimps are brown there will also be a sprinkling of the others, and vice versa.

The prawn, apart from being much larger, is distinguished from the shrimp by its saw-like spine and by its enormously long external antennæ, which are half as long again as the fish itself. A live prawn is a most beautiful thing: steel-grey, marked all over with purple spots and lines; its eyes are its most extraordinary feature, for they stand out like spots of flame or of the most brilliantly burnished copper. In their adult condition prawns are less fond of deep water than shrimps, though a few are generally taken in the shrimp-net. They rather prefer the still, clear pools among the rocks, where they play and hide among the seaweed. They are caught in two ways: in traps like the ordinary lobster-pot on a smaller scale; and in a sort of landing-net, made by hanging a net-bag on an iron hoop fixed at the end of a long pole.

When fishermen have nothing better to do, another branch of the trade is open to them whenever the weather permits—musselling.

Sea-water mussels are divisible into many classes, but the two best known are the common mussel and the horn-mussel; the latter differing slightly from the former in shape and in its habit of digging and burrowing in the sand. As an article of food, these animals are probably as nourishing as oysters, though they are so often said to be poisonous. Whether they are so, or not, must, as with snails, depend largely upon the feeding; a mussel that has passed a good part of its life clinging to the copper bottom of a liner can scarcely be wholesome as food. In any case the fish should never be eaten during the summer months.

But why "go after" mussels when so many millions of them are to be picked from rocks, breakwaters, and mud- or shingle-banks?

The question is reasonable enough, though it would never be asked by any one who had the least idea as to the number of mussels that are used in the United Kingdom alone, every year. Hundreds of thousands, not of mussels, but of *tons* of mussels, are gathered annually and sold; and, absurd as it may sound, there is little difference between the profits made on them and those derived from the oyster-fishery. To France alone, the Belgians export over twelve million francs' (half a million pounds') worth every year.

Then who are the consumers?

The ground, in the first place; all the small mussels, and those which may have been tainted with sewage or poisoned by the copper bottoms of ships, are sent away by the barge-load for manure, or for lightening heavy clay soil.

Secondly, the poor. Apart from those mussels that are eaten from choice, or those which the fisher-people out of work are sometimes glad to make a dinner of, many tons of them are eaten by the London poor alone, every winter; buying them at a penny a quart, a family can have a meal for twopence.

Even then, we have not accounted for a third of the numbers given above. The prime mussels are required as bait for line-fishing, and are sold at the rate of rather less than £2 a ton (over 51,000 fish go to the ton). Many boats' crews of the Scotch and North Country fishers who go out into deep water for cod, haddock, etc., will use over four tons per boat, in a month, in this manner. Wherefore let it no longer be wondered at, that a shrimp- or oyster-boat, in her otherwise idle spells, should go a-musselling. Mussels used in the pearl-industry will be discussed in a subsequent chapter.

Not only are these useful bivalves gathered for sale, but, in some parts of the coast, they are collected and transplanted to special beds with as much care as if they were oysters. Those taken from the beach, it may be noticed, are rarely fat and full; perhaps the constant out-going of the tide disturbs their feeding. Therefore it is necessary to find those that frequent moderately deep water; and these are obtained by dredging. The dredge used is very like that employed for oyster-catching; it is thrown overboard from a barge or smack, and the mussels that it brings up are picked out from the accompanying mud and rubbish and stowed in the hold.

Musselling is much more irksome than shrimping, for the men are often away for several days without a break, their object being not to catch so many boxes full or so many gallons, but to fill their boat till she cannot possibly find room for another mussel. Nevertheless, the work has its compensations: there will certainly not be a telegram when the crew get ashore to say that their cargo is not wanted; mussels are always wanted; if not by the ordinary consumer, by the breeder.

If the fishing has been done from a smack, there are barges waiting for her cargo to be shovelled into; if a barge has been used, she will either let herself be landed high and dry, when she will unload into carts, or else she will carry her fish straight away up north or wherever they are wanted. A stranger looking at one of these flat-bottomed, ungainly craft close at hand, as she lies on the Thames mud, would be as surprised when he saw the same barge out at sea as he would if told the number of miles she travels in the course of a twelvemonth. Looked at from a distance when she is out at sea she seems as graceful a ship as sails, in spite of her funny little mizzen. When you see her empty and realise her storage accommodation, you do not wonder that she is used in mussel-dredging, considering the enormous numbers that must be caught before the profits can be appreciable; for, as bait or manure, the catch will fetch less than a penny a hundred.

Mention of mussel-bait brings us to the consideration of how, and by whom, it is used to such an extraordinary extent.

Line-fishing is probably of far more ancient date than netting; for that matter, there are savages that have used that method for centuries, and still have not dreamt of catching their fish in quantities, by means of nets. As a branch of the civilised fisherman's trade it can never be superseded until the fish have ceased to frequent those parts of the ocean-bed where no net will go, and till such fish as conger-eels will allow themselves to be taken in respectable numbers by the trawl.

The simplest form of this fishing is by the use of "hand lines"—single lines, carrying one or more hooks, the upper end being kept in the hand while fishing is going on; such lines are pulled up as soon as there is a bite, the fish gaffed off, and the hook rebaited. Naturally the hooks vary in size and number according to the fish sought. They may be seen all along the South Coast in use for whiting, which, belonging to the cod family, are more easily taken by hook than any other small sea-fish.

The southern whiting fishery is mainly in the hands of individual fishermen, each man going off in his small rowing-boat and working on his own account, subsequently selling the fish at the local market.

The same kind of line is used off the Norfolk coast for cod, with a bit of cuttle-fish as bait.

Far more pretentious and important is the "long-line" fishing which we find going on in the north and east, and in Scotland; turbot, cod, ling, and haddock are caught by the thousand in this way, both from small and from large boats. The smacks from the Northumbrian fishing villages go out towards the "bad" parts of the Dogger and work as long as their bait lasts. Rowing-boats, too, do a lot of coast work off Norfolk and Lincoln, going out and coming in with the tide.

When a smack's crew is going off long-line fishing, it

THE MUSSEL-BAITERS

Mussel-baiting is a constant occupation with the children and women-folk of the North-Country long-line fishers.

may be noticed that each man has a small supply of baskets, otherwise known as "skeps" and "creels." Each of these contains a line, with hooks ready baited; in fact, mussel-baiting is a constant occupation with the children and womenfolk of these men. When the baits have been fixed, the line is carefully coiled round and round, with the hooks in the middle, laid in the skep, and fresh grass or moss sprinkled over the bait to keep it from drying. Some of the lines bear as many as 600 hooks, and each has been artfully concealed with a mussel or, in default, a bit of herring. Every member of the crew must contribute a certain number of such lines; generally three or four.

When the boat reaches the ground she shortens sail (or steams gently along, for there are now many steamers engaged in this work) and preparations are made for sinking the lines. First of all, an iron weight or heavy stone tied to the end of two lines is thrown overboard; the upper end of one of these which, when the weight is down, just reaches to the surface, is fastened to a buoy which carries a flagstaff. To the other line—the beginning of the "main-line"—one of the baited lines has been joined, or "bent on," at some distance from the weight, and is now allowed to run itself out as the boat drifts gently on.

During this proceeding one of the men is standing at the bulwarks holding a short metal bar at arm's length over the side of the boat, for the line to run over; by which precaution the hooks are prevented from possibly catching in the boat-side. Before the whole length of this line has been run out another is bent on by its free end, and, in its turn, has a third joined to it in the same way as before, till all the lines are used up and stretch perhaps two or three miles out to sea, lying across the tide so that the ends of line that bear the hooks are kept by the force of the current at right-angles to the main line.

But before the last of the lines has been allowed to sink, another weighted cord has been fastened to it a few yards from the hooked end and secured to a second flagged buoy as before. Now comes half an hour's—perhaps an hour's—rest for the men; it is probably all they will get till the fishing is ended for the day; for many boats carry an extra set of lines ready to be shot as soon as these are pulled up. At the end of the half-hour or hour, one of the buoy-lines is dragged up, and brings with it the first part of the main-line. These men are now pulling up from eight to ten pounds' worth of fish, and the lines are worth even more; no wonder they haul in carefully. The fish are coming to the top at last—haddock, halibut, skate, ling, cod, gurnard, turbot, eels, and plaice; rarely soles, for they can seldom be persuaded to bite at a bait; they prefer a diet of mud, sewage, and seaweed.

Some of the hooks are destitute of both fish and bait, which means that the "five-fingers" and the crabs have been indulging in an easily acquired meal; other hooks bear mere useless lumber: sea-spiders, crabs, and star-fish that have been led to their ruin through over-much greed. Occasionally the jawless "hag-fish" appears;

this elegant creature has swallowed the hook entirely and is trying to digest it.

To gaff and sort this collection is almost a day's work in itself, even if there were no second set of lines to see to. But at last it is done; the fish lie in the hold sprinkled with salt, and the smack runs for the shore. There are plenty of people waiting for her; wives and children of the crew, small salesmen with donkey-carts, perhaps a big dealer or two from the towns. She comes in as near as she can, then throws out a tow-line, which is grabbed at by every man, woman, child, and dog that is without other occupation, and the boat vigorously hauled up by them, unless the beach happens to boast a capstan. None so ready to bear a hand to help another as the fisher-folk. When did you ever hear a fisherman *ask* for help in beaching his boat? They have been used all their lives to aiding one another in that as well as in more substantial ways than the mere lending a pull to a boat or rope.

One of the dealers casts a calculating eye over the catch, and makes his offer—which of course is not accepted; but, after a good deal of haggling, or perhaps of auctioneering, the catch is sold.

Now the barrels of the dealers come rolling down the shingle; every one pulls out a knife and begins cleaning the fish as if his life depended on it; and, in less than no time, they are packed and on their way to the railway station, while the baskets of lines are carried home by the fish-wives to be patiently cleaned and rebaited for the next day's toil.

Before we leave the subject of long-line fishing we must notice that done in winter by the Yarmouth and Cromer deep-sea fishermen when they are not trawling or after the herring. Most of it is done from "hatch-boats," large single- or two-masted smacks like those used for trawling, but differing in that they have a well—a part of the hold into which water can be run; for the men are often away some days at a time, and the fish—cod and ling—have to be brought back alive.

If the North Countrymen's lines were "long," those found here are unspeakable as regards length; from seven to ten miles of line are paid out by the hatch-boats, often carrying five thousand hooks at a time. The ground is the Dogger, the bait whelks and cuttle-fish. The method of setting the lines is the same as that already described.

There is another kind of tackle—a short long-line, worked on the same principle, and known as a "bulter." The Sussex fishermen use it with cuttle-fish bait for congers, skate, and hake, shooting it from large rowing-boats.

CHAPTER V

SALMON-FISHING AS AN INDUSTRY

The salmon—Annual migration—Jumping—Spawning—Fry, smolt, and grilse—The Columbian grounds—Trap-nets—Seines—Hauling in by horse-power—The fish-wheel—Salmon-fishing among the Indians—Canadian moored gill-nets—Scandinavian fishery—The Sogne and Hardanger fjörds—Natural Salmon-traps—Seines and net-weirs—Lapps and Finns as fishers—The sea-swallow—Salmon-netting at home—Close-time—Stake-nets and stow-nets.

IN this chapter, be it understood, we are approaching the salmon from a strictly business point of view; the salmon as he is caught for sale and export, for the benefit of persons who are content to purchase six-pennyworth of him at a time and in a tin, or of those who buy him fresh or dried at their fishmonger's.

The supple, elegant form of the salmon is as familiar to every one as is the delicate pink of its flesh. No fish has been so written about, legislated about, experimented on, undigested, and misunderstood; few are more profitable from the fisher's, tradesman's, and doctor's point of view. The fishery has been known at least as far back as early in the Christian era, and the trade in dried salmon is, at any rate in Scotland and Northumbria, a very ancient one. At the time of Edward II's conflict with Bruce we find orders being given by the English

King for three thousand dried salmon for the use of his soldiers. Bergen, too, on the Norwegian coast, traces its fishery back to mediæval times.

The West Canadian and United States fishery, with which we shall first deal, is the newest, and at the same time the most profitable and most productive of any; more than half a million cases of tinned fish being exported every year from round about the Fraser River alone.

The annual migration of these fish is very remarkable. They enter the rivers in spring, as soon as the waters have become more or less swollen by the rains, swimming in great numbers and usually in mid-stream and near the surface. At the beginning of the migration the shoals seem nervous and easily frightened; so much so that a floating spar or bit of timber, or any shock such as the blasting of rocks near at hand, has been known to drive them out to sea again. But, once well in the stream, their conduct is reversed; nothing will daunt them; nothing will turn them back; rapids, currents, and whirlpools are matters of little moment to them; they will spring from the low level to the top of a cascade ten or fifteen feet high. Their perseverance is astounding. On reaching a cascade, a fish, making a bent spring of its body by taking its tail in its mouth, will suddenly shoot upwards, higher, perhaps, than the upper level, yet often at an insufficient angle to enable it to reach it, and back it falls with a crash, only to "get breath" and then make another, possibly successful, attempt.

Sometimes, after a score of fruitless tries at jumping

up, the salmon will apparently abandon the attempt, remaining somnolent at the foot of the rapid; but all it is doing really is harbouring its strength for a further attempt, which the plucky creature will make after a few days' rest.

Another interesting point relating to the up-river journey is the much-debated question as to whether the fish possesses a memory. Scientific men are now satisfied that the same fish frequently, though not invariably, visit the same rivers for the spawning season; and many authorities are of opinion that this is due to the exercise of memory and preference; albeit others still maintain that the salmon does not know the coast-line (being in the habit of seeking deep water as soon as it reaches the sea in its outward journey) and so enters the first river-mouth it meets with, which often happens to be the same.

The Fraser, it may be remembered, is an exceptionally swift-flowing river; yet salmon will swim up it at an average rate of forty miles a day—a pace which they can increase to nearly two hundred in calm water.

Having at length reached the shallower parts of the stream near the source, the fish choose their spawning grounds from the sandy river-bed, plough up the sand with their snouts, working all the while against the stream; for if they worked with their heads down-stream the water, running into their gills, would choke them. In the furrow thus dug they deposit their eggs, carefully covering them again with gravel.

By this time their appearance has undergone a curious change; they have become thin and flabby and, if eaten at such a time, would be unwholesome if not poisonous. The females have become almost black; the cheeks of the males are striped a red-gold, the body covered with the same tint, and the lower jaw strangely elongated.

The spawning has occupied about a fortnight, at the end of which time the fish lie about in the stream taking the return journey by easy stages, till their strength is recruited. Meanwhile the ova lie undisturbed, covered up till about the end of the following March, when they may be said to be hatched and have become "fry"; tiny, ugly things, pale brown, crossed by a few grey marks. The fry will remain in the river for perhaps another year and, by then, they have become grey-green on the back and silvery below, are nearly six inches long, and are known no longer as fry but as "smolt."

After two or three months in the sea they reappear at the river-mouths weighing from three to four pounds, which weight rapidly increases as they ascend the stream. At this stage they are called "grilse." Grilse remain up-stream till the next winter, when they spawn and henceforth are dignified by the title of salmon.

The bulk of the American salmon comes from two rivers—the Fraser and the Columbia, and from a huge land-locked, natural harbour—Puget Sound, which, a hundred miles long, runs southward from Juan de Fuca Strait into the State of Washington. Thus the salmon fishery of that quarter may be said to be divided almost equally between ourselves and the Americans, Canada having the Fraser, and the States the Columbia; while the fish that leave the mouth of the Fraser become

NETTING SALMON FROM COLOMBIA RIVER, OREGON, U.S.A.

The horses have just drawn the net and its contents ashore. The value of these fisheries is enormous. The fish are cured or canned and despatched to all parts of the world.

American property if they follow the southern current down into Puget Sound, Canadian if they turn northwards into Queen Charlotte Sound.

There is little hope for the fish when they swim southwards, for, as may be seen from a map of Washington, Puget Sound is a natural salmon-trap on a very large scale, having but the one outlet, and that split up by a small island; and it is doubly delusive on account of its great depth, which leads the fish to suppose that they have reached the open sea.

The fishing, which lasts about five months, begins in April, and, in the Sound, is done chiefly by means of trap-nets, consisting of a wall of netting, sometimes double with a narrow space between the two. These are moored across current or are let down from platforms in the quieter parts of the harbour.

In proportion to its size the salmon is one of the strongest fish in creation: therefore only a stout net will hold him; the meshes of such nets are made of what is known as Barbour's twine, a single thread of which would hold a hundredweight and a half.

The trap-net is set late in the afternoon and left down all night, and the fish, swimming with the tide, go straight at the net, which, well weighted below, hangs perpendicularly; small fish will be allowed to pass through the meshes, but the larger ones soon find that where the heads will go the shoulders will not follow; they can proceed no further and, naturally, as soon as they try to withdraw their heads, the cord slips itself under one of the gills and they are "unavoidably detained" henceforth.

Next day comes the hauling up, which is done by cords or levers; in the case of moored nets the catch is hauled alongside the boats from which the nets were shot, but traps are pulled straight up to the platform from which they have been lowered, and are left hanging while the net is cleared; the fish as they are taken out are heaped in boxes, sprinkled with salt, and taken ashore for drying.

Before leaving the Washington fishermen, we must look at some of the work which they share with the Oregon men on the Columbia River. Between Astoria at the mouth of the Columbia and Portland, sixty miles inland, is another valuable salmon ground; here the seine, which has been briefly described in Chapter II, is used in addition to the gill-net. As will presently appear, the seine, even when used for little things like anchovies and pilchards, is a weighty apparatus to draw ashore; when it contains salmon it is almost ponderous enough to call for steam-power.

The leaded net having been shot in a half-circle from a couple of small boats, the tow-lines that are fixed to the two edges are carried to the bank; as the seine has probably been shot across stream, the rope attached to the edge nearer the bank is naturally shorter. This one is tied down as soon as it is landed, while the longer line is hauled very slowly inwards, in such a manner that the farther edge or wing of the seine is made to describe a curve, and until the two wings are in line with the stream and the tow-ropes of equal length again. During this time many of the fish which have been going towards the sea have come in contact with the net and, in their confusion, have been swept round by it; and, before they can escape, it appears to them that they are walled in on every side; the real fact of the case being that the left wing of the seine has now been pulled round to where the middle was at first, and the right wing has cut off the retreat up stream. Well for those that have the sense to see that so far escape is still, in reality, as possible as it was at first, for the net has but changed its position.

But now the chances of freedom have begun to diminish, for the left-hand tow-line being now crossed over the right, the men on the bank begin to pull in two different directions till the half-circle has become a whole one. Above the net there is no escape, for the upper edge is buoyed on the surface with bladders or corks, and now that the edges are together, every step taken by the haulers is lessening the opportunity of flight *viâ* the bottom. At last the seine-weights touch the mud, the salmon are trapped beyond all hope of freedom, and such a crowd of prisoners is there that the combined efforts of the three or four men, who could easily tow it while it was a floating concern, can now scarcely move it an inch further. But two or three stout dray-horses are in waiting; a rope or chain connected with the tow-lines is hitched to them and the net-full drawn up high and dry.

A little higher up the river a very curious form of trap is in use—the fish-wheel, which is shaped and worked just like an ordinary water-mill wheel, and over which the fish are swept into a staked enclosure; but most of the up-river fishing is still in the hands of the remnants of the

Indian tribes. These catch the salmon more for their own consumption than with a view to selling, though some of the younger men make a good living by the sale of their catches in the towns. Some of them use a kind of landing-net, which they dip in front of any fish which may come near enough to the surface.

But the spear is the more scientific and—among the young Indians—the more popular implement. When you get a couple of hundred miles up the Columbia it is full of rapids, and at the foot of any one of these is the happy fishing-ground of the natives. During the upward and the downward migration the redskins, with light spears, some tethered, some free, sit in their birch canoes and watch for the jumping or the dropping of the salmon. The accuracy with which these fellows aim is extraordinary; some will stand and throw harpoons at the curved, glistening bodies as they shoot through the air; others, more deft, will spit them as they rise or fall, never leaving hold of the spear.

The Fraser fisheries are carried on in much the same way as those of the Columbia, but a word or two ought to be said about the Canadian river-mouth fishing, which is done by moored gill-nets. The work connected with it makes the river-bank fishing seem very safe and easy, for it is done in small, two-manned boats, and often in as choppy a sea as the Pacific can boast—which just here, almost within the sweep of the Japan *kuro shiwo* current, can be very ugly when it likes. Here you may see a couple of thousand small boats—for at least that number is employed in the British Columbian fleet—tossing about in Queen Charlotte Sound or Hecate Strait, setting or hauling up nets, the only outward and visible sign of which (while they are down) is a moored buoy. The full nets, on being dragged to the surface, are towed ashore or to larger craft, others being left in their place.

When the fish have been taken to land, whether from sea or river, sorting and cleaning begin. Doubtful or unsound fish are thrown aside with the waste; indeed, so plentiful are the salmon that only the pick of them need be saved; and, when it comes to the boiling, only the prime parts cooked. Those for drying and smoking are taken to a special warehouse for the process, which will last some weeks; the others are boiled, often on the river-bank itself, and are then handed over to Chinamen, by whom practically the whole of the canning is done.

The Scandinavian fisheries, too, are profitable and splendidly managed. An English fisherman once told me that the Norwegian fishers were "the frightenest people" he had ever seen, but the statement is libellous—or, at any rate, untrue; for they are hardy fellows with older sea traditions than our own and, whether working in the sheltered fjörds or in the open sea, accept the dangerous side of their trade as part of the day's labour. Though as business-men they are keen enough, there is a suggestion of romance about work done amid some of the most exquisite scenery in the world, that is somewhat lacking where the ultra-practical salmon-slaughter for dollars of North America is concerned.

Here the river salmon-grounds are largely let to British

sportsmen, so that the business part of the fishing is done mainly in the fjörds and at the river-mouths.

How should a salmon know the difference between a river-mouth and long, narrow openings into the land such as the Sogne and Hardanger fjörds, which, from the open sea, look exactly like estuaries? He doesn't, until he has explored such openings; and this is a work of time, for the Sogne Fjörd is "all arms and legs." Thirty miles down it widens, basin-shaped; a little further on, a river-like opening runs up into the land on either side and, beyond these creeks, are five others, two of them nearly thirty miles long, very narrow, and winding away into the Jotunfeld group, so that there is nothing but salt water to distinguish them from short mountain rivers. And not always that, for little streams of fresh water empty themselves into one or two of these, and are not infrequently used as spawning-grounds.

The narrower and more ramified fjörds, then, are even more effectual salmon-traps than Puget Sound, for by the time the fish that have escaped netting on their entry from the Atlantic have finished their researches, they too have become a prey to the snares and nets laid for them in other parts of the opening.

For mid-fjörd and open-sea fishing the Norwegians employ the same kind of seine as that used in the Columbia River, though a good deal smaller, and worked by a few small boats, which tow the gradually closing net into the shallows for cleaning.

But a seine is a valuable article, not to be dragged haphazard against rocks that, in less than a minute,

Stereo Copyright, Underwood & U. London and New York

SALMON-NETTING IN NORWAY

This huge stand is fixed on the shore of the Sogne, the biggest of the Norwegian fjords.

would tear it to shreds; and both shores of the Sogne Fjörd are girt with such rocks, which at high water are treacherously hidden; so that to sweep the fish ashore as in river work would be impossible. Here, then, some other contrivance is called for, and the Norwegians supply the deficiency by means of a trap peculiar to themselves. A very rough, narrow-gangwayed pier is built out from the beach, generally inclining upwards, so that to walk to the far end of it is like going up a ladder. The gangway ends in a broad platform, and from one of the two sides a net can be lowered. A gill-net—weighted, or tied to the stanchions that support the platform—is sunk from one of the sides, its lower edge reaching to the sand, its upper covered at high water, but visible as soon as the tide has run out. It is weighed up at intervals and cleared from the platform or from the boats below.

While we are in the neighbourhood, we must take a peep at the salmon-fishery as worked by the Lapps and the Finnish peasant fishermen.

The Lapps use spears; also a small and very elementary seine, and do their fishing from tiny, skin-covered canoes. Before the boats go off, the men keep a careful eye round for the sea-swallows, or the "luck-bringers," as they call them; small marine birds that, for some reason or other, elect to follow the outward or inward course of the salmon, and so are infallible guides to the fishermen. Where they fly the boats follow; and so tame are the birds, that many will take scraps of fish from the men's hands.

The Finns go in for trapping; making a form of weir which, at least in the last hundred years, has altered in no particular, for the traveller Acerbi describes just such a contrivance, writing in 1801. Across the mouths of the streams and small rivers they erect a palisade, extending from bank to bank, leaving only a small opening. Between the posts, bushes and branches are thrust down, and so the fish in their inland migration are forced to pass through the single opening. Beyond it is a three-sided net or moored seine, the middle of which is elongated, folded, and made to lie flat. At intervals of a couple of hours the net is lifted out bodily by men standing on either bank, cleared, and put back.

We must now notice such of the British salmon-fishing as does not come within the scope of the next chapter.

A fish at once so valuable and so plentiful would, if left to the tender mercies of the public, have long ago been extinct in these islands. Only legal protection could save it; and from the signing of Magna Charta to the present day, Sovereigns, Parliaments, Committees, and Commissions have been busy drawing up and enforcing regulations for the prevention of ruthless and indiscriminate salmon-taking. Yet in spite of artificial breeding, such as that carried on in the Tay, the salmon fishery has decreased in recent years, partly on account of the fouling of waters by land drainage and factories. Without going into tedious details it is sufficient here to say that the law as it stands has fixed a close time for the fish, has forbidden the use of what are called fixed engines, i.e. permanent salmon-traps, and insists upon the registration of all nets.

The close season, whether for nets or rods, varies slightly in different parts of the country; but for nets it may never be less than 154 days; and no fresh salmon taken from any part of the United Kingdom may be sold between September 3 and February 1, and none exported between September 3 and April 30. Heavy penalties are attached to the taking or selling of salmon, either immediately before or immediately after spawning.

For the further protection of the fish, a weekly close time has been settled of from forty-two to forty-eight hours of each week-end in England, thirty-six in Scotland, and forty-eight in Ireland.

Another legal point worth noting is as to the proprietorship of the fish. In England they are common property as long as they remain in the sea, and while in the rivers they belong to the great landlords; but in Scotland the sea-salmon, found between the shore and a mile beyond low-water mark, belong to the Crown or those who hold from the Crown.

The North Country fishing is done with a kind of seine called a sweep-net, which the men shoot from small boats (cobles). In towing ashore, the net is brought in half-moonshaped instead of circular, and swiftly instead of gradually. These nets are the only ones allowed in estuaries, but others are used for shore-fishing and for English and Scotch deep-water work. The stake-net, as it is called, is found on various spots on the coast south of the Tweed, and comes perilously near being a salmon-trap. Two parallel rows of stakes covered with netting are placed between the high- and low-water marks in such a manner as to serve as a channel up which the fish swim with the current till they are driven, through openings at the end, into a "court" or enclosed net, whence there is no escape.

The catching done in deeper water is by stow-nets or "bags," which are sunk from smacks, and are like those which some of the Scotch fishermen use in the estuaries for mackerel, etc. In shape there is little to distinguish the "bag" from the ordinary trawl-net; it has a beam as described in Chapter III, and is shot in a somewhat peculiar manner. When the boat is ready to drop the net, she is hove-to, and a couple of bridles which are attached to the mouth of the net then have their free ends fastened to the anchor which, on being dropped, helps to sink the net, and eventually moors both net and boat. In this way the mouth of the net is held comfortably open for the fish to swim into; and, as has been already shown, their intelligence is seldom equal to the task of showing them a way out again.

All English and Irish salmon-nets are taxed, the rates ranging from £3 to £20; in Ireland up to £30.

CHAPTER VI

FISHING AS A SPORT

Angling—Salmon-fishing—Tackle—Ireland and Norway—*Piscator fit, non nascitur*—Casting—A real bite—A long spell of hard work—"Sulking"—Gaffing—Fishing in the Jotunfeld—High jumpers—To America for sport—The tarpon—Tarpon-tackle—A nasty sea—A big leap—Towed along—Fairly hooked—Sharks!—Other sport.

ALTHOUGH this book deals chiefly with the fisheries which are important industries, space must be found for a few pages on the subject of fishing as it is undertaken by *amateurs*.

If there is an angling that is the lazy man's sport—an excuse for spending tranquil hours in pleasant scenery—there is also an angling that requires undivided attention, perseverance, skill, endurance, and often physical strength, and those who devote themselves to it may justly rank as higher-grade sportsmen, the equals and often the superiors of the deer-stalkers.

Salmon-fishing comes under the second class; in fact it stands well ahead of all other branches of angling. From the details given in the last chapter it will have been seen that this fish spends the greater part of its time in rivers, and that much of that time is taken up with spawning. The close season for rod-and-line salmon-fishing does not begin till two months after that for netting, though it ends at the same date; ninety-two days is the minimum. As many salmon do not spend more than two or three months out of the twelve in the sea, the angler has about half the year wherein to pursue his sport.

Two typical salmon countries are Ireland and Norway, though their rivers have little in common, for those of Ireland flow through a country that, in comparison with Norway, is flat and even, and they have very little of the mountain-torrent about them. Norway, on the other hand, is a land of strong-current rivers, often marked by waterfalls and cascades, where only the strenuous fisher will dream of angling. Scotland as a salmon country has been discussed in the last chapter; for sport most men prefer it to Ireland.

Salmon tackle varies much, according to the use that is going to be made of it. Are you going to fish from a boat on a lake, or from the bank of a river; or are you prepared to don thigh-boots and be almost washed off your feet by the torrent, and possibly get a box on the ears from a jumping salmon?

The rod used is generally seventeen or eighteen feet long, with ashen butt, the two middle joints of hickory, and the top one of a tough, elastic West Indian wood, commonly known as lance-wood. The line, which, of course, may be of any length, is made of specially prepared oiled silk, or of a mixture of silk and horse-hair; the casting-line—usually about nine feet long—is of twisted gut, and tapers towards the end. One angler will carry fifty yards of line, another a hundred; for boat-fishing

SALMON-FISHING FOR PLEASURE IN A HIGHLAND RIVER

most men will take a couple of hundred. The same with baits; will you have a fly—and, if so, of what sort?—a spinning-bait, a prawn, a minnow, a lob-worm, or a cockle? Many anglers prefer a small, sober-coloured fly; but in the Irish rivers you are almost sure to find a large and gaudy red-cock hackle, ribbed with gold, with wings of drake's, woodcock's, or mallard's feathers, set very wide apart. But there are special considerations that, in the main, determine the question of the sort of fly that it will be best to pin your faith to; the time of year, the depth and degree of clearness of the water, and many other varying circumstances, not forgetting individual preferences; every man who has fished for several years should be the best judge of what suits him personally.

All the Irish rivers are more or less salmon-yielding; so are all the fresh-water loughs that are the source or the outlet of rivers—Neagh, for instance. The Shannon, which is so fertile in salmon as almost to rival some of the North American streams, has rapids below Lough Derg; many of the smaller streams, too, have their "salmon-leaps," enticing enough to the fisherman who cannot get as far as the more exciting Scandinavian grounds. The fishing in both countries is now almost entirely proprietary.

A successful salmon-fisher is made, not born; nor can he become one by reading books on the subject. For the beginner who has grit in him there is always hope. Let him serve his apprenticeship to an old hand and, with a little common observation and a good deal of patient practice, the learner will at last become a fisherman.

True, the talk about having "an angler's eye" is not all cant; but generally the man who is observant over the things of everyday life will be so over his sports; intuitive knowledge alone never yet caught a salmon, though with luck added it might.

The complete salmon-fisher is the man who knows properly where and how to throw his fly, how to control it when it is in the river, how to hook the fish when he comes within reach, and finally how to manage and play him till he is landed or brought within gaffing distance. In throwing the fly, accurate judgment of distance is very necessary, and this again is largely a question of practice. In bank-fishing the angler, holding the rod in both hands, the left some little distance above the winch, the right below it, carries rod and line in an easy, gentle sweep over the left shoulder, till his left arm is raised in a line with his body, and he feels that the line is stretching behind him in the air; then, as though he were going to hit something with his rod, he brings it smartly forward, and this, neatly and properly done, the forward progress of the rod being checked at the right moment, has the effect of dropping the gut-line lightly on the water with the fly as near as may be to the desired position. If he happens to be fishing from the left bank, the positions of the hand and body as just given will be reversed.

For many reasons the salmon-angler will fish against the current; chief among these being, first, that, as already stated, the fish can only lie with their heads pointing up the stream, and therefore cannot see the angler when he is behind them; second, the salmon-fly, being usually large and heavy-winged, would, if carried along by the current, topple over and look unnatural; whereas, properly guided up stream, it deludes the fish into the belief that it is some gaudy creature swimming spasmodically against the tide. Therefore, the moment the fly touches the water it is pulled round without delay into the line of the current.

Next, the fly must be made to show itself to its best advantage and in all its glory. The rod is gently raised, and the fly, rising with it, has its possibly ruffled plumes smoothed down to its sides by the pressure of the water above it; then, lowering the rod again just as carefully, the angler sinks his fly once more; and this time the water resistance being under it, the fibres of the wings are spread open in a natural manner, displaying the brilliant colouring of the fly, which is now in a condition to beguile the first salmon that comes within sight of it.

Henceforward the conscientious angler has no thought to bestow on temperature or scenery or hunger or fatigue; eye and thought are both riveted on the graceful silvery creature that is following the fly. He has heard—as who has not?—of the lucky fisherman who once took, with small trout tackle, a salmon in the Shannon that weighed over forty-five pounds, and that required five hours' playing before it was exhausted. There are salmon weighing over fifty pounds in this river and, by the help of the gods, he means to catch one of them.

Talking of weight, it must be borne in mind that the age of the salmon is no guarantee for its size. There are some Irish rivers in which ten pounds is a good weight for the adult fish; there are others, the Shannon, the Suir, and the Blackwater, for example, where even grilse attain that size. The weight of the fish depends mainly on the length of time that he is content to remain in the sea, and on the sort of food in which he indulges while there. Undoubtedly he has spells of greediness come over him from time to time, but he does not always choose the most "frame-forming" food. The stomachs of those taken from the sea are often found to contain eels and other fish, though those of fresh-water salmon rarely show anything but digested food, which seems to point to the fact that, while in the rivers, they eat more sparingly and at more lengthy intervals.

Now let us suppose that a salmon has taken the bait, for, if bent on it, he will assuredly have it sooner or later. Unlike most river fish, he will rise over and over again to the same fly, seldom leaving it till he has taken it; but, if he should happen to be only partially hooked, the angler may as well say good-bye to him, as he will scarcely be likely to venture near the bait a second time. As soon as he is fairly hooked, the difference between the experienced hand and the learner shows itself very markedly; the former keeps cool and watches his opportunities, the latter will probably lose his head; though this unfortunate condition is not confined to the beginner, for some tried and mighty fishers will confess to experiencing a sudden fit of "nerves" whenever they hook a fish of any size.

As soon as the fish has taken the fly the angler's first

care is to see that he is properly hooked, and then to tire him out. The fisher gives him a minute in which to swallow the fly comfortably; and then, with a subtle twitch, he fixes the hook firmly. What will follow is problematical. The fish, at the first touch of pain, may double himself up and spring into the air, kicking and plunging, to get rid of his tormentor; he may rush about backwards and forwards as if possessed, not knowing which way to turn; again he may, and probably will, dash up or down the stream for all he is worth; in any case, "give him plenty of line," say the authoritative anglers. Whatever course his unfortunate victim may choose to follow, the sportsman has now a good hour's hard work before him if the catch is of any size; perhaps three or four hours.

His excitement must be tempered by watchfulness and judgment and dogged perseverance. The fish is darting up or down the river at lightning speed, and the sportsman, utterly unable to control it, is meekly following. Suddenly, perhaps, it turns and courses at a similar pace in the opposite direction, thinking nothing about the costly tackle which it is jeopardizing, except to rid itself of it. At last it pulls up short; it has found a projecting bank on the other side of the stream. Here it can "sulk" at its leisure; and it does, perhaps for an hour, till the exasperated fisher begins to long for a stout hempen cord with which to haul it in, hand-over-hand like a cod-fish. Tugs and jerks will not move it; the only sign of life that it gives is an occasional start, and an unqualified and persistent refusal to be "wound up."

The angler begins to speculate; he may have hooked the traditional anvil or ploughshare (every Irish guide knows a man who once landed something of the sort); what is far more reasonable to suppose is that he has hooked a powerful and wily salmon which, unless closely looked after, may lie still till it has chafed the gut-line through against the stones. Desperate at the bare thought of losing a possible forty-five pounder, he nerves himself once more to the effort and, this time, the fish allows itself to be dislodged and drawn into mid-stream; then, with new life, endeavours to spurt off up the river again. But, taking in the line, a little now and a little then, "putting the strain on" whenever possible, the angler at last brings the monster within reach of the gaff —if he does not actually land the catch, as his sportsman's *amour propre* bids him at least try to do.

Even over the gaffing there will often be a keen struggle, for the fish has a trick of being just an inch or two beyond the reach of the hook, and the hapless keeper or other person to whom falls the duty of manipulating it, discovers that he can only do so by throwing one half of his body over the stream at the risk of finding the other half over-balanced by it. When he has at last succeeded in getting the gaff under the fish, he strikes swiftly up, fixing the hook behind one of the breast fins, or, if possible, under the gills; and then, by means of his feet, wriggles back and back till he and his struggling prey roll over one another to a safe part of the bank, as likely as not entangling themselves in the angler's line in so doing.

FISHING AS A SPORT

Hitherto we have only considered the fortunes of the man who fly-fishes a river from the bank. Many sportsmen would consider this tame work, preferring the excitement of wading waist-deep up a mountain stream in Norway that has no tow-path; in the rocky beds of the Jotunfield streams or lakes, for instance, where the water is walled in by sharp crags, and cut off from the rest of the world by snowy mountain-peaks. Such beds suit salmon that are of a sulky turn of mind; for they can lie between a couple of large stones, or in an unsuspected hollow that leads abruptly out of the shallows, and meditate to their hearts' content. Nowhere, in fact, if they can help it, will these fish stop to rest on a smooth, shallow bottom, any more than they will remain in long, straggling streams that begin and end nowhere, as one may say; a short, rapid, broken-bedded stream leading to a lake, or not far from the sea, is an ideal ground for them.

In fishing among the rocks and sunken tree-roots, many anglers consider a mussel, cockle, or prawn a very killing bait. An unweighted line is cast into the meeting point of two currents formed by rocks that stand opposite each other, or into the shallows near a hole, and is allowed to be carried by the force of the water among the stones or over where the salmon lies in hiding. In all probability the fish will not be able to resist the temptation long, for the angler is offering it the kind of food on which it was wont to fatten while in the sea. All in a moment the line is jerked furiously and the salmon springs with all its force out of the water, drops again, and dives back among the hollows or stones. At such a time it behoves the sportsman to be very wide awake if he is not to lose the catch; he must sneak every half-inch of line he can, and so proportionately reduce the chances of the salmon's tumbling across the slack of it in its fall; for such an accident seldom fails to jerk the prisoner free again; in any case, if it jumps up repeatedly, it is pretty safe sooner or later to free itself.

But with all its changes and chances, and in spite of cold unspeakable and wettings that suggest rheumatic fever, the sportsman to whom the choice is open—Norway or Britain—will not hesitate to decide in favour of the former.

Salmon-fishing is a sport full of excitement, but many people say there is another more exciting still. Since facilities for quick travel have increased, sportsmen have been diligently seizing the opportunity of fishing or hunting for game whose *habitat* is so far removed from their own homes that at one time the pursuit of it by Englishmen was only dreamt of when they happened to be "on their travels." A few generations back, to go fishing in Norway or Russia was looked upon as pushing sport to the limits of wicked waste of time, on account of the distance; and a person who talked of going even to America for shooting, would have been regarded as a maniac. But all that is changed, and now the man who can afford the requisite time and money is allowed to plan a fishing-trip to the Gulf of Mexico and round about Florida Strait without having his sanity called in question by his friends. To run over to America to fish for the flying or jumping monsters that in past ages fell to the harpoons of races that the world no longer knows, has become as popular an amusement as an Indian tiger-shooting holiday was to our fathers.

Among these American wonders the best known to twentieth-century folk is the tarpon, a salt-water fish at one time erroneously called the Jew-fish. (The Jew, it should be stated, is a creature much longer than the tarpon, and often three or four times as heavy.) He is a magnificent blue and silver monster, a close relative of the herring; is from five to seven feet long, and may weigh anything from one to two hundred pounds. The body is covered with scales, some of them three and four inches wide; the back fin is very high, with a filament behind, the eyes and mouth very large, the latter oblique. As food the flesh is of doubtful value.

Like the salmon, it has the power of springing out of the water at will, though its method of doing so differs. In fact, it is often included among the flying-fish; fish, that is, that on account of the extraordinary length of their breast-fins, are able to leap from the water and make some show of supporting themselves in mid-air for a brief period. If the tarpon does not strictly come under this zoological species, it at least spends its days in the company of fish that do; for though its home is well above the Tropic of Cancer, the reader will, no doubt, remember that the Gulf Stream, which leaves the Gulf of Mexico *viâ* the Strait of Florida, gives almost a tropical character to that part of the Atlantic and its inmates; for the temperature of the water at the surface is 81° F.

FISHING AS A SPORT

To talk of catching a hundredweight fish with rod and line sounds rather absurd, till we come to look closely into the sport. The tackle required is a stout eight-foot rod, a line made of linen, from one to two hundred yards long, and a hook baited with a bit of fish. Obviously there is no scope here for the angler who wants to loaf at his work. The fishing is done from light rowing-boats, generally at low water, and, by the more earnest sportsman, at night, for then the tarpon more readily seizes the bait.

The season is a short one, lasting but two months (April and May). Perhaps there is no reason why it should not begin a little earlier, but after May, apart from such minor inconveniences as mosquitoes, sharks, and excessive heat, tropical cyclones are liable to come and trouble the waters, sending heavy storm-tides ashore and making things uncomfortable even for large ships. At the best of times it is unwise to venture far in a boat without a guide who knows the current, as well as the lie of the fish. Some men risk going out alone, anchor their boat and wait for a possible bite, taking their chance of what may happen when the fish begins to kick, if indeed they ever hook one.

Experienced tarpon-anglers maintain that there is little to learn in the sport; that the man (by the way, many ladies go tarpon-fishing nowadays) who has nerve and muscle and some notion of managing his winch, possesses all the stock-in-trade required. And sure it looks easy enough; all you have to do is to sit on a thwart, or in a chair, with the butt of your rod supported by a holder slung from your belt. At least that is the first part of the programme; in the second you may get a bite. When this occurs the tarpon does not leave you in doubt for long; for, as often as not, as soon as he is hooked you hear a splash and a rustle, and the giant springs up into the air to a height of eight if not ten feet, shaking and clattering its gills as though with fury, jerking with all the force of its hundred or hundred and fifty pounds to rid itself of the hook; then, before you are quite clear as to what will be your—and his—next move, falling back on the water with noise enough to deafen one. Did you ever see, and hear, a very fat swimmer who had not the faintest notion of diving, throw himself from a high diving-board? The tarpon's drop is just such an ear-splitting crash, and woe to the oar whereon it shall fall, or the boat either, for that matter; for if an eleven-stone man falls into a light boat from a height of ten feet, the odds are in favour of a breakage or a swamp; and an eleven-stone tarpon, though not exactly "a like cause," will probably produce a like result.

Night-time may be better for the sport, but the person who wants to get a good insight into it, and who has never seen the marvels of that quasi-tropical sea, will go by day, taking with him a guide who knows what to do with a pair of sculls, and who will keep his "fare" as far from other boats as is convenient. To have your own fish, or one that is jumping for refuge from submarine enemies, drop on to your head is quite bad enough; you do not want to be troubled with other people's. Perhaps your first cast is a lucky one; you are in deep water with a tide that is beginning to run in smoothly and gently;

and the sudden, rapid rush of the line over the multiplier (a winch whose inner cylinder revolves three or four times to one turn of the handle) tells you that you have made a strike, even if the fish fails to jump. Let him have line—a hundred yards if he wants it; and let him tow you as far as he feels inclined.

Suddenly he makes a leap, and you had better obey to the letter the guide's injunction to "hold on"; for, when the fish kicks, there is reasonable probability of the rod's being unceremoniously jerked out of your hands. You have no time to notice other smaller flying fish that whizz past your ears; someone in the next boat has just fired a gun, and you do not even speculate as to whether you were the target or no, for you are carried away by excitement and a ten-stone fish. The tarpon drops again, but springs up once more almost before he is down, tugging more desperately than ever.

This time, however, he does not come up unaccompanied. What are those things bobbing about where he has just left the surface? Shark-snouts; three of them! You have no longer any need to wonder at that gun-shot, and at present you have not time; you cannot even stop to weigh your own chances of finding yourself in the midst of those vicious-looking muzzles; for, with a final, fruitless jerk, the tarpon signifies his acceptance of the inevitable; drops, reduces his speed, and allows himself to be drawn alongside for gaffing—for only an experienced fisher will try to run his catch ashore.

Then, when the excitement is all over and you have leisure to think of what might have happened, you decide not to put off your sport another year till the end of the season, when the sharks are coming close in to shore.

Other exciting sport in this neighbourhood is afforded to anglers by Jew-fish, king-fish, gar-fish, and other strange creatures that leap or fly; and, to harpooners, by the devil-fish, or whip-ray.

CHAPTER VII

THE COD-FISHERY (I)

The Breton "Icelanders"—Seeing the fleet off—A twelve-hundred mile voyage in a cockle-shell—Life on board—Iceland in sight—Cod-fishing—An average catch—A big catch in a calm—Cleaning and salting—Breaks in the monotony—Homeward bound.

ONE may expect to see the cod in almost any part of the ocean; it is always putting in an appearance; we find it in the trawl, in the shrimp-net, even in the oyster-dredge. Perhaps there is no more popular table fish, for it is wholesome, digestible, satisfying, and usually reasonable in price. So popular is it (even apart from its value as an oil-producer), that few southern countries can keep their markets supplied without going further afield than their own waters. Our Scotch and East Coast cod-fisheries are by no means inconsiderable; yet our annual importation of cod is something enormous.

The bulk of the world's supply comes from (*a*) the Iceland Banks, (*b*) the Newfoundland Banks; and it is with these grounds that we shall specially concern ourselves in this and the next chapter.

How is it, we may well ask, that, after so many centuries of fishing, the cod has not become a rarity for

for which epicures would be prepared to pay fabulous prices? For a thousand years the industry has been pursued pretty regularly off Iceland; for four hundred off the American Banks; yet, at the present day, the supply is most likely larger than it has ever been; the fishery giving employment to 150,000 vessels and 700,000 men.

The reason is that the cod reproduces its species at a rate that is out of all proportion to that of most other fish. If the reader will bear in mind that one roe contains at the very least somewhere about six million eggs, he will see that there is nothing particularly outrageous in the boast made by an old French fisherman of having caught five hundred cod with hook and line in one day of ten hours.

The fishery off the Iceland coast is carried on by a few Danish, Norwegian, and British crews, but mainly by French, the season lasting all the summer long. The majority of the French boats taking part in the trade are from Brittany—broad-beamed, substantial-looking yawls, manned by the strongest and sturdiest fellows to be found in the country. Brittany, indeed, has its special hereditary Iceland fleet; men whose fathers, grandfathers, and great grandfathers have, like themselves, worked on the Banks year by year from February to August or September, and who, from boyhood to old age, have never enjoyed a southern summer.

For Brittany is a district of granite and moorland, where agricultural labour is at a discount; and from time immemorial the inhabitants have been obliged to expect their harvest from the sea rather than from the land; and inasmuch as the proceeds of the sardine and herring fishery are insufficient to meet the needs of the population, it is not unnatural that the bolder fishermen—men into whose very blood the sea seems to have worked its way—should be willing to risk their lives in one of the most paying branches of their trade, even though it is carried on twelve hundred miles away from home, and even though that particular kind of fishing is attended with greater danger than any other.

Twelve hundred miles of the Atlantic! And in a craft that, by the side of a steamer (which itself requires ten or twelve days for the passage), looks like a toy boat! Yet the light-hearted Bretons appear to see little to fear in the venture. In some cases they are buoyed up with their piety, and their trust in the Higher Powers; in others, they feel secure in their belief in some little pet superstition of their own. Doubtless there is a good deal of fiction about the "dangers of the deep." Perhaps most of us have a very exaggerated idea as to the number of seamen who are drowned in the course of a year; nor is it to be denied that many of the deaths which do occur can be traced to carelessness or foolhardiness on the part of someone or other. At the same time, there is unquestionably a large loss of life every season, and no fishermen contribute more to the sad list than the cod crews.

Before the Breton fleet starts, the crews make every effort to invoke the protection of Heaven. If a boat is going out for the first time it must be solemnly consecrated by the parish priest. The smack, decorated and covered with sail-cloth or a tarpaulin, is blessed and sprinkled with holy water in the presence of the *armateur*, i.e. the owner, or the man at whose expense she is fitted out—and of the crew; then follows the ornamenting of the cabin with religious and other pictures, a crucifix, or an image of *La Sainte Vierge*, and—alack!—paper flowers. This little function is followed by a meal of bread and jam, cake, and wine; and, later, by what Englishmen would call a sing-song.

The final preparations for departure in February or March are picturesque in the extreme, and, by contrast, the start of an English fleet seems prosaic and unromantic. The stores, the barrels of salt, the lines, and the handkerchief-wardrobes have all been taken aboard; the boats are gay with flags; the tugs are lying off the quay, waiting to tow them out to sea, two, three, or four at a time; and the men are now only waiting to receive the Church's benediction, and to bid farewell to the relatives, friends, and sweethearts who have flocked down to the harbour. From a little temporary altar set up on the quay, the priest, preceded by *enfants de chœur* bearing lighted candles, incense, and holy water, carries the Sacred Host round the harbour; the fleet is solemnly blessed, good-byes are said, and the boats are soon off on their long voyage.

With fair weather, the "Icelanders" have two periods of comparative leisure to look forward to; the journey out and the journey home. The crew consists of seven or eight hands, and an Iceland yawl can be managed moderately comfortably by three men and a "mousse," or cabin-boy; therefore the fishermen can take "turn and turn about." The spare time is filled up with gossip, draughts, dominoes, or cards; with sorting and inspecting the fishing-lines, or washing and mending of clothes. Laundry-work aboard is a very simple matter. Stockings and shirts are rubbed and wrung in a bucket of water and hung on the boom to dry; *blouses* or "jumpers"—the short, coarse linen dress worn over the jersey—are spread out on deck, liberally soused with pails of water, and scrubbed with the deck-brush.

The days pass quite quickly enough, each seeming colder than the one before as the vessel gets further north. England, Ireland, and Scotland have been left behind long ago; the Faroe Islands are passed without even being sighted; the boat has come within the region of the "midnight sun." Often rain, fog, or snow envelops each smack, perhaps cutting it off from sight of its nearest neighbours. The men have packed away their woollen or skin caps and donned their sou'-westers—head-gear picturesque enough to the artist and the landsman, but abhorred of all sailors, for that the heat of them makes a man bald before his time. The Bretons have given up expecting calm weather for the next month or two; at 60.0 N., 20.0 W., they know little about smooth seas; the boats are nearing the Iceland and Greenland Banks. Away to the east a few Norwegian whalers are pitching and heeling; now and again, from behind or in front, sounds the hoot of a steamer, bound from Copenhagen, Leith, and the Faroes for Reikjavik;

sometimes a hollow, uncanny shout comes across the water from a neighbouring smack: "Who are you? Is that the *Rose?* How do you like *this*, *mon vieux?*"

Suddenly, perhaps, the mist clears, and the rocky, cheerless coast of Iceland comes in sight. Bearing north-west, the boats make for where the sea seems smoother, yet is bubbling and boiling and seething with white foam. Now the lower western point of the island is on their right; if the air were a little clearer the outline of the nearest of the hospitable fjörds, whither the fishers must retire in exceptionally dangerous weather, would be visible; as it is, all that can be seen is the lava plain south of Reikjavik. Further still to westward, the little corner peninsula is almost out of sight again; the Banks are reached at last—the home, for the next five months, of the cod-crews.

There is bustle enough on board now: sail to be taken in, salt-tubs to be dragged out of the hold, knives to be sharpened, hooks and lines to pass final examination. To-morrow fishing will begin.

At first the catches seem poor; either the season has not really begun, or the men are out of gear and have not got back to the old working groove yet. Codding is not work for weaklings. On the Iceland Banks the muscular labour is even greater than on the Grand Banks, where the fishing is mainly done from small boats; here the line must be hauled up every time on to the deck of the smack. A cod sometimes measures three feet from tip to tail; it weighs from half to three-quarters of a hundredweight —often nearly a hundred pounds. Think what it means to haul up two or three hundred of such burdens a day; or, at busy times, to work for fifteen hours with only a short break for dinner, pulling up, on an average, one fish every three minutes! Unless unusually stormy weather forces the boats to seek shelter for a time in the natural harbours of the Breidifjörd or the Faxafjörd, you may say that the fishing never stops as long as the season lasts, except when in fairly slack times, the crew meet over the cabin fire for an hour's chat and smoke before one half "turns in" and the other half starts on the night work.

While the catches do not rise much above the average, a couple of men can be spared to do the cleaning and salting as the fish are drawn up. Watch the fishers at their work. The main-sail has been pulled round to leeward, and on the opposite side of the deck are four line-men and two cleaners, the former standing about ten feet apart in order to avoid fouling, i.e. getting one line entangled with another; the latter squatting on the deck, waiting for the others to give them something to do. That "something" will soon come. The long, plummeted lines, scarcely the thickness of a blind-cord, slip merrily through the men's fingers; at last one slackens—it has touched bottom—then a second. A third does not reach the bottom at all; a hungry cod, swimming downwards from a little below mid-water, has spied the bait—probably a bit of cuttle-fish—and, the next moment, the fisherman shouts proudly: "Good; I've got the first fish!"

"You think so?" asks a stronger, older man, as he feels

the little vibratory "nubbling" that experience has taught him is a bite. With a loud laugh, he begins to haul in like fury, hand over hand, the sodden line falling in snaky, oval coils between his sea-booted legs. The cleaners lean over the side, laughing, too, at the friendly rivalry between the fishers, and watching with a sort of gambler's interest to see whose fish will come up first.

Plomb! Splash! The stronger man has won after all, though he had to pull from the bottom. Up comes a cod as big round as his thigh, "kicking" and struggling and wriggling as it falls on the deck; and before the hook is disgorged another, equally big, lies by its side; and in less than a minute a couple more are jerked out of the water and left near them. Down go all four lines again, but the cleaners calmly go on finishing their pipes; they want to see something of a heap before they begin; hard work will come quite soon enough without going to meet it. The minutes drag on; the four fish have became eight, and the eight sixteen. Some are lying motionless, others are gasping and flapping their tails as if in feeble protest; poor creatures, their flapping days are nearly over.

The cleaners have to bestir themselves now. Near them is a barrel of salt, the head of which has been knocked in; each scoops from it sufficient to make a good heap which he deposits at his side, and the task of salting begins. Every fish is carefully ripped up, gutted, and well coated inside and out with salt; then laid out flat, and stacked one above another in an ever increasing heap. Presently one of the crew will come along with cases, into which the piles of fish are carefully packed with yet more salt, and all will be safely stowed within the hold.

By mid-season the fish have increased in size and seemingly in number. Naturally no two weeks' catches are alike. In most fishing fleets, no matter of what sort, you will nearly always find one skipper who is more knowing, or has the *reputation* for being more knowing, than his fellows. "Show me where old So-and-so fishes," says one of the crew, "and I'll tell you where to get a good haul." Wherever he goes, others will try to follow. Some of the more independent, however, are content to roam over the otherwise neglected ground—and as often as not it is *they* who get the haul, and not the knowing ones or their followers. We know, of course, there are old stagers so shrewd and so observant that they know, almost literally, every square yard of the ground; and such men will catch a boat-load while others get nothing. But cod are not like oysters or sponges; they want to move about, and at times move very swifty; so that the boat that toils in vain for several hours may at any moment have a shoal of fish under her, so eager for prey that they could almost be caught with the naked hook.

Once in a way, as summer advances, the sea round the Banks condescends to lie still for a space. The wind drops; there is a dead calm; the sunlit water looks as if it could not be rough if it tried, and grows so clear that you can almost see to the bottom. One of the men pauses in his fishing to jerk a remark over his shoulder to the skipper, who has deserted his useless helm. The "patron" looks over the bulwarks, turns away again rubbing his hands, and shouts to the two or three lads or men who are resting: "Now then, come on! No skulking; it's harvest-time!" The tired fellows know what is meant, and every-one pulls himself together with a good will. Ejaculations of joy or surprise escape them as they look over the gunwale and mechanically uncoil the lines, or bait the hooks. For down below are thousands, nay millions, of full-sized cods, with steely backs and silver bellies, dashing up and down in line, or lying motionless and looking upwards as if they had come to be fed.

There is no talk of cleaning or salting now; that must all be done afterwards. Every man throws in his line, knowing that long before the hook reaches the bottom he will feel the sudden little shock that announces a capture; and this must go on hour after hour, perhaps all through the night, in spite of stiffening muscles and aching backs. At last the shoal thins down; half the crew falls out and, by way of rest, sets to work on the gigantic mound of fish; obliged first to kneel, then stand, then stoop, in order to keep themselves awake;

> "Achin' for an hour's sleep, dozin' off between,"

as Mr. Kipling hath it. Already the day is dawning, not as we understand dawn in England, for it has not been really dark all night; but the ghostly yellow light is growing of a whiter shade. Presently the sky will redden, the dun-coloured clouds will part, and it will be morning.

Meanwhile the wind has got up; the halliards rattle petulantly and there is a mournful creaking and sighing in the shrouds. A summer storm is coming on; maybe only a squall; maybe one of those terrible tempests that, before the fleet can run towards Reikjavik, will have put an end to more than one of the plucky little Breton yawls. But, be it squall or tempest, it will interfere with the fishing for the time being, so it is no wonder that the men have been anxious to profit by the recent calm.

There is another aspect, too, of that calm and the ensuing storm. They are *incidents*—events coming in relief of what would be, to most people, a dismal sameness. Even a fisherman is human and likes a change at times as well as his neighbours; and a lull, or a storm, or a fog, or an extra large or small catch are the only changes the "Islandais" can look for, except the periodical visit of a Danish or French steamboat, which brings him his letters and his newspapers, his medicines, tobacco, and fresh water.

A few more brief calms, another fog or two—happily the fog does not interfere much with the fishing—and the men begin to count the days, then the hours, that must elapse before they start for home. The boats that have had the luckiest season are the first to go; some, less fortunate, stay as long as the late August and September squalls will allow them. Often there is a sort of understood race for home; for the boats that are the first in will get the best market for their fish. Most of them will probably sail straight away for Bordeaux and the neighbourhood, where prices may be better than in the large northern towns, buy their salt for the coming season and then turn homewards, each member of the crew with perhaps a thousand francs (£40) in his pocket, his share of the sale of the fish. Similar ceremonies to those which attended his going out are being prepared for him at home; and for some weeks after the first crew has landed, his little native town will be *en fête*. Then for a few months he will settle down to the more peaceful coast-fishing, and by February will be quite ready to set out again on just such a voyage as the last.

CHAPTER VIII

THE COD-FISHERY (II)

The American cod-fishery—The Newfoundland Banks—Dory work—Hand-line fishing—Drawbacks to it—French trawling—No piracy allowed—Pulling up the trawl—Clearing and rebaiting—Cleaning and drying—The gill-net—Its special utility—Its mechanism.

NOW as to the American cod-fishery, an industry far more important and extensive than that discussed in the last chapter, and pursued on the largest cod-grounds in the world—the Grand Banks of Newfoundland. These, forming one immense submarine table-land, lie more than fifty miles to the south of Cape Race, more than three hundred to the east of Cape Breton Island, and are covered with water that varies in depth from ten to a hundred and fifty fathoms.

Sealing, the industry only second in importance to codding in Newfoundland, finishes about the middle of April, and within six weeks of that time the ground is crowded with cod-crews, drawn from almost all nations under heaven. Naturally the first to arrive are our own hardy colonials from various parts of Canada, with a sprinkling of Frenchmen from Miquelon and St. Pierre, —two little islands belonging to France, which lie a few miles north-west of the Banks. Before June is far advanced, these have been joined by large fleets from the United States and even from France and Holland, and for the next five months these men, drawn from everywhere, will fish together more or less amicably, for the Banks are a sort of "No-man's land," beyond the jurisdiction of either Great Britain or the States.

In the height of the season there will be something like seventy-five thousand vessels on the grounds—not including steam-tugs, carriers, and the like—of from 50 to 200 tons burthen; many of them schooners (two-masters, with square fore-topsail and fore-top-gallant), but the majority of them cutters and yawls. Each of these vessels carries half a dozen or more small boats—dories, as they are termed—from which most of the fishing will be done. And therein lies the danger of the work; for the dories are often obliged to travel a great distance from their ship, and are only too easily swamped through carelessness in overloading, or lost in the darkness or the fog.

The most popular quarters of the district are Flemish Cap, Brown's Bank, and St. George's Bank—the last-named, situated in the far south-east corner of the ground, producing the finest cod-fish in the world.

Until lately two methods of catching were in vogue; by hand-lines and by the French trawl. For a great number of years the second system struggled hard with the first and older plan, and, as will be seen from the last chapter, many French crews still prefer the hand-line. By the time French trawling had gained the sway among British and American fishermen, a third contrivance—the gill-net—had arisen; and a few of its advocates maintain that in course of time it will completely supersede line-fishing, except where inshore work is concerned; a statement which affords great amusement to the older fishermen, for they know better.

As has been already said, the Banks hand-line fishery differs mainly from that carried on by the "Islandais" in that it does not usually take place from the deck of the smack. Each member of the crew has his own cock-boat or dory and, having sculled himself out some distance, with his tackle and his bait-store, throws in his line. From a sportsman's point of view, what could be finer? The little boat is being tossed in any and every direction; often the fish come up as fast as ever the angler can haul them in; often, again, there is the increased excitement of irregular bites, when our man will catch two fish in three minutes, and then has to wait three hours before he gets another bite; then succeeds again, by fits and starts, pulling up sometimes one per minute, sometimes one per hour. Further excitement comes at the moment of "landing" the fish. True, a cod is not a tarpon, to jump upon you unawares or pull you out of your boat or tow you along, the moment he is hooked; but he is a heavy, muscular beast, all the same, and in a boat that was never intended to hold more than two men, you can't "wrastle" with a thing that is in a very great hurry to get away, and that turns the scale at three-quarters of a hundredweight, without meeting with an occasional upset.

But there is a less sporting view of the matter to be

considered. A storm rises suddenly just when the boat is well-nigh full of fish—representing the whole of a man's day's work. A slight slip, or stumble, or roll on the part of the fisherman—just the least little bit of awkwardness that, in a somewhat larger craft, would pass unnoticed—and the hapless dory capsizes, no matter how carefully the fish have been stowed. At least there is a day's pay thrown away and—God help the poor boatman if, encumbered as he is by oilskins and thigh-boots, he is not man enough to reach and right his boat again!

Or there is that awful fog for which the Banks are celebrated, caused, so the geographers tell us, by the meeting of the warm water of the Gulf Stream with the current which is called the Cold Wall, and is really a stream of melted Arctic ice brought down by the Labrador current. The unfortunate dory-man is not only cut off from sight of everything, but, if he has finished his fishing, will soon be chilled to the bone through inaction; for he can do nothing but sit still, listening anxiously to the sirens and hooters of larger craft that may be in the vicinity, and wait, either till the fog lifts or till he is run down by a passing steamer—unless he has the luck to drift towards some friendly smack that will take him aboard.

Yet, despite such drawbacks as these, it is easy to see why hand-line codding dies hard; take the year through, an individual fisherman can earn more money at it than by the other means mentioned, though owners and master-men may gain less; for the dory-man, being alone in his boat, has not to share the proceeds of his catch with a companion.

French trawling, on the other hand, requires a crew of two; one to attend to the tackle, the other to scull and "make himself generally useful." In many respects it is only a development of the old Scotch and French long-line fishing. From each smack about half a dozen dories go off in the morning; arrived at the part where the trawls are set, the men can see a number of small tarred kegs floating, that look like the ordinary buoys to which boats are moored, but for the fact that each of them carries a tiny flag which is of some distinctive colour, or else has a name or number painted on it. With the same keenness of perception that enables them to recognise their own vessel among the thousands that drift or lie at anchor on the Banks, the boatmen quickly pick out certain buoys which they know to be theirs.

And here let me say that, among the fishermen of civilised countries, there is surprisingly little piracy; i.e. interference with, or robbery of, other men's tackle. Of course if a Frenchman or a Yankee "goes and puts" his lobster-pots on a Canadian ground he must take his chance of the trouble that ensues. But, generally speaking, the fisherman, when not restrained by honesty or fear (and, on the Grand Banks, to pull up someone else's gear is to get a knife into your ribs sooner or later) is held back from this deadly sin by his superstition that if he steals another man's catch or tackle "it will come home to him."

To return to our dories—a very close observer might

notice that the buoys go in pairs, in some cases each two being joined by a thin line, and the distance between the two being anything from a hundred and fifty yards to a quarter of a mile. On reaching these the dories separate, one boat—or perhaps two—rowing towards either end of the connecting line; the others lying between, and waiting to bear a hand as soon as they are wanted. One of the men responsible for the tackle now leans over the gunwale, seizes the buoy by its iron ring and drags it aboard. It may now be seen that, from each of the kegs—another line—the "buoy-line"—runs downwards, and on this the men at either end begin to haul for all they are worth, as though they were weighing up an anchor. In point of fact, that is just what they are doing; for presently the intermediate men make a grab at something under water with hands outstretched and, everyone pulling together, up comes a line equal in length to the connecting cord, with a little anchor fastened to each end of it. From this line, branching in all directions, are others only a few feet long, each bearing a hook—from two to three hundred of them in all; and more than half of these have caught a cod. This is what is meant by French trawling.

Very speedily the dorymen release the fish, packing them neatly away in their boats. Sometimes there will be more than they can find room for, and these must either be left on the hooks or thrown back into the sea. Another method of clearing the tackle is, as in the seine-netting, to tow the whole catch back to the vessel. The coast fishermen of Miquelon and St. Pierre now use no other system than the French trawl, going out daily from the shore to tow the laden tackle home and to set fresh lines. Many of the Canadian mainland fishers do the same; and their inshore catches are so large (although the cod are comparatively poor) that they manage to keep the whole of the West Indian market supplied.

As soon as the hooks are cleared, the lines have to be rebaited and sunk again. The favourite bait on the Newfoundland ground is what the Frenchmen call a *capelin*—a kind of haddock or pigmy cod. As river anglers are well aware, fixing "live-bait" is not a task to be approached lightly or carelessly; yet the speed with which the cod-men bait hook after hook is simply incredible. When the task is finished the main line of the trawl has a most weird appearance; fancy a cord, nearly a quarter of a mile in length, from which, at intervals of about five feet, hang short ends of line, each terminating in a fish rather smaller than a herring.

With very great care the trawl is sunk again, the weight of the two little anchors being sufficient to carry it to the bottom; the buoy-lines are made fast to the kegs again. If we were able to see through the water to the bottom, we could now make out an immense four-sided linear figure, perpendicular to the plane of the sea; everything has been made ready once more for a new catch. If the boats are very heavily burdened they will now row back to their schooner or yawl to be hauled up and emptied before proceeding to clear the next trawl. The lines just set will be left for at least twelve hours, sometimes even twenty-four, before they are pulled up again.

The cleaning and salting processes are the same, no matter what means of catching may be in use. As soon as the evening meal on the smack is finished—a meal usually consisting of fish-pie or "tinned rations" with tea, coffee, or cider—boards are laid out on trestles below decks, thus forming a long table, and all hands take a share at the splitting and cleaning of the day's catch. Boats coming from a long distance will stow their fish away as we have seen the Iceland Bretons do. Those that have put off from Newfoundland, however, will either run into shore periodically with their cargo or else hand it over to carriers; for the Newfoundlanders have not only to salt, but also to dry their fish. The drying is a laborious though very simple process, consisting in laying the opened cod on sloping wooden stages in the sun. If figures and statistics were not rather tedious, the reader might be interested to know that Newfoundland alone exports five and a half million dollars' worth of dried cod every year, in addition to cod-oil to the value of about half a million dollars.

Now for the gill-net. I have left it till last because it cannot be considered as a feature of the June to November season. Generally speaking, it does not come into use till about a month after the line-fishing for the year has finished. The cod, though one of the easiest fish to be taken with hook and line, is not readily caught by a net, except at spawning time when it is more unobservant and heedless of its surroundings. It has a rooted objection to a net, and a countless shoal swimming at top speed would wheel like lightning on coming within a few feet of one.

THE COD-FISHERY

For more than a hundred years the Canadian fishermen have firmly believed that, during the breeding season, the cod are short-sighted. They maintain that when the fish go down and bury themselves in the mud at spawning, Providence supplies them with a special film-like growth which covers the eyes, thus protecting them from particles of grit and sand that would otherwise blind them; and this membrane, they say, does not disappear till about the end of March. Now, as from November, when line-fishing ends, till the middle of March, when sealing begins, was a slack and often moneyless time for the fishers, some of them began to think how it could be turned to account; how fish, which would not be persuaded to leave the bottom where they had a plentiful supply of cockles and shrimps for food, might still be ensnared against their will. The gill-net is the result.

A stranger, sailing over the ground in winter, would assume that French trawling was going on as usual, for the flag-bearing buoys are still in evidence; and, if he took the trouble to pull one out of the water, he would find a buoy-line running down from it, differing from the trawl-lines only in being considerably stouter. Moreover, if he took a dive to the bottom, he would see that the gear is held down by a couple of small anchors, just as in the other method. Or, again, he might see only one keg instead of two, for often the second buoy-line is made fast to a boat lying at moorings.

But the two little anchors that will sink a set of lines are not sufficient to weight this sort of tackle, and to help it to preserve its perpendicular with a strong current running; and if we pulled up a buoy-line, we should see that it is weighted at regular intervals by three large glass balls. At the lowest of these, which would be nearly down to mid-water, the single line becomes two; one running down to the anchor, at an obtuse angle; the other continuing in the same straight line with the buoy-rope till it reaches a fourth ball which hangs within a few feet of the bottom. Forming the third side of a triangle, another line runs upwards from the anchor to this fourth ball and, beyond it, to a fifth, placed at the upper corner of the net. This fifth one is the first of a long horizontal row which is threaded upon the whole length of the upper edge of the net, whose other end meets the second set of anchored guide-lines in precisely the same manner as given above. The net thus hangs perpendicularly, with but little freedom to move backwards or forwards, its lower edge lying along the mud, and kept there by another row of glass balls, each of which hangs from a separate short cord tied to the bottom edge of the net.

One might think that, at such a time of year, the net must needs lie a long time before it is anything like full. On the contrary, it fills very speedily, and can be pulled up any time within twelve or fifteen hours; for the fish will come out from the mud as soon as they are hungry; and, considering their vast numbers, the odds are that wherever the net may fall, some hundreds of them, too occupied with family cares to notice where they are going, are bound to swim into the snare laid for them in the course of a few hours. To guard against taking young fish, the meshes of the net are so wide as to allow all but the most full-grown to pass harmlessly through them. But woe betide the parent fish if they once get their heads into the meshes; by the time the cords touch them where they are roundest and plumpest, they can go no further, and the first backward movement drives the thread well under both gills, and then all hope of freedom is gone for ever.

CHAPTER IX

THE OYSTER

Where the oyster is, and is not, found—The Essex and North Kent "flats"—Development—Restocking the beds—"Brood"—A day of a dredger's life—Description of the dredge—Hauling up—The oyster's companions in the dredge—Its enemies—Measuring up the "wash"—The collecting boat—Other kinds of oysters—Typhoid!

IT is not possible to say for how many centuries the oyster-fishery has existed; before the Christian era had begun, Roman epicures were turning up their noses at Italian oysters because those from Gaul and Britain were finer and more succulent. Certainly in the North Sea, the English Channel, the Bay of Biscay, and various parts of the Mediterranean, dredging in one form or other has been practised from time immemorial.

The fishmonger's price-list leads us to suppose that oysters are found in Scotland, Colchester, Whitstable, Holland, and America; but, as a matter of fact, they are taken in very great numbers almost everywhere. There are, it is true, some few parts of the ocean where we might dredge for ever without catching one. Professor Huxley tells us the reason, viz. they cannot live and breed in water containing less than three per cent. of saline constituents; and he quotes the Baltic, where the tasty little creatures are almost unknown, as an instance. But equally there are particular quarters of the ocean-bed—the Bay of Arcachon, for example, or the Essex and North Kent "flats"—that scientists say are specially adapted to oyster-culture; and, as the last-named is the better-known ground, as well as one of the oldest and most important in the world, we will take a glance at the kind of work that goes on there.

The law forbids the sale of English and Scotch oysters between the middle of May and the beginning of August, partly to prevent undue clearing of the beds, partly because the oyster is at that time more or less poisonous, —"sick," as the fishermen call it; it is spawning. The spawn, or "fry," falls in tiny particles on the stones, shells, and rubbish at the bottom of the sea and soon develops into small white protuberances: "spat"; these in their turn become little bivalves which are found lying independently, or with one shell tightly stuck to some foreign body. Such baby oysters are called "brood," and more than half of the fisherman's time is given up to collecting them.

Oysters are dearer than other shell-fish for pretty much the same reason that pheasants are dearer than rabbits; they are a proprietary article, and their rearing is a somewhat expensive matter. The beds from which the fully developed fish are taken belong to companies or private individuals, and are severely marked off by buoys. But such preserves are very small when compared with the immense surrounding space on which anyone may fish; and it is from the outside spaces that millions of brood oysters may be obtained.

It stands to reason, with the vast number of native oysters that are eaten or exported within a twelvemonth, that the beds from which they are drawn require to be continually restocked; and this is done by the owners buying of the fishermen the brood which they have gathered from common ground, and laying it down in their own "parks," where it will gradually come to maturity.

Brood-getting, then, is the chief occupation of the fishermen in such a place as Whitstable; supplying not the fish-market, but the fish-breeder. While the close season is on, and perhaps two or three days a week during other times, the dredgers are to be seen going off in their cutters for a task that will occupy from eight to twelve hours, and during that time they will go ten and even twenty miles away. With no quay and no tugs, the smacks are dependent on the tides for getting out to sea; thus, if the tide is ebbing at—say—one in the morning, the men must be away within an hour or so of that time, though—as in winter—they may not be able to begin work till six or seven, for their task cannot be performed in the dark.

Arrived at a likely spot, a trial dredge or two will be thrown over and left to trail for a few minutes; then pulled up and examined. If the sample be promising, work begins at once; if not, up goes the fore-sail again and the smack sails away towards better ground. In Chapter II, for the sake of convenience in classification, the dredge, (*drag*)—generally pronounced "drudge"—has been included under the head of nets; but a more minute description of the instrument may not be out of place here. The front meshes, we saw, are composed of string, and the back of stout wire. The wire meshes are linked on to a slip of iron about two feet long, the "bit"; while those at the front are lashed by a cowhide thong to a slip of wood similar in size to the bit, the "catch-stick"; and at either end, connecting the two, is a "side-stick," half the length of it. Thus we have a deep net with a rectangular opening, that will hold as much as a good-sized portmanteau. The side- and catch-sticks are but loosely hinged at their ends, so that the front and the sides of the mouth are comparatively free in their movements; but each end of the bit is fixed to a bar of iron as thick as a kitchen poker and a little less than three feet long. These two bars, or "limbs," bend back till they meet in a point, two and a half feet from the bit. As stays to the limbs are two more bars, one running down from the meeting point, halving the angle, till it joins another at right angles, which connects the limbs half a foot above the bit and parallel to it. All told, then, you have an iron triangle, bisected from apex to base, with its two sides produced till they meet a second base, the bit. At its apex is a stout iron ring through which the lowering rope is tied, and below this is a projection, the use of which will be seen directly.

An oyster-smack crew consists of three or, at the most, four men. As soon as a good spot has been found, the boat is brought round to the wind and left to look after herself, and the men arrange themselves to windward, one at bow, a second amidships, and a third near the stern. The minutes being so precious to the fishermen, everything has been made ready while the boat was still travelling; the dredges fastened to their warps; a little wooden bucket placed near each man to hold the brood; and no time is wasted now in throwing in the six dredges, two to each man. The upper end of every warp, or coil of rope, is secured by being tied to a stout block which lies on the deck, while, to prevent more rope being paid out than will reach to the bottom, a short bridle or regulating cord is tied from a cleat inside the bulwarks to the part of the warp that is just above water.

Henceforward everything depends on the wind; if there is not enough the smack will not move, and the dredges will be scraping thereabouts the same spot over and over again; if too much, she will rock and drift to such an extent that no sooner have the men found a good "pitch" than they are washed away from it. Give them a light breeze and they are happy.

The pulling up and landing of one full dredge requires little experience, but a good deal of breath and muscle; the pulling up of twenty or thirty per hour demands considerable staying power, and hands as hard as leather. The rope, a good inch in diameter, must be hauled straight up, hand over hand; to pause for breath is to risk being pulled overboard, or, at least, to have the rope jerked out of the hands by the tremendous weight at the end of it.

When at last the top ring comes above water the worst of the strain is over; to the beginner it has seemed as though the rope would never end, though in reality the depth is nothing as compared with deep-water fishing; the "flats" of the Thames estuary are not, as a rule, covered by more than five to fifteen fathoms of water, even at high tide. The use of the limbs and the little iron projection—the "heel"—is now apparent. The final pull has brought the ring well above the bulwarks; but it goes without saying that weight in water and out of it are two widely different things; out of the water a loaded dredge is sometimes so heavy that only a strong man can lift it; and the wet, slippery, sloping deck is not the standing-ground that even he would choose for the task. Instead, therefore, of lifting the catch bodily over the side, the fisherman continues to haul on the rope till the projecting heel hooks itself on the gunwale and he is released from the strain. The rest is a mere question of knack; seizing the ring, and using the limbs as a lever, he drags the iron frame over till the net rests on the gunwale, mouth towards the deck; and by a deft twist of the right limb empties the whole, then flings the dredge back into the sea.

And what a collection he has brought up from Davy's locker! Such an one as would make the mouth of a naturalist water if he saw it for the first time, and as might incline the curio-hunter to poke about in the heap on the chance of finding treasure. A complete list of the objects, other than young oysters, that appear in the dredges in the course of a day would fill a page of this book; everything from dead men's bones to fossil remains; from a lump of rock weighing half a hundredweight to a silver pencil-case; the young, and sometimes the old, of twenty different kinds of fish; mussels and whelks by the gallon; a score of varieties of seaweed. I have a sixteenth-century tobacco-pipe that was landed in this manner; and myself once pulled up a lively sole weighing over a pound and a half, in a dredge.

Before we discuss the brood that has come up, we must specially notice two objects that have not been included in the collection outlined above, but which will almost invariably be found wherever there are oysters; to wit: the "five-finger" (star-fish) and the dog-whelk. These are the young oyster's deadly enemies against which, poor wretch, he is powerless. The star-fish grips him with its terrible arms and suckers, and eats him up, shell and all. The dog-whelk goes to work in a more subtle manner; having fastened himself on to the shell, he patiently bores a hole through it with a sort of drill wherewith Nature has provided his mouth; and, having effected an entry, gradually demolishes the soft body within. You may see scores of empty brood shells neatly perforated in this manner.

Strangely enough, the dredgers wink at the depredations of the star-fish; if they do not want to take a bag-full of them home for the garden (they are splendid manure for cabbages) they throw them back unharmed into the sea. Yet not many dog-whelks are ever allowed to escape; the heel of a sea-boot or a bang with a stone speedily cuts short their days. They can easily be distinguished from the common whelk by the white and purple or yellow and brown shades of the shell, as well as by the lengthy spines with which the latter is covered.

From such a motley heap, then, the brood has to be sorted, or "culled"—for the Kent fishermen still use the good old word; and here is labour more irksome and, in the long run, more tiring, than the hauling up; for the men are down on their knees, or bent double over the heap, gathering up the little shells faster than the stranger could pick them out with his eye. Brood shells are of a pearly white till they are about a year old, and at that age their size is anything from that of a sixpence to that of a halfpenny; older brood are of a delicate pink on the round valve, and brown on the flat. They may be said to increase in diameter about an inch each year, up to the age of three; after which time the growth is more a matter of the shell's thickening, and there is not necessarily any great difference in circumference between a three-year-old oyster and a fully matured one.

In a very few minutes each dredger has singled out from his heap everything that he wants and has thrown it into his bucket; and now, with a couple of bits of board he rakes together all the mass of weed, stones, and rubbish preparatory to shooting it through a port-hole. Before he throws the heap away there is one more item of it that it will not be going away from our subject to glance at; the sea-urchin or, as he would call it, the "burr," for whose creation he firmly believes the Evil One to have been responsible. Most people are better acquainted with its shell-like skeleton than with the living creature itself; it is a greeny red, globular object, any size from that of a marble to a small orange, and looking exactly like a coiled-up hedgehog. According to the dredger there are three grounds of objection to it; it pricks the fingers most painfully; a prick from it is poisonous; it eats the oysters. Nobody who has handled one will cavil at the first statement; the second is nonsense; the third open to debate, for zoologists seem to agree that the urchin is a vegetable feeder. It certainly has a trick of getting in the way of the fingers while the brood is being culled, and a pleasant little habit of sticking one of its spines between the nail and the flesh—and leaving it there. So long as it behaves, the dredger shoots it overboard with the rest; but should it prick him, the bystander will see that the savage is not altogether dead in our fishermen; for the offending burr must be slowly hammered to death with a stone, or gently dropped into the cabin fire. You might tell the dredger that the urchin does not feel anything, has no evil intentions, and was not made by the devil; and being the naturally courteous fellow that he generally is, he would not contradict you—till you were out of hearing.

Now out through the port-hole are swept the pipe-fishes and sea-mice and the half-dozen or more varieties of crab—noticeably the ghastly spider-crab—with an avalanche of stones; and the fisher hauls up his second dredge, empties it, throws it back, and sorts as before. If it is a lucky day with him, after a few such hauls he has filled his pail, emptied it into a larger one and started to fill it again. If you take the trouble to examine the contents of one of the pails you will find a curious mixture; young oysters in clusters of two or three; a stone or an old shell with as many as a dozen little ones adhering to it; perhaps a few oysters that, in spite of the continuous dredging, have by chance been allowed to come to maturity in their native beds.

On a busy day the pails are soon filled again, and it becomes necessary to pack away some of the brood. The men gauge it very carefully before they empty it into sacks—it will be measured again by the buyer, but they like to know how much they are earning.

"Two wash already!" A "wash" is five gallons, and will be bought by the cultivator for four shillings. On two wash, then, our three men have earned two shillings apiece, and the boat another two shillings; if the owner is the skipper, so much the better for him.

After a while it is seen that the supply of brood is dwindling; the patch, over which the dredges are being towed by the gently drifting boat, is exhausted; or perhaps only mussels are coming up—a sure sign that there is little brood about. Then the helm is unlashed, the boat puts about, and makes for another likely spot. Here, perhaps, the brood is more plentiful than ever, and very soon another three or four wash are put into the bags. But now the men are beginning to grumble; the wind has dropped, and the boat scarcely moves at all, hampered as she is by the heavy dredges. There is just the hope that, though she may not bear six, she can yet manage three, so each man tries working with but one dredge. The plan answers perhaps, but the crew are only earning half as much as they otherwise might do. And maybe the tide has been flowing for some time already; they have but an hour or so before they must put back. Happily the wind is getting up once more, and all six dredges are thrown in again. The men may well be anxious to make hay while the sun shines; when they are not after brood they are either kept ashore by unfavourable weather, or are "oystering" at four-and-sixpence a day. Oystering, I may remark, is exactly the same process as brood-getting, but that the men are working on a private ground and are rejecting everything but the fish that are ready for eating.

At length, good luck or bad, they dare stay no longer if they are to get in before the tide turns again; for very likely they are miles away from home. As they come in sight of the town we see the same kind of thing happening as we witnessed with the trawlers; two of the men jump into the little boat, the sacks of brood are handed out to them and they pull rapidly away to a smack labelled "collecting-boat." Round this are scores of little boats, their crews waiting to give up their catches and have them measured. In some cases however the catch is taken ashore to a sorting house. The brood thus procured will be replanted in some special part of the oyster park, dropped down from smacks by the handful as if one were sowing seeds.

This is an average day of a dredger's life in good weather. In winter-time he must necessarily earn but little; the hours of daylight are very limited; there are fogs about; and, more, if a frost sets in, he can take himself home as soon as he likes and stay there till the thaw comes; for frost kills the brood the moment it comes in contact with it, no matter how quickly the catch is stowed away. You can see the little oysters open of themselves as soon as they are taken out of the water on a frosty day.

Hitherto we have dealt with but one class of oyster, but there are others that may be of interest. As youngsters, most of us have been told by our travelled elders that oysters grow on trees; and we have had the uncomfortable feeling that we were being "chaffed." Yet we live to find out that in some parts of the world, such is the case; in the West Indies, at the heads of inlets and natural harbours where the mangrove grows freely under water, oysters may be found by the hundred, clinging to the branches.

There is an interesting point, too, relating to the colour of oysters; those from Spain are red; from parts of the Adriatic, brown; from the Bay of Biscay and parts of the Channel, green; from the Red Sea, opaline and rainbow coloured.

There is, though not to the extent that once prevailed, a good deal of exchange in the matter of brood. In bad years—that is years when the fall of "spat" has been poor—brood has been brought over from Cançale or Dieppe or Arcachon, and planted in English beds; similarly, though the Dutch have large beds off Zealand, they will buy young oysters of English fishermen to ripen in the grounds at Petten. In recent years the Australian beds have proved so fruitful that an attempt has been made to transport brood oysters to Europe; but so far the promoters of the scheme have not been successful.

Dredging for oysters, and from boats, is not always necessary; most of the American fish are picked up from the beach like cockles. At Arcachon, perhaps the finest natural bed in the world, the tide goes out so far that what, at flood-tide, is a large bay, becomes at low water a vast sand-track, intersected, however, by narrow streams from two to seven fathoms deep. At the bottom of these streams lie some of the best oysters, and dredging can be carried on from land.

The Arcachon fishermen have to wage war against what is called the whelk-tingle, as do ours against the dog-whelk; and the Americans find almost as great a scourge in the oyster-catcher or sea-pie, a stork-billed bird that eats oysters as thrushes eat snails.

One more word about the British oyster-fisherman. He cannot be brought to believe that oysters produce typhoid fever, and doubtless he would find medical men ready to back him up. According to his own account he has seen a man's head swell to the size of a bushel-basket through mussel-poisoning; he has had his own hand in a sling for weeks, through being pricked by a burr; he has seen someone else helplessly drunk, merely through eating a few red whelks; he may even have seen the sea-serpent; but never, never has he known of a case of oyster-typhoid. And surely he is in a position to know!

CHAPTER X

UNITED STATES FISH AND FISHERMEN

The States fishermen — The " foreigners " — The spring mackerel-fishing—The " purse-seine "—Fishing by night—How the net is cleared—Shore-weirs—Line-fishing for mackerel—The herring—The mullet—A big catch—The " red snapper "—Other American fish.

THE life of the American mackerel is a busy but not an enviable one, for it is passed in a futile effort to find a resting-place "between the devil and the deep sea"; in other words, between the artfully designed coast-traps known as "shore-weirs," and the attacks of the sharks and blue-fish that lie in wait for him as soon as he flees into deep water. It is just possible that he might find a happy mean, if it were not for a third danger that pursues him in his flight from the coast, and is waiting to meet him on his return there to the fishing-fleet. For, all the way down the Atlantic coast of the United States, from Maine to Louisiana, are fishing stations, some rivalling in importance our Lowestoft or Grimsby, and catering for a greater population and a far wider area.

The States fishermen might be divided into two classes:

foreigners, and "odd hands." In a new country one does not expect to see a fishing race, sprung from untold generations of sea-going folk, such as Britain, France or Denmark can show; and but for the immigration of European fishing families, one might seek in vain for anything like a hereditary fleet. But when English and French, Swedes and Portuguese settled along the east coast of North America in the sixteenth and seventeenth centuries, attracted by the tales of their sailors as to the prevalence of the cod, they went a long way towards endowing the new country with such a fleet as they had been accustomed to see at home. On Cape Cod, for instance, there is, to this day, a complete colony of Portuguese fishermen who still retain their own language and customs. All these different settlers, then, with Lascars, Coolies, and an occasional Chinaman, make up the "foreigners"; while the "odd hands" are landsmen —labourers, negroes, etc., or their descendants, who have drifted towards the coast in search of work, and are looked upon with a certain amount of contempt by the more blue-blooded fisher-folk.

Such of these men as are not engaged on the Banks fishery, may be found during March and April fishing for mackerel; in the late autumn and winter for herring; then, till mackerel-fishing begins again, for mullet. Their ground may be said to lie anywhere between the coast and a line parallel to it, fifty miles distant; and, lengthwise, between the Gulf of Mexico and the Bay of Fundy. Further north they dare not go except for mackerel—the only fish which they are allowed to take from British waters—or when they are making for the common ground further east.

A favourite spot for the spring mackerel-fishing is off Cape Hatteras, where the water reaches a remarkable depth; and here a fleet of yawls, and even schooners and brigs, is to be seen working day and night—really more night than day—as long as the shoals of mackerel remain. A large vessel is necessary, if only as a storehouse, for the catches are so enormous that only big craft could find room for them.

The net used is a development of the old-fasioned *seine*, probably introduced by the French and Portuguese *émigrés*, and known as the "purse-seine"; it requires considerable depth of water and, like the trawl, a sandy or shingly bottom, free from rocks. As a rule it is single, i.e. a plain sheet of netting, with cords at top and bottom which will draw it together in the form of a bag; sometimes, however, it is pocket-shaped. To cause it to hang perpendicularly, the upper edge is buoyed with a cork-line, while the lower is weighted with lead; it can either be moored to a couple of boats or anchored buoys, or it may be towed gently between two or more boats.

The fact that mackerel are not essentially a bottom fish will explain why the work is more easily accomplished in the dark than by daylight. In the daytime the fish are rather shy of coming near the surface, with the result that only the lower meshes are to be relied upon as long as the light remains. By night it is different; a man standing at bow, or stationed at the mast-head, can easily follow the movements of a shoal, which, seeing nothing to fear, swim hither and thither among the fleet, unconsciously betraying their whereabouts by the phosphorescent track they leave behind. Following such a track with his eye, an experienced skipper can give directions to the men who are waiting to shoot the seine from the small boats, and can even tell when the net is in danger of being overcrowded.

The clearing of the net is a case of "the mountain's going to Mohammed"; not of the net's being brought to the ship, but the reverse. The moment the seine is full, the vessel pulls round alongside of it; the cords are drawn up and hitched to the bulwarks, so that the whole catch is taken in tow; and a fresh net is shot. If the crew are busy, the fish caught can stay where they are till morning; then they are baled out of the purse at intervals, as occasion offers, and stacked below, to be taken ashore either immediately or when the call-boat comes round. The reason why the net is not hauled bodily on deck, as in trawling, is pretty obvious when we bear in mind that. at one shooting, the seine is sometimes found to contain as many mackerel as will fill a thousand good-sized barrels.

But what is the result of such enormous catches? Year by year the mackerel-fleets find themselves forced to go farther and farther away from the shore; for the spring fishing disturbs the shoals in their northward migration, causing them thereby to take a wider sweep from the coast, so that, in time to come, mackerel-seining must become as much an ocean-fishery as codding.

The shark and his various amiable relatives are rarely the fisherman's allies; yet, where American mackerel are concerned, they must be considered as such; for one of them will pursue a whole shoal—swallowing a mouthful now and again as opportunity arises—for fifty and sixty miles, coming as close in to shore as he dares. It is then that the shore-weirs mentioned above come into play. They are of two sorts: shoal-(shallow)-water weirs and deep-water weirs. The first are simple enclosures made by walls of stakes, bushes, etc., into which the fish swim helter-skelter, on the "any port in a storm" principle, where they are either cut off from retreat by a sliding door of hurdles as soon as a big capture is made, to be left high and dry when the tide goes out; or are baled out by the score as they come into the trap.

The deep-water weir is considerably less primitive, and is composed of a series of net walls cunningly arranged so that entry is simple enough, but exit—to the dull-witted mackerel—a matter of impossibility. Parallel to the shore is one long sheet or wall of netting, buoyed and weighted like a seine; from one end of this, running out into the sea at right-angles, is a similar wall, from a hundred and fifty to two hundred yards long; the "leader," as it is called. At the other end of the first net is a third wall, about a quarter the length of the leader and parallel to it, at the end of which is yet another, which goes more than half-way towards making the fourth side of a square, leaving, however, a good wide opening for the fish to come in at. Sometimes the fourth side doubles back, parallel to the leader, and has yet another net perpendicular to it, inside the square, making the beginning of a sort of key-pattern labyrinth.

When a shoal of mackerel in full flight from a shark encounters the "leader," it hesitates, wheels, and swims steadily alongside the net wall till it is caught in the maze prepared for it. But shore-weirs, take them how you may, are even more destructive to the fishery than the purse-seine, for hundreds of thousands of mackerel can be caught in the course of a few days; and the sooner such a wasteful method is entirely abolished the better.

There is one more way in which the mackerel may be caught—again an importation from Europe; that is by means of hook and line. All sorts of bait have been tried, but experienced mackerel-anglers say that none is so satisfactory as a bit of scarlet flannel, cloth, or ribbon, tapering downwards to a point. As there is no marine animal, so far as one knows, of which such bait could be an imitation, it may be assumed that this is yet another instance of the inquisitiveness of fish upon which scientists have so often remarked.

Next in importance to the mackerel, where the States coast-fishery is concerned, is the herring; and the catching of it is one of the special industries of the shore people of Maine and Massachusetts; but, as the next chapter deals specially with this fishery as carried on in Europe, we shall here only touch upon such points as are peculiar to the American branch of it. Gill-nets, such as we saw used on the Banks for cod, are frequently employed, though the buyers are much against the use of them; for they say that the redness round the eyes of herrings is caused by the strangulating effect of the meshes; and consequently they prefer those fish that have been caught in weirs or purse-seines. Weirs are very successful in late autumn, when the fish come close in-shore to spawn.

The more distant herring-fishery, which extends as far as the British waters round New Brunswick, is carried on in smacks, and principally by means of purse-seines. The season is a long one, lasting at least three months. Often the catching is done in exactly the same way as mackerel-seining, the full net being towed aft; but, where small purses are used, the catch is sometimes hauled up on deck. Collecting-boats are often dispensed with, for many smacks carry a plentiful supply of ice; and the herring, packed carefully in this, will keep good and fresh for months at a time; other boats give up their catches daily to a steamer.

Before the herring-fishery has ended for the year, another industry begins farther south: mulleting. The great mullet-ground is the Cedar Keys, off the Florida coast, and the season lasts from the beginning of December to the end of the first week in February. Gill-nets and even trawls are used for these; but again neither is so popular as the purse-seine. The fish taken average two and a half pounds, and they are caught in astonishing profusion. A seine worked by eight men has been known to catch ten thousand of them at one shooting. Reckoning at the rate of thirty fish to a cubit foot, this represents a solid mass measuring about seven feet each way, and weighing over eleven tons.

Coming a little further south and then sailing westwards into the Gulf of Mexico, we light upon another important fishing-ground; the home of the "red snapper." This is a gorgeous creature, averaging 7 lb. in weight, which is regarded by the people of the Southern States as a great delicacy. It is found in depths of from ten to fifty fathoms, and swims over a bottom that is everywhere dotted with rocks and lumps of coral, where no fisherman dare dream of shooting a net.

Snapper-catching does not greatly differ from cod line-fishing. Each smack is manned by a crew of seven or eight men, who go fifty miles out and as much as two hundred and fifty along the shore. On reaching a favourable spot the boat is either anchored or brought to heave-to, and work begins. As the snapper happens to be a particularly voracious fish (he has earned his name from his practice of snapping at everything that comes within his reach), very long lines are not necessary, for he spends a good half of his time chasing small fish that swim near the surface. Each man's line is furnished with two large, thick hooks and is weighted with four or five pounds of lead; and, as a rule, before the weight has sunk more than a couple of fathoms, one, and sometimes two fish have swallowed the bait, not to say a hook as well. Bait, indeed, is a secondary matter; hundreds of snappers are caught in a day with naked hooks; a pebble lowered on a string would be sufficient tackle to draw them; it might even be worth a sportsman's while to try them with an alder-fly or a cockchafer.

A snapper boat carries no ice, no salt, and has no dealings with steam collectors. Under hatches is an immense tank filled with water, and the fish, having been carefully made to disgorge the hook, are put into it; the tank will hold a week's catch and, at the end of that time, the boat puts back to shore, and the fish are killed by a slight blow on the head when they are handed out to the buyers.

Beside those already mentioned or yet to be discussed in other chapters, the Americans have many fish which are unknown in our own waters; in most cases their names are descriptive, e.g. the horse-eyed jack, pork-fish, hog-fish, goat-fish, moon-fish, etc. Another individual that almost calls for separate mention is the menhaden, more commonly known as the "porgy," once in great favour at the tables of the poorer classes in the States. This fishery is now spoken of as a lost art, though menhaden make excellent bait for cod, and have, in time past, been so plentiful as to be netted for field-manure.

CHAPTER XI

THE BRITISH HERRING FISHERY

The herring—The lugger—Night-work—Signs!—"Lythe"—Shooting the tackle—How the drift-net is worked—The trial shot—Shooting a "fleet"—The net filling—Hauling in—The first strike—A second shot—More than they can carry—"Maze," "cran," and "last"—Getting rid of the catch.

AS a popular dish, where the poorer classes throughout the western world are concerned, the herring is hard to beat. If it were not such a prolific—and consequently cheap—fish, it would no doubt find favour even in the eyes of wealthy epicures; for, in all its forms, fresh, salted, kippered, or red, it is more appetising and sustaining than many of the more expensive fish.

Herring are in season whenever they can be procured, which is at almost all times of the year; though during the first three months they are not at their best. Roughly speaking, from June to October is the season for the British fishery.

All round our coast are herring boats of some sort or other; but the important fleets hail from sundry Scotch and North Country ports; from Yarmouth, of course; from Ireland and the Isle of Man, and from North Devon. There is not a great deal of difference between the craft and methods in use in these various districts; and perhaps the only distinction between a herring-fisher and any other is that the former grows rich more quickly and more surely than his less favoured brethren; for where both supply and demand are abundant and fairly constant, there money must be made.

The boat most generally employed is the Scotch or two-masted lugger, open or decked, as the case may be; more often the latter. The luggers found on the coast of Scotland usually have a little cabin forward, but the rest of the vessel open. The North Country boats are long and narrow, with a pointed stern; the foremast is placed as near as possible to the prow, which practice, though it may render her awkward and sulky when sailing against the wind, makes a very fast boat of her with the wind behind her. The vessels in the west and south-west are, as a rule, broader in the beam, and not uniformly so fast. The special advantage attaching to the use of the double lugger is that, while fishing is going on, the foremast can more easily be stepped (lowered) than could the main-mast of a cutter or yawl. And this measure is very necessary because, when once the nets are shot, even though there be no sail up, the least wind will add tremendously to the already heavy strain on the tow-rope; and it is the skilled fisherman's one endeavour to keep such strain at a minimum.

Herring-fishing is night-work, and the darker the night the better the men like it; for the fish are much too wide awake to run their heads into the meshes as long as these are visible. To say that the boats go out every night in the season would be to imply either that the

Photo, Jenkins *Lowestoft*

FISHERMEN LAYING-OUT HERRINGS FOR SALE AT LOWESTOFT

fisherman is an ass—and he is not—or that luck is always with the fleet. The herring fisherman, especially he of the North, is an exceedingly astute person, and will not risk his valuable tackle unless there is reasonable hope of gaining something thereby. True, there are times when he comes back with an almost empty boat, but such a calamity is more often than not due to some unforeseen accident, such as a trawler's having split up a shoal; and it is made up for by the next lucky night. He has very reliable indications of a shoal being in the vicinity—the systematic flight of the sea-birds, a peculiar boiling up of the sea in isolated patches, the presence of porpoises or an occasional whale; perhaps his wife or children have spent half the day watching for the appearance of such signs; or he has done well at a certain spot on the previous night and means to try his luck again at the same place; in any case he will not go unless there is something to go for.

Sometimes a shoal moves from district to district with such rapidity that only the boat which happens to be on a certain spot at a given moment stands the least chance of making a capture; other craft that have put off a little later will come up to find that the coveted shoal has swept onwards from—say—the Firth of Clyde, southwards; and to-morrow one or two fortunate Manx or Irish crews will have netted the fish that to-day have circumvented the Scotchmen; what remains of them being, perhaps, snapped up by the Devon men a night or two later.

When the "signs" are sufficiently promising, the boats

put off as near sundown as tides will allow, making what sail they can; often rowing as well, if current or wind be adverse, or if there be no tug handy. At this time of day the demeanour of the men is markedly the reverse of what it is when they go off at midnight or early morning; as then their spirits and hilarity gradually rise, the farther they get from the shore, so now they begin cheerily and noisily, growing more silent and subdued as the darkness gathers. By the time it is dark not a voice will raise itself above a whisper; will scarcely utter a single sound other than an objurgation on the moon for shining, or on a juvenile member of the crew for snoring.

A faint light streams down on the deck as the lamp is run up the mizzen-mast, and the hands—six or seven—prepare to lower sail at a word from the helmsman. That personage has for some time been watching the flight and occasional downward swoop of a flock of sea-gulls; where they are dropping, fish of some kind or other are sure to be near the surface. As the gloom deepens, another and more certain proof of the presence of a shoal appears, for sheets and streaks of phosphorescent light begin to show themselves on the surface; that means that the fish are stirring, and in very considerable numbers. Still our skipper does not seem to excite himself. Fish are there, sure enough; but they may not be the fish that he is seeking. Suppose the luminous flashes should be caused merely by a shoal of "lythe"! It is not at all unlikely.

Lythe are fish that swim in shoals off the Scotch coast and are practically useless as food. The oyster-dredger is not alone in holding heterodox opinions on the subject of creation; for the Scotch herring-fisher devoutly believes that the foul fiend created the lythe and invented the trawl-net—the one to give occasion for many disappointments and much consequent swearing; the other to drive away and break up the shoals of herrings which otherwise would swim obligingly towards the net spread for them.

As the lugger draws near to the first of the phosphorescent splashes, a whispered word goes round; the skipper means to shoot a trial net, and we shall have an opportunity of seeing how "drift" tackle is worked. (Some of the more up-to-date men use a trawl-net or purse-seine for herring.) The drift-nets are lying amidships, carefully coiled up; each about fifty feet long and from nine to twelve deep, and as innocent of pockets, purses, or folds as a tennis-net; the meshes, which go about thirty to the yard, will do all the work of themselves. The prudent skipper is determined not to act rashly; the depth of water here is not much more than four fathoms, and there are gigantic jagged rocks about.

"Try three, first," he mutters.

A pull at the helm throws the boat round in order that the gear may be shot at the proper angle, i.e. across the current, so that the shoals will strike it in their course up or down; and some of the hands stand by to pay out the first net. As it touches the water the tendency of the heavy twine meshes is to sink, even if the lower edge be not weighted with lead.

"Let her go; mind the corks, and easy with that foot-rope."

The first thing that has touched the water is a good-sized bladder, which the waves toss up and down like a feather; this is tied to the end of a stout rope which forms the upper edge of the net. As the meshes disappear we can see that the net will not be allowed to sink to the bottom, for, along the line that ends in the bladder, is an array of lumps of cork, which, with the bladders, will keep the upper edge—or "back"—on the surface, while the net itself hangs perpendicularly. As the cork line comes to an end we see another bladder, and beyond it enough rope to connect up the beginning of the second net. This is quickly joined on and paid out, and then the third. The trial net has been shot.

Meanwhile one of the crew has been engaged with what is termed the foot-rope or foot-line, a strong cord independent of the cork line, fastened to the "back" of each of the nets by a connecting cord, and so much longer than the cork-line that, when the nets are all shot, it sinks well below the under edge of them. It is on this rope that much of the strain of hauling-in will come; moreover, should the cork-line be broken by a passing vessel, as not infrequently happens, everything would depend upon it; therefore it must be kept safely out of the way of accidents. The ends of the lines are made fast to a tow-rope, which can be lengthened or shortened according as the boat wants to ride close to or away from her nets; and the tackle is all ready for a strike, or catch.

Now the foremast, taller considerably than the mizzen, has to be stepped; sails and ropes are hauled down and

Photo, Jenkins *Lowestoft*

ESTIMATING A CATCH OF HERRING IN NORWAY

The fish are either sold by the box or in one lot. If the latter method is selected by the merchant, he calculates whilst the fish are still in the water, by means of a water-glass, what amount the catch is worth. The man at which the white arrow is pointing has such a water-glass in his hand. The fish are plainly to be seen in the water behind him.

the mast is gently lowered backwards till it lies like a dividing-line along the middle of the vessel. At present nothing more can be done, and the men adjourn to the cabin-stove, or huddle round the fire-bucket if there be no cabin, and smoke their pipes or eat their supper in dead silence. Boat and nets are drifting, and, so long as they drift away from the rock-bed, the skipper does not worry himself; he can keep a certain amount of control over the vessel with the rudder, and, if he considers it necessary, he has kept up his mizzen-sail in order to hold her nose to the wind.

Presently he gives a little chuckle of satisfaction; the gleams and flashes in the water are broadening; the surface is bubbling and frothing in places; here and there the flashes break up from time to time into innumerable points of light; and little clucking sounds are heard, like the popping of corks at a distance, or the fall of hailstones on a pond. Shall he risk putting out more nets? By this time they must have drifted to a safe depth away from the sharp rocks that would make havoc of the gear. Why should he have only three when the boat will stand a dozen or more?

"Hullo! Blue light to le'ward! May happen the *Argyle* 's made a strike," says one of the men; and every-one looks in the direction indicated, where, among the sparse train or group of yellow mast-head lights, one blue flame stands conspicuous.

The skipper still watches the little islands of foam, making up his mind that he too will soon be in a position to run up a blue light, and gives the word to haul in the nearest net for examination. The warp comes in so easily that a stranger to the work would conclude that nothing has been done; surely only an empty net could weigh so little!

True enough, as the first meshes rise above the water, nothing can be seen in the net. But wait; near the lower edge is an irregular row of herring, whose presence suggests that there are more where they came from. The bulk of the shoal has not yet started to rise.

"That's near enough," says the skipper. "Let's run out the whole fleet"; and speedily extra nets are fastened on, one after another, till there is a wall of them, many hundreds of yards long, trailing out into the sea, the cork-line waggling and coiling till it looks like an endless worm.

Other boats are running up blue-lights now, but no one troubles to comment on the fact; there is silence again, only broken by the *plop-plop* of the fish as they rise, or by a sudden wild shriek from the gulls as they announce to their friends the fishermen that the herrings continue to play near the surface. Following the track of the cork-line with our eye, we can see that it is now illuminated all along with streaks of greenish light; every now and then, too, we may see the bladders rocking and bobbing in a curious manner; now one goes completely under and comes up again; the corks are swaying hither and thither irresponsibly. The advance-guard of a shoal is being safely snared.

But, before there is time to do more than arrive at this conclusion, a whole wave of phosphorus flashes along in the direction of the net-fleet, and bladders and cork-line are dragged under; the tow-warp groans, and strains on the boat. The main body is encountering the nets, and the crew no longer care whether the *Argyle* has made a strike or no; at any rate *their* boat has. They shuffle to their feet without a word from the skipper, for experience of him and his methods has taught them that, if he is not one to be in an unnecessary hurry, he equally is not given to letting his nets get fouled or sunk, through a foolish desire to catch more fish than he can possibly carry away.

Seizing the sodden warp, they drag and strain till sufficient of it is hauled in to go round the windlass; and not till then does one of them untie the end of it from the cross-bit. Irish or South Country fishermen would bid him hurry himself, in no measured terms, for the strain is unspeakable, even on these tough muscles and strong-knit frames; but the more phlegmatic Northerners just bide their time and wait patiently while the end of the warp is hitched to the windlass or the capstan, and till the click-click of the ratch stops, telling them that the man who is turning has taken in as much rope as, unaided, he is able. Then one or two of them join him at the windlass, while the rest stretch themselves and prepare for the further task of drawing the nets over the gunwale. A few more turns of the winch and the first bladder is lifted in and the top corner of the nearest net comes into view. Again the streaks of greenish light, more tangible now; again the popping, buzzing sound; then you realise that hundreds, or thousands, of the herring, caught fast by the gills, are wriggling for freedom, so close to you that you can touch the polished little bodies; more, you can see cod and other big fish jumping above water to snatch a mouthful.

"Yeo-ho; oo-up! Now, all together—oo-up! Now—oo-up! *All* together!" murmur the hands in a sort of doleful chorus, as they bend to their labour, and with muscles strained to their utmost, hoist in coil after coil of net, so stuffed with fish that, in places, it is difficult to find a hand-hold. Here and there may be an empty mesh, where a slender youngster has been able to squeeze itself right through the little inch-and-a-half opening; but the majority of the middle and lower squares have tenants.

"We'll have to be lively, lads," says the skipper, who has left the helm and is bearing a hand with the nets; "I'm thinking there'll be dead stuff in the last three, else."

When herring have been held by their gills for some length of time they are apt to die—in fact, no fish dies so quickly, whence the saying, "dead as a herring"; and dead fish means dead weight; a net filled with such a catch will sometimes tear itself away from the "fleet" and be lost beyond the hope of recovery. Therefore the men waste no time in working their way through the seemingly interminable series of nets, for the last three to come up were the first three to be shot, and they will be lucky if they find them unbroken. The last lot are more crowded than ever; every now and then there is a little jerk as half a dozen meshes break; and some of the men lean over the bulwarks and, getting their arms under the net, lift in whole bundles of living and dead fish.

"Last lot," says someone who has been mechanically counting the nets as they come up. Now the jerks and rips are growing more frequent, for here are more dead herring than live ones. That last net will require a lot of patient mending when they get it ashore. But, in spite of breakages and unusual weight, it is pulled aboard at last. While the men nearest the gunwale have been hauling in, others behind them have been busily shaking and twisting the nets in order to clear them as far as they can of their silvery load; and now that all hands can be spared for this work the hold is getting fuller and fuller, till, to the inexperienced eye, it would seem that the vessel must either founder or else take about a day and a half to wander home, lame duck fashion. But the crew cast almost a disparaging glance over the catch; all of them have seen twice as many to one strike.

"Unship the last three," cries the skipper, "and let's try another shoot."

The three nets at the top of the coil are untied and laid aside, considerably the worse for wear; and, as the water still glitters, and it will be long before daylight appears, the remainder of the fleet is re-shot. Then careful hands spread out the pyramids of fish so that those at the top fill up the spare corners of the hold and leave room for the next batch.

Now that the nets are shot for the second time, a bystander has an opportunity of noticing that a peculiar *cheep-cheep* sound, like the squeak of mice, is coming up from the hold. If the skipper be facetiously inclined he will reply on being questioned as to the noise—

"Ou, it'll just be the haerin' greetin' to gae back."

Such an informant must needs, one would think, be own brother to the crab or lobster-boiler who announces that his fish scream when thrown into the hot water. As a matter of fact the noise is caused by the escape of the air from the herrings' swimming-bladders.

"All right; pull up—and shairp!" cries our skipper suddenly; and the same weary work has to be gone through all over again. And this time the meshes seem fuller than before; the net must have shot clean in front of a shoal that was driving down with the current. The skipper measures the contents of the hold with his eye. There are still two more nets to be emptied, and the boat won't stand another barrel-full. He takes a philosophical view of the subject; the rest must go back. A grasping young skipper would perhaps load his vessel till she was like a coal-tramp, but this fellow has more sense; he has done what he came to do and he means to get home. The superfluous fish are shaken out of the net overboard, and the tired fishermen withdraw to the fire, except those who are occupied in unstepping the mast and fixing the lug.

Dawn is coming on; many of the mast-head lights have disappeared and the fishing fleet show signs of gathering together.

"Twelve maze," or "Fourteen cran," cries the skipper of the *Argyle* exultingly. "That'll beat ye, lad."

"I'm thinking we've gotten as many," says our skipper

Photo, Jenkins *Lowestoft*

HERRING-DRIVING IN NORWAY

In order to frighten the fish into such a bay as this, Norwegian fishermen lower wooden imitation whales into the water behind the fish, and literally drive them into the bay, where they are netted. The steamer carries the catch to the market, which is generally Hull.

diffidently, knowing full well that his catch amounts to nearly half as much again.

"Maze," "cran," etc., it should be explained, are semi-local terms. The measure for herrings differs according to the neighbourhood. The three generally recognised are the *maze* on the west coast of Scotland and the Irish Sea generally (*mease* in Devonshire); the *last* on the east coast of England, and the *cran* on the east of Scotland. The last-named—equivalent to $26\frac{2}{3}$ gallons—makes the fish sold by bulk; the other two by numbers. The east-coast fishermen reckon the warp (i.e. 4 fish) as their unit; and 33 warps, or 132 fish, make a "long hundred"; 1320 fish go to the thousand, and ten thousand (13,200) = a last.

The west-coasters reckon 123 to the long hundred, and 5 long hundred (615) to the maze. Mr. Frederick Pollock, however, makes the Devonshiremen arrive at their maze in a totally different way. Their unit is a cast, i.e. 3, or as many as can be held in the hand; 51 cast = a quarter maze (153)—the number, he points out, of the miraculous draught mentioned in St. John XXI. 11; and 4 quarter maze = 612.

Now that the sails are set the men are free to breakfast; for, unless they have come a long way from home—in which case the fish has still to be sprinkled with salt—there is nothing more for them to do till the question of selling arises. The getting rid of the fish will also differ in various districts. In many parts the boats will have a good-sized harbour to run into, and the fishwives will be waiting on the quay to buy up the catch as fast as it can be thrown out to them. At a big port like Grimsby it will be hurried off to the market and sold by auction, or at current market-price. In many places the steam-carrier is requisitioned. She comes out to meet the fleet at dawn, and the agents on board buy each boat-load (or undertake to dispose of it at the market) as it comes alongside.

As far as the picturesque is concerned, one cannot help regretting that the account of the herring-fishery as outlined above must soon be decidedly "out of date." Following American and Norwegian examples our herring-fleets have gradually congregated in the big ports, have substituted the purse-seine or the trawl for the old gill-net, and are even abandoning the luggers of our childhood in favour of ponderous steamers.

By means of the purses mentioned in the last chapter an entire shoal will be taken (amounting sometimes to hundreds of thousands), necessitating the employment of extra deck-hands and the erection of huge store and clearing-houses.

In addition to those herring caught here, millions are brought to Hull and Lowestoft from Norway. The Norwegian fishermen, on sighting a shoal, lower into the water an imitation whale, made of wood and weighted; and, terrified at sight of this, the herring swim into a bay which forms a natural trap. Huge purse-seines are then shot and the whole shoal is rapidly netted. The catch is sold by the box or in one lot; in the latter case the buyer bargains while the fish are still in the water, and estimates the value with the aid of a water spy-glass.

CHAPTER XII

FISHING IN THE MEDITERRANEAN

Possibilities of the Mediterranean fisheries—Migration of the anchovy—Shooting the seine for anchovies—The moored net—Some of its occupants—The fisherman's friends and enemies—Sharks—Saw-fish and sword-fish—The tunny—Setting the nets—Slaughtering the catch—Another Sicilian industry—Line-fishing.

A SEA that is over two thousand miles long and considerably more than a million square miles in extent, that never experiences a temperature of less than 50° F., and scarcely knows the meaning of tides; above all, that abounds in fish of every description, as well as turtles, sponge, coral, and amber, sounds like a fisherman's Elysium; and such, in the hands of more energetic people than the North Africans and the Southern Europeans, it might be. Unfortunately the Mediterranean washes the coasts of nations that, for the more part, have ceased to believe much in hard work; and even our own poor Irish fisheries are better managed and relatively more productive than theirs. Exceptions must be made in the case of France, and of Austria, which has her Adriatic fishing navy of twelve thousand men; also in that of the East Mediterranean sponge-fishers, of whom more anon.

FISHING IN THE MEDITERRANEAN

The reader may ask, What about the Andalusian and Italian fisheries? What about the sardine industry?

Spain and Italy import far more fish than they ever catch, and Cornwall and Brittany send pilchards by the million to the southern sardine factories every year. Italy, it is true, has in late years taken more interest in her fisheries, even to the extent of going in for artificial fish-breeding; but comparatively few of the men attempt deep-water work.

Starting eastwards from Gibraltar, the first important fishery we meet with is that carried on by the Andalusians, French, and Genoese for the anchovy. This little fish is about three inches long, bluish-brown on the back, and silvery white on the belly. Strictly it is a tropical fish, but the variety known as the common anchovy may be found anywhere south of Ireland. By the end of April, shoals of them collect off the south-west of Spain, and sweep through the Strait of Gibraltar in millions. By far the greater number of them, as soon as they are in the Mediterranean, seem to take an almost straight course north-east, shaving the under side of the Balearic Islands and making steadily for the north of Corsica, and up to Leghorn. Arrived here they circle round the little island of Gorgona, remaining till the end of July, when the survivors return to the Atlantic, swimming along the Portuguese and French coasts, and even as far north as England and Holland.

The Spaniards and the Majorcans thus get first shot at the visitors; they use the seine principally, working it from small boats close in to shore. Some, however, put out to sea in smacks something like the old Algerine xebecs, rigged with two and three lateen or triangular sails, and furnished with a bag-net that resembles a shrimp-net without the beam. Many of the Genoese anchovy fishers use the same kind of tackle, shooting it from a boat whose build would astonish English fishermen; for it is a short, broad, clumsy little thing with a double curve along the bottom, leaving her with no keel, or rather with a keel that is buried between the two curves; nevertheless, experienced persons say that no better boat for the class of work could be found.

The seine-catches are necessarily enormous. The shoals, which can be seen from a great distance, announce their presence by the pale tint which appears in patches on the water; and at sight of these patches the boats put out. Sometimes the Andalusians have no need to do more than lie in wait on the shore, for the shoals come in so near that it seems as if you could wade out and catch the fish in buckets. Going leisurely to work, the rowing-boats pull out to the far side of the nearest shoal, each two carrying between them a seine a couple of hundred yards long, six to eight fathoms deep in the middle, rounding off to three or four at each end or wing.

When a pair of boats has arrived at the desired spot the seine is shot as soon as they have separated to a distance equal to the length of the net, each end of which is made fast to a long tow-line, the other ends of these being tied one to each boat. Then the rowers pull back very gently, the boats gradually getting nearer one another again, and carry the tow-lines ashore, where women and children, or horses, are waiting to haul up. It will be seen that the net, being pulled in by two forces that gradually approach each other, thus converts itself into a kind of bag in which the fish are swept along willy-nilly.

As soon as the seine is within a few yards of dry land it is moored, a smaller net is shot inside it, and baling out commences—a task that sometimes lasts a whole day and more; the fish are then packed in kegs between layers of salt and taken to the factories.

The anchovy industry is a very ancient one; the *garum* of the Roman banquets was merely another form of anchovy sauce, and the condiment which Hindu cooks call red-fish is obtained from the anchovies caught at the mouth of the Ganges.

In the Adriatic and in the shallower parts of the Gulf of Lyons, we find the moored net a good deal in use for mullet and dory. With and without a beam, it is shot across tide from small boats, which are held by the same anchors that moor the net. The net is sunk half doubled or "mouthed," that is to say the ropes attached to the upper corners by which it will ultimately be pulled up, are first carried through rings at the lower corners so that, when once it is anchored, it lies bowed; and, on the ropes being tightened by the upward pull, will become completely closed. Such nets are cleared the first thing in the morning and the last thing at night, the fish being taken ashore by tugs or large two-masters.

A frequent tenant of these nets is the *dragonet*, which is beautifully marked with blue and yellow on a white ground, and is of the same family as the Scotch "gowdie."

Its peculiarity is that, instead of the ordinary gill-opening, it has two holes in its neck; its eyes are situated on the top of the head, so that the fish always looks upwards; its skin has no scales. With it will probably be found the *jaune dorée*, or yellow gilt fish, which has been vulgarly anglicised as "John Dory." It may be remembered that this fish, like the haddock, has an oval black spot on either side; from which the pious southern fisher-folk argue that it was from the dory's mouth that St. Peter took the tribute money, the marks being the impress of his finger-tips; unfortunately for the truth of the legend, there is neither dory nor haddock in the Sea of Galilee or in any other fresh water. Another fish of the same family, which only the poorer Italians will eat, is the boar-fish, whose head is shaped like the snout of a hog.

The fisherman of the south of France has a valued friend in the maigre, a doubtful one in the pilot fish, and a deadly enemy in the shark. The least known and most interesting of these, the *maigre*, can be taken with long lines, but quite as often goes of its own accord into a net and stays there. Its average length is four feet, though fishermen boast of having taken many six and seven feet long. When it finds itself among a number of other fish, it emits a humming or buzzing noise that is plainly audible through fifteen fathoms of water, and in this way it is an infallible guide to the men as to where they should shoot the nets. It figured in Roman feasts as the *umbrina*, and is still a great delicacy in France and Italy, especially its head. Its internal hearing apparatus was worn, set in gold, in the Middle Ages, as a charm against colic.

The pilot-fish, as our sailors call it, resembles the mackerel in size, marking, and flavour, and can be trawled with more ease than anything except a herring, for, in small batches, it will follow a ship for a thousand miles. But fishermen have a superstition that there is a secret understanding between itself and the shark, for where one is the other is usually not far off.

Almost all varieties of sharks, except the Greenlander, are represented in these waters: the fox-shark, the hammer-head, the white, the blue, etc. The last is the fisherman's pet abomination, for it not only eats the fish that he is wanting to catch, varying its diet with a human meal when circumstances permit, but it will bite a mouthful out of a full net (generally about half the catch), and swallow fish and meshes with gusto. The shark is shot and harpooned for the sake of his oil and the well-being of the community, and the Levant traders make a considerable sum annually over the sale of shagreen, which is supposed to be shark-skin dressed, but is more often the hide of camels, donkeys, and horses.

Two other net-destroyers are the *pristes*, or saw-fish, whose toothed snout is familiar to most of us; and the celebrated sword-fish. This giant—his body is fourteen feet long and his proboscis another seven—is an unreasonable beast. He does not care about fish as food, in fact, he lives on seaweed, yet is never so happy as when breaking up a shoal and frightening fish away from his neighbourhood; and, when he happens to take up a position in front of the net, this propensity of his has rather a disastrous effect, for other fish dare not come near. He is a wonderfully fast swimmer, as may be seen when he is fleeing from a shark, and is perhaps the most powerful of all fish. He will swim straight through a full net, tearing up the anchors or snapping the tow-lines; sometimes he is shot, and his flesh is supposed to be particularly nutritious, especially if he is young.

Passing downwards to Sicily and Sardinia we find the inhabitants possessing a monopoly in tunny-fishing. That monopoly, by the way, is only of recent date, for these curiosities used to be caught in great numbers by the Andalusian fishermen and also by the Turks.

The tunny (Greek *thuno*, to dart along) is a giant mackerel, dark blue above, white below, and silver on the sides, measuring anything from ten to twenty feet long, and sometimes weighing as much as half a ton. It is not quite peculiar to the Mediterranean, for there is a species found off the east coast of the United States which the Americans call the albicore and the horse-mackerel.

In Sicily and Sardinia it is caught very much as the Sicilian Greeks captured it, seven hundred years B.C., only with perhaps less assiduity, by means of nets and harpoons. Like other creatures that shoal, they cannot do without betraying their whereabouts, and a man perched on an eminence can detect from a great distance the pale brown blotches which a crowd of them would create on the water-surface. In spring and summer the fish come within a mile of the shore for spawning, and it is then that the tunny-harvest is made.

A coarse-meshed net, more than a mile long, is carried out to sea, and one end of it moored, the other being made fast ashore or to a smack; a second, almost as long, is then shot parallel to the coast, making with the first net either a T or a cross, and these are left in that position for at least twenty-four hours. When a sufficient number of fish have been covered, the towing-in begins; the anchors are pulled up, and a line fastened to each wing is rapidly carried ashore by boats. The towlines being pulled very swiftly—often by horse-power—not only the fish that are already caught by the gills are brought in, but also those that happen to be within reach of the two wings.

The moment the net is drawn into a specially prepared shallow, the fish find themselves enclosed above and below, and there is no possible escape for them. Then the killing; this is unsportsmanlike, but all fishing is apt to be so when money is the sole end in view. The poor fish, mewed up so closely that you can't tell one from another, are speared at leisure from the boats with harpoons till all are dead. They are then disembowelled and quartered and taken ashore for boiling, for the sake of their oil, which is valuable and plentiful, one fish alone sometimes yielding twenty gallons. Tunny-fishing gives employment to more than three thousand men in the two islands, much of the work in Sicily being done by convicts.

Another Sicilian industry, now on the wane although popular among the ancients, is pinna-gathering, the "pinna" being a member of the pearl-mussel family. The shell is immense, about the size of a very large meat-dish, and is gathered by wading and rock-scrambling. The fish itself is a secondary matter, though it is largely eaten by the poorer classes; but the filament or *byssus*, by which it attaches itself to the rocks or other objects, is about two feet long, and is used for making fabrics, being very tough and glossy.

The Greek and East Mediterranean fisheries are so sadly neglected that there is really nothing to say about them, all such work being overshadowed by the importance attached to sponge-diving; while the fisheries of Austria do not differ from those of Italy except in magnitude. On the African coast of the Sea, fresh-water fish are more sought after than those from salt water, for the reason that they are more easily come by. The fishermen of Tripoli are industrious, and France has infused a certain amount of energy into those of Tunisia; but, while a hand-net lowered haphazard into a pool or river will bring up a day's supply of fish for a whole family—nay, while live fish are even thrown at a man's door, as sometimes happens in North Africa when an artesian well is sunk, coast work is liable to be neglected.

A word about Mediterranean line-fishing among the French, Genoese and Venetians. Hand-lines are used principally for maigres, eels, and rays, the work being done from quays and small boats. Among the rays thus caught is one which commands more sale to conjurers, naturalists, and practical jokers than to ordinary consumers—the torpedo, or electric ray, which is so like the skate that it is often mistaken for it, and which has under its gills, two organs wherein is lodged an electrical apparatus capable of giving twenty or thirty violent shocks per minute.

CHAPTER XIII

THE PILCHARD—THE STURGEON

The Cornish fisherman—The pilchard—Shoaling—Drift-nets and seines—The "seine-boat"—Shooting the net—The stop-seines—Sharks!—"Tucking"—Taking the fish ashore—The factory—The sturgeon—Russian sturgeon and sterlet fishing—Isinglass and caviare.

CORNWALL and the pilchard are as closely associated in one's mind as Devonshire and cream, and any one who has seen the coast-line between the Lizard and St. Ives will also unconsciously connect pilchard-fishing with danger. Certain spots do not get such names as the Devil's Frying-pan or the Lion Rocks for nothing.

The Cornish fisherman takes himself far more seriously than the happy-go-lucky fellows of the south and east coasts. Instead of their quaint survivals of Saxon paganism, he holds certain gloomy predestinarian views, and devoutly believes in the ultimate perdition of the Devonshire trawlers. But he is a fine man all the same, and if his opinions give him the courage to face a rock-studded sea that, even in the brightest of weather, would be uninviting to most landsmen, he had better stick to them.

From October to July he is occupied as fishing jack-of-all-trades—spratting, crabbing, mackerelling, trawling. But, when July comes, every other interest is put on one side by the men of St. Ives and Penzance for the sake of the pilchard-harvest, which will last till the equinoctial storms of late September have begun to drive the fish to the ground, or further out to sea.

The pilchard, or the "gypsy herring" as the Scotch fishermen call it, is merely a large sardine or a small herring, and may be of any length up to nine inches. Really it can be found off the Cornish coast at all seasons of the year, though in December and January one would have to go down to the mud after it; in March it begins to shoal, but to no great extent, and the fishery seldom starts before the end of June or beginning of July. For some good reason the pilchard has, through successive centuries, decided that that particular quarter of the Atlantic is best adapted to spawning purposes and to the special class of food which it most affects; and thus, year after year, it chooses almost the same spots for shoaling. It is a most voracious little creature, its food consisting mainly of a kind of shrimp scarcely larger than a pin's head, or of the roes of dead fish when it can get them.

A shoal of pilchards must be seen in order to be fully realised. It has been likened to an immense army, with wings outstretched in line with the land, and composed of contingents which are continually taking up a new position. Wherever the shoals move, they give the appearance of a cloud-shadow to the water-surface, and by this the pilchard-watchmen profit; for men are placed on rising ground to look for these signs, and the moment they see them they signal by means of a white canvas ball to the boats that are lying in wait below.

Ever since the reign of Queen Elizabeth this fishery has been closely protected and governed by Acts of Parliament; the law even decides as to the dimensions of the nets, every one of which has to be registered. St. Ives has over three hundred nets, and is the centre of six specially appointed fishing-stations.

The net most in use is the seine—and that of gigantic proportions; the smallest allowed for out-fishing being a hundred and sixty fathoms long, eight fathoms deep at the middle, and six at the ends. These belong principally to companies nowadays, but a few private individuals still embark in the trade. Fleets of drift-nets, seven fathoms deep and three-quarters of a mile long, are also used, and are worked like herring-nets.

The old-fashioned "seine-boat" is a ponderous craft thirty-two feet long, manned by a crew of eight—six to row and two to manage the gear. Before sunset she is lying off the shore, awaiting the signal from the men on the look-out, and, the moment that comes, she pulls away as directed by them. With her are two shorter boats, each with six men aboard, and behind her she tows a third—a little cock-boat or "lurker," from which the skipper gives his orders and superintends the manipulation of the net; thus a pilchard-seine takes four boats to manage it.

At such work as this there is little time for spells of idleness; hard, heavy rowing, often against wind and current, is the oarsmen's portion; unceasing vigilance that

Pilchard-Fishing

"Tucking" is clearing the seine with the aid of a tuck-net, which is shot inside the larger net. The tuck comes up concave, bringing a large number of the fish to the surface, and it only remains to bale them out.

of the skipper and the net-minders. At times the skipper seems to be giving as many and as rapid directions as though he were a coach training a racing crew. This is because there is no reliance to be placed on the position of the bodies of the shoal; at one time the fish will appear to be making straight away from the boat's course; the minute after, the rowers must suddenly slow up, because it seems as though the entire shoal is driving as quickly as possible towards them.

At last, at a shout from the skipper, every one stops pulling and rests on his oar, and the two net-men in the seine-boat, one at bow and the other in the stern, throw the ends of the seine to the two smaller boats, and all three begin shooting. The "bunt" or deepest portion of the net is sunk from the large boat and requires careful handling, being the most heavily weighted part. As soon as the lower edge of this has touched the water it is maintained in that position while the other two crews arrange the tow-lines that are to be attached to the wings.

"Right," and "Ay, ay!" come hoarsely from first one boat and then the other, and the men in the principal boat lower the bunt gently, parallel to the coast-line, till only the cork-rope is visible.

Now that the main net is down the seine-boat pulls rapidly back towards the shore for a minute and then stops again, waiting to complete the work. Meanwhile the boat at each end has been joining one wing of a second and a third net—the "stop-seines"—to the principal seine, and is now pulling towards the bigger craft in order to throw the connecting line at the other end on board of her, paying out part of her stop-seine as she goes. The lines are seized by the waiting crew, drawn together, and the two stops joined so that they are like one net; and then the meeting-point is lowered like the rest. The result of this manœuvre is that a second seine has been shot—making, with the first, an oval or a letter D, according to the length of the stops—in *front* of the shoal, thereby arresting the fish that had been swimming towards the shore away from the large seine and driving them back to it.

Now the three boats, all pulling together, begin slowly towing in till shallower water is reached. Then another halt is made, for the area covered by the nets is larger than is necessary, now that there is no longer danger of the fish swimming under the net. The small boats again make for the "joins"; each one separates its own end of the stop-net from the wing of the seine, and between them they rapidly draw these wings together till the whole forms a rough circle; then the stop-net is removed and towing begins once more, and continues till some time after the lead-line has begun to scrape along the bottom, when the net is moored.

By dawn the men will be off again, for sunset and sunrise are the two favourable times for catching. The nets are paid out as before, the morning work being perhaps a little more leisurely done, because light is coming instead of going. Occasionally while at this morning fishing, the cork-line is suddenly seen to sway and bob, and perhaps to be drawn under altogether, as though a shoal had been caught by the gills and were carrying it down with their weight.

"A shark, lads," roars the skipper. "Look to your tow-ropes."

Again the cork-line ducks, then comes up again, and floating with it is, alas! a jagged strip of netting several yards long. A blue shark that has wandered up from the Bay of Biscay has helped himself to a mouthful of the fish.

"Pull up sharp," is the order, which is quickly executed and the net examined. Perhaps the mischievous monster has but bitten a hole big enough for its unwieldy body to pass through; if so a fold is made, the edges are deftly joined up without useless lamentation, and the net is taken aboard till another shoal presents itself. But where drift-nets are used, and the pilchards therefore a fixture in the net, times have been known when, on starting to haul up, the hapless fishermen have found little to haul beyond the cork-line and a strip of net, for the shark has passed along the entire length of the "fleet," cutting out the catch as though with a pair of scissors, with the result that the lower part of the net—or as much of it as has not been swallowed—has been sunk irretrievably, together with the fish that it contained.

During the past five-and-twenty years many of the old seine rowing-boats have been displaced by steamers, but it may be questioned how far this is a change for the better. Certainly larger seines can be used, and towing is made easier, but here the fishermen will tell you that the advantages end; for a great part of the work must still be done by small boats, so that there is no appreciable decrease in the danger involved, and when the men add up their profits they find themselves no better off than before.

We left the full seine moored close in to shore, awaiting the operation known as "tucking." When so many thousands of fish are packed together in this manner they cannot be taken from the net all in a few minutes, or even hours. A good-sized catch of pilchards will often take several days to move, whence the notion of keeping them in the water alive. Where the fish have been taken in drift-nets they are removed on board the smacks from which the nets have been shot, and sprinkled with salt.

"Tucking" is clearing the seine with the aid of a tuck-net, which is just half the length of the principal seine. It is shot from a small boat, inside the large net, and when it is down we notice that in addition to the two end lines which are being drawn together, a third and stouter one is sticking out of the water. This line is fastened to the lower edge of the smaller bunt, and is now hauled on till the middle of the tuck comes up concave, drawing a large proportion of the fish up to the surface; and it only remains to bale them out. This is done by scooping them into large baskets, which are placed in the boats that are waiting round the moored seine, and sent ashore.

The crowd of watchers for the boats is composed of two classes: "blowsers," or licensed porters who carry the bulk of the catch to the curing-yard; and the wives and children of the fishermen, who will take home as many fish as they can, for there is scarcely one of these industrious Cornishmen who does not do a certain amount of curing on his own account in his spare time.

Let us now take a glance at one of these curing-yards, where almost all the work is in the hands of women. In the first place the pilchards have to be sorted, the larger ones to be exported to the West Indies or sold for local consumption, the smaller to be sent to the Mediterranean to be made into sardines. Then a large square space on the stone floor is covered with a stratum of the fish, and over it is sprinkled a generous supply of coarse salt; then other layers of fish and salt alternately, till a pile five or six feet high is made. The heaps are left in this condition for a month, the oil, water, and salt gradually draining out of them into gutters communicating with tanks.

By this time the fish are "cured"; they have now to be carefully washed, after which only the packing remains to be done; the latter is the most important and lengthy part of the business, for improperly packed fish and bad fish mean the same thing. The pilchards must be placed in layers in barrels, and, when each barrel will hold no more, a weight is placed on the top of it and the bulk is steadily reduced by gradual pressure till the tub is only two-thirds full, the oil thus squeezed from the fish oozing out of the seams. When the barrel has been filled up once more, the pressure is repeated; and so on, till it will hold no more, and the fish are ready for export. The liquor drained and squeezed from the pilchards was at one time allowed to run away and breed fever, but it is now collected with great care and sold as manure.

THE STURGEON

I do not include the sturgeon in this chapter because zoologically it is a close relative of the pilchard, but because it too has to pass through a factory and export phase. So far from being connected with the pilchard, it has little but gills, fins, and tail in common with it, for it is a cartilaginous fish, like the shark, having gristle in place of true bone; it is devoid of teeth and has a long tapering snout, whence its name is derived (Latin, *stiria*, an icicle). Like the salmon, it divides its time between the sea and the river, though there is an entirely fresh-water variety which is found in the shallows of Lakes Michigan and Erie. Generally speaking, it passes the greater part of the year in the sea, entering the rivers in spring for spawning, and occasionally in the autumn for some purpose at present unknown. Its length is from six to eleven feet, and it is believed to live for two and three hundred years.

South Russia and parts of North America are the special localities for this fishery, though the sturgeon appears in all the temperate quarters of the world. Most readers are probably aware that in England it is a "royal fish," and when found in the Thames within the Lord Mayor's jurisdiction can be claimed by the Sovereign.

In the Caspian, Azov and Black Seas it is sometimes taken by long lines, but the Russian fishermen mostly rely on the spring up-river migration; at one Volga station alone more than ten thousand fish are often caught during that fortnight. The modern method is by double-walled nets moored across the current at the river-mouths, or by stake-weirs; but the peasants higher up the river still go in for the mediæval process of "snatching" the fish—sturgeon or sterlet, for the only difference is that the sterlet is smaller—with a cork and bare hook.

As soon as the thaws have finished, quite a fleet of the little home-made boats may be seen dotted about the quieter parts of the Volga, two men to a boat, one rowing and the other fishing. In spite of the sturgeon's being a ground feeder, he can often be persuaded to come to the surface, for he possesses a double portion of fish-inquisitiveness; therefore long lines are not absolutely necessary. Ordinarily the peasant ties a piece of cork or light wood on his line, and, a few inches below it, a barbed hook as stout as a pot-hook. This he throws a good distance from his boat and waits till a fish rises. In the thick of the season he need not wait long, for a fish quickly comes up to investigate, and a skilful fisherman will have jerked the hook into some part of its body long before its curiosity is satisfied. The larger fish are also harpooned.

To a poor Russian the catching of a big sturgeon is almost a fortune, for every bit of it is valuable. It is no uncommon sight to see a peasant-fisherman rowing or rafting down-stream to the nearest station with quite a cargo of these giants. Eaten fresh, the flesh is white and somewhat resembles veal.

At the factory the fish is first carefully opened and cleaned; the air-bladder and the roe being set aside, and the entrails removed to be boiled for oil. The bladder, after being freed from all greasy matter, is rendered down, and yields the purest gelatine that is to be found in the animal kingdom—a substance better known commercially as isinglass, which name is taken from the Dutch *huizen blas*, sturgeon bladder.

A more important process relates to the roe; the procuring of *caviare.* The roes, after they have been properly cleaned, are lightly beaten with twigs so that the eggs may be dislodged and separated; then the whole mass is rubbed or pressed through a sieve till the eggs have all filtered into a tub below, the tissues of the roe remaining in the sieve. The eggs are then dried and salted.

Lastly, the flesh is cut into strips which are laid for some weeks in brine-tanks and, when sufficiently salted, are smoked like bacon.

CHAPTER XIV

THE CATCHING OF LOBSTERS, CRABS, AND WHELKS

Fish that are caught in pots—The lobster—Colonial fish—The Bergen and Christiansund lobster-fishery—Cray-fish—Crabs—The hermit—Land crabs—Tropical and fresh-water crabs—Crabbing—Whelks—Fishing with "trots"—Whelking as a trade—The boats—The pots—The fish.

LOBSTERS, crabs, and whelks are fish that, on account of their habits, their formation, and their general preference for deep water, require special gear before they can be taken in the large quantities that the market demands; the name given to that form of gear is *pots.*

None of these animals possess a very high degree of intelligence where escape from captivity is concerned, and all of them are as greedy and insatiable as sharks; therefore the trap that will catch them need not be a marvel of ingenuity. A lobster-pot is generally a wicker cage with a small opening; sometimes it is dome-shaped, sometimes oval; often, again, it is formed like a soiled-linen basket with the middle or waist narrowed down to about a third of the original circumference. The lobster's own curiosity is sufficient to encourage it to "step inside"; but to stimulate desire, a piece of meat or fish is laid or suspended in the "belly" of the pot, and the result is that, when the tackle has been down for a few hours, a store of struggling lobsters will be found lying at the bottom, for not one of them will have the good sense to try to get out by the way he came in.

Lobsters are by no means so plentiful round these coasts as they used to be, no doubt because it is only comparatively lately that the law has troubled to protect them; and the greater number of those sold at the shops come from Scandinavia. Nearly three-quarters of a million fish are imported from there every year. Scotland, however, still seems to maintain her position as a lobster country, and the Orkneys and the Hebrides send from one to two hundred thousand fish in the course of a twelvemonth to Billingsgate.

The canned lobsters, apart from those from Scandinavia, come from Newfoundland and British Columbia. Latterly South Africa has also embarked in the tinned-lobster trade, and it is probable that the Cape Colony will not stop at lobsters, but will, in years to come, develop into one of the world's great fishing centres. Why not? It has hundreds of miles of coast-line; its latitude is about the same as that of Western Australia or Queensland; above all, along the bank that runs out from Cape Agulhas, is the end of the cold current which sweeps down the east coast from Madagascar, and which ensures a perennial and bountiful supply of fish.

The chief Norwegian lobster export centres are Bergen and Christiansund, which two towns form the limits of a curved line of the oldest and perhaps most productive lobster-grounds in the world. Here thousands of small boats are at work during the greater part of the year, for there are still few restrictions in regard to this fishery, though they are now being increased; the bulk of the Norwegian lobsters, however, are caught between March and September. Most local by-laws forbid the taking of spawning fish, and of those which measure less than eight inches from "beak" to tail.

There is no inducement to the fishermen to take small fish, for the large ones are generally plentiful enough; the infant lobsters, moreover, are very careful to be out of the way. When a little one leaves its mother its shell is still unformed, and its body therefore unprotected, and, while in this condition, it is liable to be snapped up by the first cod or conger that comes along; and if it should attempt to remain in a lobster colony it may expect to be eaten by adult fish of its own species; therefore it wisely swims away to the shallows, finds a strong position for itself in a rock-crevice, and there remains till its shell hardens and the animal can return to open water without fear. Every year it will go back to this or a similar hiding-place, for lobsters lose their shells annually, and are, for three or four days, defenceless; and it is during this shell-less period that much of their growth takes place. From the time a shell begins to re-form till it is quite hard, the lobster is said to be "soft," and if one finds its ways into the trap it is thrown out again, for the fishermen believe it to be poisonous. This is unlikely, although an animal that is about to cast its shell is undoubtedly sickly, and can scarcely be wholesome as food.

The pots are generally roped together, half a dozen or a dozen at a time; a weight or a stone is put into each, and one after another is allowed to sink; to the last one of the series a buoy-line is tied and its upper end fastened to a cork or keg. Sometimes the fish are so plentiful in one spot as to keep a large fleet of boats occupied the whole day in setting the tackle, and the catches are brought ashore literally by the boat-load.

A cargo of live lobsters are not the most desirable of companions in a small boat; an animal that has eight legs, and fangs like pincers, is a sort of thing one likes to keep at a distance; for a nip of a lobster is rather like a burn from a hot iron. The legs are a very variable number, for the lobster seems to have power to part with one when he likes; take him by the claw and he will wriggle away, leaving the limb in your hand rather than allow himself to be captured. One of the most curious facts about the fish is its extreme sensitiveness to loud noises; if a gun be fired close to it, it will shed some of its claws immediately, and the same thing will often happen during a thunderstorm. These limbs grow again in course of time.

A very close relative of the lobster is the cray-fish or craw-fish, which most of us, as children, have caught in the rivers. Most of this species are small, but those of the Indian rivers as well as the celebrated Tasmanian cray are very large, and are eagerly sought by the local fishermen.

Far more variety exists where the crab is concerned than among the lobsters. In common with the lobsters it has four pairs of legs, and a fifth pair which are converted into nippers. Many naturalists are of opinion, from the shape of its feet, that it is properly a land animal; and this argument is strengthened by the fact that certain varieties live entirely on land. The common crab is nearly always a deep-water fish, except where, as for example, on the Cornish coast, the deep rock-pools on the shore promise it reasonable immunity from trespassers; and the same may be said of most of the inedible crabs, the spider, the red crab, etc., many of which are never seen except on board a fishing-boat, when they have allowed themselves to be scooped up by a dredge, or have got themselves caught on a cod-hook.

For some reason or other most of these fish seem to be inedible, for, beyond the common crab and its little shore brother, no British crabs are ever eaten. The others are nevertheless valuable as bait, and though they are not regarded as a special bait-fishery like mussels or whelks, the shrimpers contrive to do good business with a very large quantity of them.

One of the finest bait-crabs is undoubtedly the hermit, or as the fishermen call it the "farmer," for its soft, unprotected body is a great temptation to all fish. Hermits may be picked up on some beaches at low tide after rough weather, but the majority of those used for bait are bought of the dredgers, for whether they interfere with oysters or not, they are always found in large numbers where oysters most do congregate. While the upper part of the animal is as well protected by shell and nippers as that of the other crabs, the lower is quite soft and pulpy. Guided by the marvellous instinct of self-protection, the little creature, as soon as it can fend for itself, seeks out some small shell into which it can fit the defenceless portion of its body, and, as it grows, it abandons the shell in favour of a larger one, changing its abode periodically till it comes to full size and can fill the shell of a very large whelk.

One day I persuaded a hermit that was trying to crawl away through a port-hole, to come out of his shell, and then dropped him into a bucket of sea-water with his own whelk-shell and another a size smaller; he crawled to the smaller one, examined it closely, but did not attempt to "fit it on"; after a minute's hesitation he pushed it contemptuously away, moved over to the larger shell and, after a brief hesitation, back-watered into it, drew in his horns and settled down to sleep comfortably. In some parts of the world—Keeling Island, for instance—these hermits are to be seen waddling about on land.

Talking of land-crabs, the largest and most extraordinary, as well as the most valuable kind, is the Birgos or purse crab, which is from two to three feet long and is an inhabitant of the East Indian Islands. This animal pays a daily visit to the sea, for the purpose of moistening its antennæ, but spends the rest of its time in its nest which is made at the root of a tree—generally a cocoa-nut palm. It burrows a large hole in the ground and lines it thickly with cocoa-nut fibre, thereby laying up a vast store of that useful material for the natives to avail themselves of. As food it is pronounced excellent by Europeans, but what is of more consequence to the

Malay fishermen is its oil; each adult contains a huge lump of fat which yields a quart of pure oil. Whether these crabs actually climb the trees after the nuts on which they live is a disputed point which does not come within our province to settle.

Another remarkable crab and, from the fisherman's point of view, the only useless one, is the glass crab of the tropical seas; this creature is transparent and, but for its staring, blue-black eyes, would be invisible in the water.

All readers may not be aware that there are such things as fresh-water crabs, quite distinct from the cray-fish. They are to be found in the Indian rivers as well as in many of those of South Europe; in the latter they are caught with pots similar to lobster-traps; the carapace or upper shell is almost square, and the antennæ are curiously short.

Here in England crabbing is scarcely a trade by itself, but is rather pursued in slack or leisure time; the Cornish pilchard-fishers, for instance, fill in their intervals with such work. The most commonly used tackle is an iron hoop with two diametrical cords, crossing at right angles; dependent from the hoop is a net-bag which bellies out till the circumference is nearly twice that of the hoop. The fisherman baits the trap with fish—generally ray—fastens a short bit of rope handle-wise across the frame, and lowers the pot by a long cord that is tied to the middle of the handle. When he feels the hoop touch the bottom he raises it again about a foot, so as to give free play to the net, and then makes his end fast to a buoy or to his boat. For small-crab fishing less care is needed; the pots are let down in a series, left for some hours and then pulled up again, and the catches thus made are sometimes enormous; I have seen as many small crabs in one pot as would fill a peck measure. By small crabs I mean such as just come within legal limit, for the law is very sharp nowadays on the crabbers; no fish that measures less than four and a quarter inches in length may be taken; fishermen are also forbidden to take spawners, and crabs whose shell has not hardened; for these fish assume a new shell every year just as the lobsters do.

I spoke of crabs as bait. Whelks and crabs "se mangent entre eux"; there are few things the one likes so much as a taste of the other; but the odds are in favour of the crab, for it is only when his shell is soft, or after he is dead, that the whelk gets a fair chance at him. The fisherman comes along and, like the stork that settled the dispute between the frog and the mouse by eating the pair of them, catches the crabs and then uses them as bait to catch the whelks. This method of whelking by means of lines is the one least commonly known, and we must leave the consideration of pots to glance at it.

Whelk-lines, generally termed "trots" or "bulters" (not to be confused with the "bulters" mentioned in Chapter IV), are great favourites with the Thames-mouth fishermen. Each main line has short lines (called "snoods") tied at right angles to it, at intervals of a few yards, and every short line has twenty tiny crabs fastened to it, each about six inches apart from the other. This tackle is shot in the same manner as the ordinary long lines, the far end buoyed, and the other either buoyed or kept in the boat.

In a very short time the lines are alive with whelks, for their movements are quicker than those of land gasteropods, and their appetites more ravenous. They fasten themselves on the unresisting crabs and, with their powerful, toothed tongues, begin to eat through the shell; when once they have taken the bait nothing will shake them off, and the little fools fall victims to their own greed. The strength of a whelk is enormous; pick one up when he is crawling about the deck and try to hold him from withdrawing into his shell; you cannot do it once in a hundred times. No wonder then that the pulling up of the trots does not shake off any of the catch from their prey.

It may be surmised, from their being caught in such large numbers, that whelks are very prolific; they are. When do you ever go to the seaside without seeing the spawn lying about? It is contained in those irregular clumps or bunches of white, spongy-looking globules that are often taken for seaweed. Dog-whelk spawn is generally seen only in deep water and, instead of being bunched together, every capsule is distinct; it is generally thrown on stones and rocks, and looks like a beautiful yellow growth or lichen, in shape and size not unlike heather blossom.

Whelking is a trade by itself; and it is a very lucrative one, partly because many men are frightened at the apparently low prices paid for the fish, and so steer clear of it, and allow the few to make their profit undisturbed; and partly because whelks are never out of season either as food or bait. They are sold principally to the line-fishers of the north and east, not by the cart- or ship-load like mussels, but by the bushel or the bag.

The most renowned whelkers are the Norfolk men, and where local feeling is not too strong against such a measure, they carry on what might otherwise be a neglected industry in other eastern and southern fishing grounds besides their own. As a rule they are not interfered with, for though fishermen are proverbially tenacious of their rights, they are seldom churlish. But the interlopers must mind their manners; you may see a hundred pounds' worth of whelk-gear deliberately sunk by the lawful tenants of the ground if it has been shot so as to do harm to the local industry. Generally, however, the whelkers are regarded as harmless lunatics who "whelk" because they are fit for nothing else.

One of the funniest things I ever saw in connection with the fishermen was their contempt for some whelkers' boats brought to a southern fishing town from the Norfolk coast; they were beautiful boats, too: large enough for lifeboats, and, when rigged with a big lug-sail, they could almost fly through the water. Then why the contempt? Because they had been brought down by rail! What good could any boat be that had arrived in such an ignominious fashion? Scarcely any of these good fellows had ever been in a train—save one old dear who went to London once upon a time, and while there (not being able to read) "steered" himself about by means of a pocket-compass and the weather-cocks, and whose method of finding a given spot was to "shape a course nor'-east," etc. After a day or two he shook the dust of London off his feet, because he was sure that wherever he went there was always a policeman following him; whereas he "knowed he shouldn't be took for a thief down home."

These despised little boats go off every day with the ebb tide, and on reaching water whose depth at high tide would be about five fathoms, make ready to clear and re-lower the gear. The pulling up of the nearest buoy-line drags up the first few of the series of pots; these are emptied one by one, and the cord is hauled and hauled till the whole row of pots—generally about fifty in number—lie empty in the boat. Then you can see that, attached to the buoy-lines, is a main or ground-rope, about a quarter of a mile in length, along which the pots are threaded at intervals of from three to five fathoms. The pots themselves are far more elaborate than those used for crabs or lobsters; the upper part is a dome made of thin strips of iron, and its base is a perforated iron disc from which depends a little net bag capable of holding two gallons. Round the dome, a cord—the "rattling line"—is laced loosely, and acts as a ladder up which the whelks climb to reach the bait that is lying on the sieve-like base, through which they will fall into the net below.

The pots are soon rebaited and thrown over again, and the boat sails away to her next buoy. You can see now why such a capacious craft must be employed; one series of pots if full would yield about twelve bushels of whelks; and a fair average catch from five series would be forty bushels. The fish are stowed in bags and sent away by rail.

It may be asked, what need is there for making a special fishery of whelks when the dredgers land such a great number? The dredgers do indeed, when their own catches are poor, pick out the whelks and put them aside for selling; but it is rather like a private householder saving his empty wine-bottles for sale; the proceeds of small quantities are so ridiculously low that only a miserly or very poor man would trouble to keep them; and the dredger who can earn from six to ten shillings a day is not likely to neglect his own work for the sake of a gain of about fivepence-halfpenny.

Whelks as seen in London on a costermonger's barrow would, I think, only tempt a very hungry man, or one whose appetite had a strange bias; yet these fish are a favourite food among the fisher people, and, from the fact that a man will often do a hard day's work on nothing else, they must needs be nourishing. Boiled the moment they come out of the sea, and eaten hot with a sea-appetite, they are certainly very good, and, inasmuch as the intestine can be removed, are much safer and cleaner eating than crabs or lobsters. There is a member of this family, called the red whelk, which is very tasty but, according to the fishermen, very disastrous in its effect on the eater; they say that a plateful of such fish will make a man absolutely intoxicated.

CHAPTER XV

THE FISHERIES OF THE FAR EAST

China, Japan, Siam, etc.—A fish-eating people—Fresh-water fishing—Chinese angling—Fishing with the help of cormorants—How the birds are trained—Good and bad divers—Two birds to one fish—The dip-net—River-fishing by hand—Sea fisheries; the junk and the lorcha—A Portuguese colony—"Archers" and "fighting-fish"—Japan's fisheries—The salmon and trout.

UNDER the above heading we may include the fisheries of China and Japan, together with those of Siam, Annam, and Malacca.

It may not be easy for us Europeans to realise that the inhabitants of these countries are even more a fishing people than ourselves. Nevertheless they are. The fact could doubtless be demonstrated and explained in scores of different ways; but it is sufficient for us to remember that (1) the people of the Far East are, as a whole, of a somewhat timid disposition, and consequently less inclined to take to hunting than the men of the West; (2) for the most part their climate is against the consumption of much flesh meat; and, in any case, a large proportion of the inhabitants would abstain from it on religious grounds. Hence a disposition to live on vegetable produce; and to eke out or savourise such diet with fish would surely be instinct to a seaboard people. Japan is surrounded by water; Malacca and Corea nearly so; China, Siam, and Annam are washed by the sea as well as drained by huge, fish-teeming rivers; and the inhabitants of the three last-named have, for centuries, cultivated the art of fresh-water fishing to an infinitely greater extent than can be seen in any other part of the world. Fish is cheap, moreover, and Easterns are economically inclined. Next to rice, therefore, fish must be regarded as the staple food of these temperate folk, and the procuring of it as one of their most important occupations.

Fresh-water fishing as carried on by the Chinese is anything but a laborious industry; on the other hand it offers ample opportunity for meditation and rest; and, as a large proportion of the population spend their lives on the water, they have not far to look for their dinner.

The approved Celestial method of angling has its peculiarities. The fisherman provides himself with two or more slender bamboo rods, each of which is supplied with rings for the line to pass through, such as our own rods have, and also with a homely attempt at a winch. His lines would make a British angler envious; they are of the finest silk, deftly twisted, and scarcely thicker than a hair; yet of wonderful strength and durability. His hooks are not so likely to be coveted by Europeans, for they are of the bent-pin order, being destitute of barbs. Each line has a short bit of wood tied on to it in place of a float, fastened only by one end, so that it will merely lie on the water instead of standing perpendicularly.

Seated on his raft, or on the bank, the Chinaman very methodically prepares for his morning's work. With the point of one of the rods he first carefully separates the weeds and leaves on the surface of the water, and brushes aside, or flicks off, the heads of lotos that may be in his way. As soon as he sees a clear field, in goes his first hook, baited with a fly; or, if ground-fishing, probably with a strip of kid or morsel of paste. Then he places the butt of the rod in a holder ready prepared and proceeds to make his second cast. This holder is a short length of bamboo, the hollow of which will just fit the end of the fishing-rod; and is driven into the bank, or lashed to the side of the raft, so that it will keep the rod at an angle of about thirty degrees to the water.

But how this casual individual ever succeeds in catching anything at all is one of the hidden things. Apparently he is asleep half his time; we do not see him make any attempt at watching bait or float, or at playing his fish; yet he seldom pulls up the line without there being a fish at the end of it. Above all, as often as not it is a dace; and anglers do not need to be told that this is an exceedingly sharp biter which requires to be struck immediately.

Each time John takes a fish off the hook he stoops and seems to put it back into the water at his feet. But if you watch him when he leaves off work you will see him drag out a large bamboo basket that has been kept in the water with only the rim showing above the surface. As the basket comes up, the water naturally is drained off, and the Chinaman has fresh fish for sale or private consumption, instead of flabby things that have been exposed to several hours of scorching sun.

A more characteristic and better-known system of fishing among the Mongols is with the aid of cormorants. Anyone who has ever taken the trouble to watch one of these curious birds dive must see that they are capable of being made splendid allies to the fisherman; and the Mongolian peoples have succeeded in taming and training the creatures till they can be relied upon to fill their master's bag in a very short space of time. Early in the seventeenth century an attempt was made to introduce cormorant-fishing into England as a sport, but it does not seem to have met with much success.

When the bird is quite young a ring, or a collar of grass, is fastened round its neck, so tightly that, though it can still breathe, it can only swallow a very small article. A cord, or sometimes a pair of reins, is attached to the collar and, with much coaxing or smacking, the master sends the little one into the water. Ordinarily its instinct will prompt it to dive and to seize in its bill as large a fish as it can lift; and as soon as it comes to the surface it is smartly hauled in, informed that it is a good bird, and made to deliver up its prey. As it progresses in knowledge the cord is dispensed with; and the bird, still tightly collared, has to learn to enter and leave the water at a sign of the hand; and when its education is complete, the collar is sometimes removed as well, by which time no well-bred cormorant would think of swallowing a fish unless its master had given permission.

The cormorant is usually started from a boat, or a moored raft, a long, low-lying construction made of the eternal bamboo, and propelled by one paddle. Each

Stereo Copyright, Underwood & U. *London and New York*

FISHING WITH CORMORANTS IN CHINA

A characteristic method of fishing among the Mongols is with the aid of cormorants. These birds are capable of being made splendid allies to the fishermen, who have tamed and trained them till they can be relied upon to fill their master's bag in a very short time.

fisherman has about half a dozen birds—among them, perhaps, a couple of "apprentices"—and these have all arranged themselves in a row at one end of the raft with their eyes solemnly fixed on their master. With a wave of the hand or a snap of the fingers, he summons the first; it waddles up to him and jumps on to his open hand. Petting it and gently smoothing its feathers, the fisherman seems to whisper confidentially to the bird; then places it on the edge of the raft and stands by to await developments.

Then the cormorant dips its bill into the water once or twice, jerks its head from side to side, gives a shake to its tail, and suddenly disappears. Meanwhile the other birds, huddled together in a perfectly straight line, look on, expectant of a summons from their master. After an interval of about a quarter of a minute the diver reappears at some distance from where it went in, holding in its mouth a struggling fish of the dace or roach tribes. It swims over to the raft, springs aboard, hops lightly on to the fisherman's knee, and is relieved of its burden; and the master, having placed the fish in the basket, goes through the same endearments as before, and again puts the bird on the raft-edge. The same thing happens again, and perhaps three or four times over, till, thinking the bird has done enough, the fisherman once more caresses it and deposits it in the middle of the raft; this is a sign that the faithful creature may take a rest; and, full of pride at its exploits, it struts away to the opposite side, where it takes up a position on the rail and stares superciliously at its friends that are still waiting their turn.

Bird Number 2 is beckoned; affecting ceremony as before; but, when its head comes above water, its bill is still empty and it looks hesitatingly towards the raft, though not daring to approach it without leave. The master shakes his head reproachfully and points downwards, and the bird dives resignedly. This time it is down longer, yet once more comes up empty-mouthed; but the fisherman is inexorable and the cormorant is bidden to dive a third time—and a third time comes up with nothing. Celestial patience cannot brook this; clearly bird Number 2 is a duffer; the man beckons it out of the water, spanks it soundly about the head, and tosses it on to the deck, whence it waddles shamefacedly away and takes a place of dishonour at the end of the rank.

Bird Number 3 obeys the call in a sprightly fashion and dives the moment it is released, without any useless preliminaries. It is down a whole minute or more. Then, some thirty feet from the raft, the surface is seen to bubble and ripple, and suddenly the little black head rises above water; bird Number 3 has caught some kind of salmon, over a foot long, and so heavy that every now and then it drags the plucky head under again. The fisherman mutters a cheering word and snaps his fingers in the direction of bird Number 4, which is started off in the usual manner. 4, however, does not dive; it swims straight at 3 and, seizing the river-monster near the tail, sets 3's mind and bill at rest; and the industrious pair paddle steadily for the raft, supporting the weight between them. Even now there is a danger lest the fish should escape, to which the fisherman puts an end by leaning over as soon as the birds come within reach and relieving them of their burden.

When it is the turn of the "apprentices" to go in, the procedure is different. Probably the cord is fastened on, and the bird is driven in by dint of much clapping of hands on the part of the fisherman. Then, perhaps, instead of diving, the cormorant will merely stare round in bewildered fashion till the master, with a long rod, guides it away from the boat, and, if it still remain obstinate, plunges it bodily under with the end of the stick. Some men, in addition to bridling the young birds, fasten a cord round the body, leaving a loop like a kettle-handle at the top to serve the purpose of lifting the creature in and out.

When this species of fishing is carried on by night, a brazier or a lighted torch is fixed at one end of the raft, where it not only enables the fisherman to see what he is doing, but also acts as a bait, appealing to the everlasting curiosity of the fish which rise "to worship the delusive flame," as Shelley expresses it.

A third variety of bank and raft fishing is by means of a very large dip-net, made of twine or spruce-fibre. The gear, weighted with stones, is lowered by a single rope which runs out over the head of a wooden lever and is left down for an hour or so; at the end of that time the lever is weighed up till the mouth of the net comes just above water, then the fishermen, armed with small landing-nets fitted to long handles, proceed at leisure to bale out the contents.

Yet another way, the most primitive of all, is by catching the fish with the hands—a practice easily possible in shallow streams and pools that are literally alive with fish. The operator wades in hip-deep, and this at once stirs up the fish that are on the bottom, which is just the reverse of what the wader wants; and, as a counterblast, he slaps and splashes the water till they go down again and hide in the mud; whereupon, using his feet as feelers, he coolly stoops and picks the fish out of it, filling the bag that hangs on his shoulder in a very few minutes.

There are few specially noteworthy features of the Chinese salt-water fisheries. All the way down the coast of the Yellow and China Seas, fleets of junks manned by Coolies, Chinamen, and Lascars, are to be seen daily; they do not go far from land, partly because there is little need, partly through centuries of habit of giving a wide berth to Japanese and Malay pirates.

The junk, without doubt the oldest-fashioned craft in the world, is a not unpicturesque, flat-bottomed vessel with one sail, similar to our lug-sail in shape, but ribbed all the way down with parallel cane yards, which apparently can be used for reefing. Some of the more go-ahead boatbuilders have during the past century attempted to improve on the junk by the construction of the *lorcha*, a boat made after the European model, though still rigged like the older vessel.

At and round Macao, on the Canton River, is a colony of Portuguese, founded as far back as 1586, and similar to that mentioned in Chapter X, in so far as many of its people are hereditary fishermen who have partially introduced European methods of working, and have made themselves the centre of the fishing-trade for many miles round.

In the China Sea and parts of the Indian Ocean is a remarkable little fish known as the "archer," and whenever it makes its appearance in the net it is jealously set aside in a pot of water by some member of the crew. In their idle moments the men will even angle for it when they are sufficiently far from land. It is about seven inches long and has a wide, ugly mouth, the lower jaw of which is considerably longer than the upper; it feeds on flies and insects and has an almost infallible means of catching them. Swimming near the surface it watches for the approach of its prey and, the moment this comes in sight, squirts a jet of water straight at it; this manœuvre brings the prize down to the surface, and all the archer has to do is to swallow it. When such a fish is caught, it is taken home and kept in a jar as a household plaything, its owner amusing himself by suspending a fly on a string over the jar, for the entertainment of its occupant.

In the rivers of Siam and Annam is a somewhat smaller creature, though none the less remarkable; the "fighting-fish," which is as carefully angled for and treasured as the archer. When taken, it is preserved in a bowl and kept for fighting. Two of them, let loose in a shallow tank, will afford as much amusement as fighting-cocks gave to our grandfathers; and, like them, the bystanders bet heavily on the issue of the struggle. In Siam such fights are specially licensed by the Government, and seem to prove a fruitful source of revenue.

Japan, more ready to follow Western nations than its neighbours, takes her fisheries very much in earnest. The European trawl-net is in use, as also the various forms of seine, though we cannot expect to find anything answering to our notions of a smack; for the Japanese fishers have no medium between the most up-to-date steam-trawler and the old-fashioned junk. The latter is slightly different in make and rig from the Chinese boat. It has no bulwarks beyond a shallow plank; is built rather high, and has immense storing accommodation below decks. At the very top of the mast is a bamboo yard from which hangs the sail, plain, oblong, divided from top to bottom, and so long that it almost sweeps the deck. Another very common fishing-boat of native build, though latterly of European rig, is the *sampan*.

The *maguro*, a large, salmon-fleshed fish, the cod, mackerel, and a variety of sea-bream called the *tai*, are the commoner fish taken in the nets; the last-named is more often eaten raw than cooked, and either way it is very appetising. I once saw the tai served up raw, sprinkled with vinegar and herbs; and the very next course was the same fish cooked,—stewed in a sort of *soupe au vin*.

The chief fishing ports are Hakodate, Nagasaki, and Yokohama; in fact, till 1859, Yokohama had no other occupation than fishing.

FISHING IN JAPAN

The fisherman may be seen seated on the raised platform. He is lowering his extraordinary hammock-like net. When sufficient fish are above the meshes, he dexterously jerks up the net, and lands his catch by means of a small hand net.

The inshore fisheries include weirs of a sort, together with a system of dip-nets not unlike those in use among the Chinese river-fishers. The fisherman erects a rough scaffolding above the water, over which a thatched roof is placed as a shelter from the sun; and from here he lowers a huge, oblong net which is drawn into concave form by cords, and kept open by a framework made of two curved, intersecting poles. Connected with the framework is a wooden lever, by means of which the whole net can be quickly weighed out of the water.

As soon as the net is down, the fisherman waits patiently till the fish collect over the spot where he has lowered his tackle, and then suddenly jerks the edges of the net above water; then, like the Chinaman, he ladles his catch out with a smaller dip-net, hauls the fish up to his platform, and packs them away in his basket.

But the Japanese are by no means mere stay-at-home fishers; almost all the Corean coast-fishery is in their hands, and sealing boats put off every season from Hakodate for the Kurile Islands at the far north, and even for Kamchatka. Moreover, the little country's exportation of fish-oil is steadily on the increase.

In their river-fishing, too, Western principles have come largely into use, though the cormorant is still very popular among the peasantry and the old-fashioned native sportsmen. Trout are found abundantly in all the streams, and in the north, salmon are exceedingly plentiful. In angling for the *ai* (a large kind of trout) and the *masu*, or Japanese salmon, before the tackle is thrown, the native fishermen catch a handful of small fry, something like our young roach, in a landing-net, and fastening a string to each, pull them up and down in the water to attract the larger fish.

The Ishikari-gawa is the favourite salmon river, and its reputation has now become so great as to cause both English and American sportsmen to make periodical pilgrimages to it.

CHAPTER XVI

SOME REMARKS ON THE IRISH FISHERIES

Comparative poverty of the western fisheries—Possible reasons—Present state of the Irish fisheries—The Irish fisherman—Trawling and long-line fishing—Congers, sharks, and sea-cats—Trawling on rocky ground—"Man overboard!"—Ling, halibut, and ray—Eels—Tory Island.

IF one had space and leisure to dive into the matter, there are doubtless good reasons to be found for the fact that the western portions of the United Kingdom cannot compare with those of the east for productive fisheries. Where is the western fishing town that can be mentioned in the same breath with Aberdeen, Grimsby, Lowestoft, Yarmouth, or even Ramsgate? Yet the Irish Sea, the Channels and the Atlantic generally are surely as well adapted for the work as the German Ocean; for if the rainfall be greater, the wind is just as favourable to the smacks as it is on the east; often more so.

It is certainly not that the men of the east are necessarily more careful over money-matters than the men of the west; for much of the talk about the "thrifty fisher-class" is so much foolish cant; with the exception of the Scotch, and of the Cornish and the Welsh—who, by the way, are westerns—a more foolishly improvident class than the fishermen scarcely exists, no matter which point of the compass they come from; if a trawler earns ten pounds in one week, the chances are that he will not have a halfpenny by the end of the next. I am well aware that there are exceptions, and that in every fishing town there are generally one or two wealthy men who have made every penny of their money in the boats.

What is much nearer being the reason is that the percentage of Danish, Saxon, and Jutish blood is far greater in the east, and that for one western Rolf Ganger or Ragna Rough-breeks, the east coast can produce twenty Hengists, and Gorm Ethelstans and Herewards; and that therefore the inclination to a sea life is far stronger in the Yorkshire man or the Norfolk man than it is in the average Kelt. To this must be added the fact that the power of steady work is sadly wanting in some of the fishing people of the west; at any rate among the Irish, Welsh, and Manx.

Five-and-twenty years ago the fisheries of Ireland were apparently in an almost hopeless condition, but to-day things are certainly on the mend. Much has been done. Government has built piers and harbours, has made grants or loans to the fishers, and, even as far back as 1875, had begun to spend large sums in encouraging the industry generally. If you ask an Irish fisherman why trade is so bad he will tell you that the mackerel have all gone away, and that the Scotch and Devonshire trawlers have broken up the herring shoals; but the Board of Trade reports say very differently; to wit, that shoals of both herring and mackerel have been allowed to pass the coasts through the indolence of the fishermen and the scarcity of nets; and that, till the "foreign" trawlers came, soles, which often abound round there, were never caught at all. Twenty years ago lobsters and crabs could almost have been shovelled on board the smacks round the west coast of Ireland, and such may still be the case.

Out of a population of four and a half millions, twelve thousand people are now engaged in fishing; the trade is controlled by a Congested Board, and the coast is divided up into centres, of which Dublin, Cork, Sligo, and Galway are the chief.

Every imaginable form of craft may be seen in these waters, cutters and luggers being the most popular; and the crews include negroes, Welshmen, Englishmen, Manxmen, and an occasional woman. The typical Hibernian fisherman is not the same being on land as he is at sea. Once persuade him to buckle to his work, once let him get on board his smack, and his seamanship and his energy would be a valuable object-lesson to some of the East Coast men. He is not infrequently a bold romancer—I have seldom met an Irish fisherman who had not, at some period of his existence, caught a conger that had at least ten other eels in its stomach, graduated and arranged like the wooden puzzle eggs that the London hawkers sell, one inside the other; and he will sometimes do what the East Coast and Cornish fishers strongly set their faces against, take beer or whisky on board; but, these peculiarities apart, he is a splendid fellow at sea, whose unfailing courage and brilliant flashes of inspiration will help him to steer round rocks and currents like the best pilot that ever sailed out of harbour.

To see him at his best you want to watch him trawling or line-fishing under an English or Scotch skipper whose rule is "no beer on board." Plaice, mullet, hake, sole, turbot, these are what he is trawling for and, with a good wind, what he will catch! If he is line-fishing he wants ling and halibut and cod. Often one gear takes fish that is expected in the other; turbot and brill will sometimes swarm on the lines; or a couple of huge congers will wriggle about in the trawl. The lines are probably hand-lines; for not many Irish families would give up a whole day or more to the baiting of a creel-full of hooks.

I have never met the man who could truthfully say that he liked conger-fishing; if a conger should come up in the trawl, nobody cares much how soon it worms its way through a port-hole and out into the sea again. One would almost as soon have a boa-constrictor for a fellow-passenger; many a fisherman can show horrible scars caused by the bite of one of these gentry. Fancy having a thing that weighs nearly a hundredweight, is thicker than a man's arm, and more than eight feet long, going about on deck seeking whom he may devour! They are as savage and voracious as sharks, and do undoubtedly devour their own brethren, though not in the orderly manner quoted above. If they once get their teeth into anything, even decapitation will not loose them, and the

Irishman was no *fandi fictor* who said that he had seen the jaws of a bodiless head prised open with a chisel and pincers before the arm which they had bitten could be set free.

The South Ireland conger-fishing is done by hand-lines, with a pilchard or a small herring as bait. The fish are caught at night, generally from luggers or rowing-boats, and a knife is driven through their heads before they can get into mischief.

The west and south coasts are only good in certain places for trawling; here and there a beautiful sand-bed will offer itself, where the trawl-heads can glide along as if they were going over a ballroom floor. Then up come the mullet and turbot and plaice as fast as you like, and our Irishman rubs his hands as he reflects that at least a fortnight's immunity from work will accrue from to-day's catch. Sometimes a small mountain of plaice only is shot out of the trawl; good, honest seven-pounders—a reasonable weight for such fish, though they sometimes reach fifteen pounds.

The reason why plaice appear more often in the trawl than the majority of other fish, is because they are such poor swimmers; they have no swimming-bladders, and consequently keep pretty much along the bottom, where they find their food—molluscs chiefly, and baby skate—and so are swept in by the foot-rope of the trawl where swifter fish would escape.

Another fish frequently taken in Irish waters is the "mackerel-guide," more properly known as the gar-fish. This is really a kind of salt-water pike, but it tastes wonderfully like mackerel; it has gained its nickname on account of its being so frequently found at the head of a shoal of mackerel that are coming into the shallows to spawn.

Sometimes, among the heaving mass that is being turned over and sorted, a broad sheet of light grey shows itself, and a big tail pokes its way through a crowd of smaller fry and lashes itself irritably up and down, thus displaying dark stripes along the lower part of the body to which it belongs. Every man instinctively snatches up his knife or a bit of wood and prepares to defend himself.

"'Tis a sea-cat; look out!" shouts everybody in one breath; and, as the spiteful monster raises its ugly head and opens its mouth, a prudent fisherman salutes it with a cut across the nose, or pins it down to the deck with a knife-blade. This unlovely creature—sea-cat, cat-fish, or wolf-fish—is a vicious beast, whose bite is "ten degrees worse," as the fishermen say, than a conger's; at any rate it is often more painful, and some even maintain that it is poisonous. The fish is about six feet long, its flesh is much prized by the poorer classes, and its skin is so tough and durable that the Scotch and Irish fishers make bags of it. It is exceedingly savage, and will snap at anyone who goes near it.

The stranger on board an Irish smack need not be astonished or alarmed at seeing an occasional monster thirty feet long, lying on the water, or even inquisitively shoving his muzzle over the taffrail.

"An' indeed it's no shark at all; 'tis a sun-fish, surr," the Irishman will tell him; generally adding a rider to the effect that it is more peaceable than any kitten. But it *is* a shark all the same, let Patrick call it what he likes; the basker, which, in warm weather, spends most of its days lying almost on the water-surface as though revelling in the sun's rays. It is as strong as a whale, but undoubtedly quite harmless, and no fisherman ever takes any notice of it.

These western and southern beds are very treacherous to the poor trawlers, and a skipper who does not know every square yard of the bottom had better keep clear of them. Sometimes, while on such a sand-bed as we have just been peacefully drifting over, there will be a sudden, violent jerk on the boat—the higher the wind the more this will be perceived. Sometimes she will lie over for a moment like a yacht tacking; the skipper springs across to the helm and puts the boat about, shouting directions to the crew and, if he be a humorist, which most of these fellows are, observing that they have "netted a rock." In a fairly high wind the towlines have been known to snap when this has taken place; then, of course, all hope of saving the gear is at an end. As it is, the smack must, if possible, get to the farther side of the rock and tow the net backwards from under it—an impossible feat if the wind chooses to be contrary; at best it will be something like trying to turn a hay-cart in a narrow lane.

Then the trawl is winched up, and the extreme lightness of it tells a sorry tale; the net is certainly empty or nearly so, and, as the beam is taken on board, it may be seen that the net hangs straight and flat in the water like a limp rag. Impatiently the men snatch at it, in a hurry to know the worst. Down in the "cod" of the trawl are a few plaice and brill, but above it is a rent four feet long, which has doubtless been caused by some sharp rock when the foot-rope was jerked free from the mass under which it had slid. Then out come the netting tools, and the busy crew hastily, yet neatly, repair the damage, thanking the saints, meanwhile, that it is no worse; and once more the tackle is thrown over.

But all this turning about has thrown some of the men off their guard, and, as the main-sail flies round, one of them gets the boom full across his chest. For a second his head is muffled in the swelling sail, and then, before anyone knows what is happening, there is a splash, followed by the shout, "Old Jack's overboard!"

That "man-overboard" cry is a far more awful sound than italics or marks of exclamation can make it appear; I have heard it once and am not anxious to hear it again. Sometimes even practised sailors seem for the moment to be paralysed by it, although it is not absolutely an uncommon occurrence in rough weather, or when another smack comes along and steals the wind from your boat so that your main-sail recoils suddenly.

One man "unships" his sea-boots and sou'-wester, another stands by with a boat-hook, a third with a rope. It is on these occasions that you realise that, however bitter enemies men may be in everyday life, one is ready enough to help another unhesitatingly when there is any fear of death. But, in this case, there is no call for sentiment or sacrifice; a very soused-looking head comes above water, makes some unintelligible remarks, and then a young fisherman leans over the bulwarks, grabs the drenched man by the neck and shouts laughingly, "I've got the old chap!" and in a minute he is hauled on deck. But such easy escapes are not necessarily the rule.

If the torn net cannot be repaired, or if the ground is too hopelessly rocky to risk another shot with the trawl, the men will sometimes make good their day's work by throwing in what lines they have on board, hastily baited with the most likely fish they happen to have caught.

Line-fishing here is fairly lucrative, for it can be done at almost any time; and in Ireland, as in other Catholic countries, the demand for fish is very great—greater than the trawlers alone could supply, even if they went off more regularly; and the huge halibut and ling that come up on the hooks are easily gutted and salted. Ling are not quite so common here as further north; the Hebrides, and perhaps the Orkneys, are the best grounds; still, a very large number may be taken by the Cork and Waterford men. "Ling" is simply another form of the Dutch or Saxon "lang," and the name was applied to this fish because it was regarded as merely a long hake; the Germans still call it the "long fish." It is of the same family as the cod, and is from three to four feet long; its markings are rather pretty; the belly is silvery, and the back anything from grey to olive-green; all its fins are tipped with white, and the tail has a black bar across it.

Halibut are a much larger fish, and weigh anything up to three and even five hundred pounds, and sometimes measure six feet from tip to tail. They are flat, ugly creatures, with teeth not only in their mouths but in their throats, and having both their eyes on one side.

The Irish fishermen devote much of their line-fishing time to rays and eels; the eels they sell, and the rays either form their own food or are used by them as bait for crabs and lobsters. Rays are better known to the consumer as skate and, to the fishermen, as "roker"; they may be seen on the fishmongers' slabs almost any time between July and April. It is said that there are no less than eleven species of them round the Irish coast. They are cartilaginous, like the shark or the sturgeon, and their flesh is very popular among the poorer classes; for some reason London and Dublin seem to consume as much of this fish as all the fishing towns put together.

The Irishmen are only administering poetic justice when they catch the ray as crab and lobster bait, for no fish plays more havoc among the crustacea; it will crunch up a big crab, sometimes shell and all, with no trouble whatever, and will lie in wait near the rocks on the chance of a meal of lobster or shrimps. No fish requires more careful handling, whether it comes up on a line or in a trawl, for most species are armed along the back with tough spines, and, in defending itself, the ray bends its body in a bow and lets itself spring back with frightful force, often causing very serious wounds with its spikes; "thorn-back" is another name under which it is known by the fishermen.

Eel-catching in both fresh and salt water is a popular occupation among these fishermen; their tackle varies with the neighbourhood and time of year. A most ghastly method is by means of "needle-tackle." One or two stout needles are buried in the body of a worm and the line is tied round the whole; this is sunk with a stone or plummet and is extraordinarily successful in working, for eels are no less greedy than other fish, and, once the bait is snapped up, the points are safe to lodge somewhere, so that the needles act as a fixed cross-bar, to which the line is immovably fastened. This is for summer fishing. In the rivers and lakes, night-lines are also let down, but this is not regarded as a legitimate form of fishing—at any rate by the gamekeepers.

At the approach of winter the eels either bury themselves in the mud or migrate to the estuaries like that of the Shannon, or sometimes into the open sea. If they stay in the mud they are soon "forked out" with an eel-spear—an instrument with several prongs, which is fitted to a long, slender handle; but if they reach the estuaries, the taking of them ceases to be a sport and becomes an industry. Eel-pots are laid down in series after the fashion of the crab-pots, across the current, and are cleared and rebaited every morning. The traps are very ingeniously constructed; they are of wicker and shaped like a narrow-mouthed gallipot; the funnel-like entrance is made of springy, flexible sticks which radiate towards a common centre—a hole as big round as a shilling. The eel has no difficulty in forcing its way through this opening, for the springs bend back most obligingly; but they shut to again after the fish has passed through, and he has no sort of chance of ever getting out any more.

The Ulster fishermen are naturally very different from

the genuine Irishmen, most of them being of English or Scotch descent; and they are far more thrifty and business-like than the men whose country has adopted them.

On Tory Island—an islet three miles long and less than a mile broad, which lies about ten miles north-east of the Bloody Foreland, there is a tiny colony of real Irish fishers; these are they who, it is reported, feed their cattle on fish. They and the Donegal men who fish between Lough Swilly and the Foreland, have an exceptionally dangerous ground upon which to work, for there, apart from the awful, rocky reef that runs out from Tory, the Atlantic can be its roughest, so much so that often no boat can pass from the island to the mainland for five or six weeks at a time. The islanders are therefore obliged to store their fish alive in salt-water reservoirs, and perhaps it is from this fact that Irish fishermen have been accused of tethering valuable fish like soles and turbots by the tail, and letting them swim about till the steam-carrier comes to fetch them.

CHAPTER XVII

SOME STRANGE FISH AND STRANGE FISHERMEN

Decay of primitive methods—South American fisheries—The *arapaima*—Harpoons and tethered arrows—The *armado*—Catching fish on land—The *diodon*—Fishing in Tierra del Fuego—African river-fishing—The Indian mango-fish—The modern Galilean fisherman—South Sea Island fish—Proas and Hawaiian "outriggers"—Australian and Arctic fishing.

BEFORE quitting the subject of fish proper, we ought to take a glance at a few of those distant fisheries that cannot well be classed under any of the foregoing heads. Colonisation by Europeans has necessarily swept away many of the primitive methods and appliances with which the native fishermen of Polynesia, the East Indies, Africa, and America were wont to astonish the travellers of a bygone age; but the fish are still there—many of them very curious and interesting—and some of the old ways of catching them still prevail.

It is only among civilised or quasi-civilised nations that much deep-sea fishing is to be found. Work of that sort implies the use of strongly built vessels such as few savage races would have the means of constructing, as well as a far more profound knowledge of seamanship than could be expected among a barbarian people. Enlightened as the ancient Egyptians were, even they had a horror of the sea, and usually confined their skill and energy in boat-building to making only such craft as would be used on the Nile. The American Indian who glides along the river, or fishes at his ease, in his frail birch canoe, regardless of deep water and alligators, is terrified at the sight of a heavy sea, and in many cases would not let himself be persuaded that fish can live amid such tempestuous surroundings.

Still, there are exceptions. Up till quite a few years ago the coast Indians of Peru would accomplish long and dangerous sea voyages in their *balzas*, which were little better than pointed rafts with a lug-sail, bringing back a cargo of fish which they had caught with hook and line and dried in the sun. Many of the Polynesians have also proved themselves successful deep-sea fishers, while the natives of Madagascar and Malay, if they did not trouble about fishing themselves, had no objection to pursuing into deep water, and molesting, anyone else who did. Another exception must of course be made where the pearl-fishers of the East and West Indies are concerned.

But those who neglect the greater depths have generally very remunerative coast fisheries, and, not infrequently, large rivers and lakes on which to expend their energies. In China, for instance, there are more river fishers than all the sea fishers in Europe and America together; while the great rivers of South America and Africa make a fishing people of races that have never been within hundreds of miles of the sea.

In some of the South American rivers there is a fish—

the *arapaima*, a gigantic fresh-water herring—the hunting of which has been both a sport and an industry among the inhabitants of Brazil and Guiana for centuries. As the average weight of these monsters is about three hundredweight—some have been taken weighing four hundred pounds and measuring fifteen feet in length—it will be seen that arapaima hunting is not child's play. The catching is done by hook and line, by tethered arrows and by harpoons, angling being only employed for night work. The line, a sort of slender lasso, carries a heavily weighted hook baited with some small fish, and is lowered from a canoe which it is almost useless to moor, on account of the immense towing powers of the fish. If the angler is wise, as soon as the creature is pulled near enough, he puts an end to its struggles with a spear.

Sundown or sunrise is the time for spearing. A boat pulled by half a dozen Indians or Zambos paddles gently up stream, everyone observing perfect silence, two or three fishermen crouching in the bow and watching keenly for a first sight of the largest fresh-water fish in the world. Suddenly a head splashes half above water and goes down again. Instantly one of the watchers snaps his fingers, at which the rowers rest on their paddles and every one waits breathlessly. The same thing happens again, the head, or perhaps just the nose of the fish appearing above the surface and vanishing again before aim can be taken.

Presently a loud splash is heard some distance astern of the boat, as, with a clumsy imitation of its sea relative, the tarpon, the giant essays a half-spring out of the water.

But the men take no further notice of him now; they know that they have lost him in any case, for the fish are all travelling down stream. Judging, however, from the number of ripples ahead, he is no great loss, for there are plenty more like him to come. At last a broad silver belly rises a good five feet. Evidently this is a monster, for, some distance beyond, the water is being threshed into a tiny whirlpool by his great forked tail. Before the arapaima can sink again, a harpoon whirls through the air trailing behind it a long leathern cord, the other end of which is made fast to the boat. For an instant it seems as though boat and crew would be dragged under, as the fish gives one convulsive plunge; but the spear was too well or too luckily aimed; it has bedded itself in the upper part of the chest, and that sudden, jerking plunge was the arapaima's last movement; all that remains to be done is to drag the dead body aboard.

But there are times when the shot is not so opportune; often the fish with three and even four harpoons bristling in its back or sides, will plunge, kick, and dodge, till there is every likelihood of the little vessel's capsizing, and leaving her crew at the mercy of the sleepy-looking alligators, that are innocently watching the sport from the muddy bank.

The tethered arrow, formerly more commonly used than the harpoon in arapaima fishing, is almost identical with the Indian turtle-spear. The head is movable, being lightly fixed in a socket at the end of the shaft; when the point strikes an object, the shaft is shaken free, though still in connection with the point by means of a long coil of stout cord or thong which has been neatly wound round the arrow. The coil rapidly unrolls itself, leaving the shaft on the surface as a sort of float, and all the fishermen have to do is to paddle up and seize this; then to draw the refractory giant to the top, as a further mark for their bows and arrows.

When caught, the fish is either cut up into steaks and sold slightly salted, or is dried and packed for transport to the large towns, or for export. The flesh is said to be excellent.

The South American rivers and pools have almost a monopoly of the curiosities among fresh-water fishes. In the Parana is another giant, called by the Gauchos the *armado ;* shorter though thicker than the arapaima, and much prized for its delicate flavour. The Gauchos angle for it with hand-lines, and hooks baited with cray-fish or meat. Two men in a canoe can work four lines—they could work forty if the craft were large enough to stand the strain; the upper end of the line is tied to the boat, and the men stand straddle-legged to guard against sudden lunges. These do not always come; often the fish swallows the hook, and lies on the bottom, scarcely moving, and only kicking when hauling-in time comes.

Then how does the fisherman know when he has got a bite? The *armado* sees to all that; for, the moment he is hooked, he sets up a rattling, grating noise that can be clearly heard even when he is at the bottom, and, if near the surface, is audible from several yards away. And, moreover, he is not always content to lie in the mud and groan. He has a trick sometimes of seizing the line with the spine of his back or breast-fin, and either snapping it or doing his best to capsize the boat. So powerful are the fins, in fact, that he will seize the blade of a paddle with one of them and jerk it out of an unwary hand in an instant.

Another member of his tribe (*siluridae*), the largest fresh-water fish in Europe, is found in the Elbe and Danube, under various local names, measuring eight feet long and weighing about three hundredweight.

Further varieties of the same family are also found in other South American rivers, the best known of which is called by zoologists the *callichthys;* it is covered from end to end with rows of small scaly plates, and on the head is a kind of bony helmet. Not only does it make a regular nest in the mud, wherein it deposits its eggs, but, if the stream or pool in which it lives dries up in the hot weather, it will make a considerable land journey to some other piece of water; and it is on these journeys that it is generally lain in wait for and speared by the Indians. One more member of this genus, common in the Essequibo, the most highly prized of all as a table delicacy, is the "broad-mouth" (*platystoma*), the most beautifully marked of any; the skin is a pale blue, and across the back are alternate stripes of black and white; from their flat snouts and wide jaws, which they are in the habit of poking above the surface, they may easily be mistaken at first sight for alligators.

Alligators, by the way, are not the only foes to river fishers here. In the streams of Paraguay are enormous water-serpents which have been known to upset a light canoe and drag one of the occupants under water.

British and Dutch residents in Guiana had at one time ample sport in fishing the Essequibo for the *dawalla*, a scaleless fish, brilliantly marked with green, brown, and crimson, two and a half feet long, with a head like our jack; but, as it has been hooked without mercy for the sake of its delicate flavour, to catch one nowadays is something for the sportsman to boast about.

The coast fisheries of South America have, except in the far south, ceased to offer anything particularly striking or unusual; the seine, worked from the shore or from small boats, is the most commonly used net. In it are taken eels of various sorts, mackerel, a species of herring, and an occasional sun-fish, globe-fish, sea-porcupine, or *diodon*, as it is variously termed—the most innocent of creatures if left alone, and one of the most formidable to interfere with, for it will bite like any wolf, and the fishermen, though they are anxious enough to secure it, for it commands a good price as a curiosity, allow it to die in peace before attempting to carry it away. It is about two feet long, very bulky and flabby, and has the power of inflating itself till it is almost globular, when its whole surface is seen to be covered with short spines. In this blown-out condition it is incapable of swimming, but comes to the surface lying on its back, and allows itself to be carried along by the tide. Sometimes while in this position it will shoot a jet of water some considerable distance, at the same time making a curious grating noise with its mouth. Sometimes a misguided shark will elect to swallow a diodon, and in doing so inadvertently commits suicide; for in nine cases out of ten the smaller fish "goes down" whole and living, and at once proceeds to bite a way out for itself through the stomach, ribs, and skin of the shark.

Its under-skin secretes a beautiful red dye, which was once much prized by the Indians of Brazil. The fish is also found in the Indian and Pacific oceans.

South American fishermen keep careful watch in the pools at low tide for the hideous octopus or cuttle-fish, which scarcely calls for a description, as everyone has seen it in pictures or aquaria. Sailors and novelists tell us horrible things about the misdeeds of the creature, though many naturalists regard it as more or less harmless. To the fisherman it is rather a "find," both for the sake of the valuable black pigment which it secretes and also for its calcareous "shield," commonly known as the cuttle-fish bone, which is reduced to powder and used as a metal-burnisher. The small northern variety, called the flying-squid, which the cod-fishers use as bait, has the power of leaping to a height of fifteen or twenty feet above the water.

The savages of Tierra del Fuego subsist almost entirely on fish, blubber, and seaweed. Here we must talk about fish-*wives*, for it is the women who do almost all the fishing, though the men sometimes paddle the canoes from which much of the work is done. Generally speaking, the women catch fish while the men gather molluscs from the rocks, or drift about in their canoes on the chance of finding a dead whale or seal. The women's lines consist, as often as not, of lengths of their own hair braided and joined; some few use a fish-bone hook, but most of them

Fishing on the Nile

In the Nile, fishing is carried on as it was in the days of the Pharaohs, by lines and dip-nets—the latter worked from the bank, and shaped something like a very long-handled shrimp push-net.

none at all: the body of a good-sized shell-fish is tied to the end of the line, and the woman, sitting in her canoe, waits till some fish is choked by the bulky bait, and then draws up. When not engaged thus, these primitive fish-wives are occupied in diving for shell-fish and sea-eggs; this they do without any such mechanical appliances as ropes or weights, springing into one or two-fathom water from the rocks just as we might dive from a boat or spring-board. Some of the more energetic of the men practise fish-spearing, pulling out to a depth of a few fathoms, and "jabbing" at the fish as they appear, with a one-barbed spear; but this is an operation which requires more judgment than the poor Fuegians possess, as any-one is aware who has ever aimed at even a stationary object that is under water.

Passing on to the African continent, we see very much the same state of things as in America—sea-fisheries mainly under direct or indirect European influence, the natives attaching more importance to the rivers and lakes. In the Nile, fishing is carried on almost as it was in the days of the Pharaohs, by lines and dip-nets, the latter worked from the bank, and shaped something like a very long-handled shrimp push-net, or by groping in the mud as the waters recede after the floods. A very popular fish that is taken in the latter way is the *bichir*, which is about eighteen inches long, and is covered with hard, bony scales. In the same manner the Arabs of the Upper Nile catch what they call the "thunder-fish," which averages a foot in length and, like that of the Calabar River in the west, is endowed with considerable power of developing electricity. A large kind of barbel named the *binny*, also found in the mud, is greatly prized by the Nile dwellers, though to English palates it would be tasteless.

In less civilised parts of the continent—on the Gambia River, for example—we find fish-spearing as mentioned above, as well as mud-searching. The West African Negroes are very fond of the "mud-eel," which, according to some naturalists, ought to be classed as a reptile on account of its foot-like fins. When the floods subside, thousands of these are left high and dry, and promptly bury themselves in the mud, which soon becomes hard and earthy, and here they would remain till the next inundation if the Negroes did not come along with wooden forks and dig them out.

The inhabitants of the Congo Free State use fish-spears, as well as long metal hooks, which they hold in their hands. The people of Madagascar are more advanced, and have for centuries known the art of making hempen nets and barbed hooks.

In the Indian Ocean is another curiosity called the "drum-fish," which the island fishermen of the Seychelles, Amirantes, etc. often take with hand-lines, and which is highly esteemed as an article of food; it has earned its name from its habit of making a booming noise when pursuing or pursued; in size and taste it is not unlike cod.

The fisheries of India scarcely differ from those of China, the only deep-sea work done by the natives being practically confined to the pearl-oyster. But a river fish greatly sought after by native anglers is the *tupsee* or *bartah*, known by Europeans as the mango-fish, from its yellowish colour. It is not unlike our perch, and always commands a high price, partly on account of its toothsomeness, but especially because its air-bladder yields isinglass. Several allied fish are found in the hotter parts of America and Africa.

In the Ceylon rivers, too, we find the peasantry still clinging to the wading method, almost identical with that practised by the Chinese; the fisherman finding his catch with his bare feet.

The use of weirs or garths has been introduced into the Andaman Islands; at Port Blair, the great convict settlement, the prisoners erect across the mouths of the creeks similar wooden traps to those mentioned in Chapter X; they are not a fixture, but are periodically moved from creek to creek, because after a time the fish grow wary and avoid the spot where they have seen their friends disappear. The seir-fish, a kind of salmon, is caught in this way. Here deep-sea fishing is almost out of the question by reason of the strong current and heavy seas.

We cannot leave the subject of Asiatic fisheries without a word or two about that carried on in the Holy Land. The modern Palestine traveller tells us that we should now look in vain for boats "launching out into the deep," and working nets all night in the Sea of Galilee. Not that the fish have disappeared; they are to be caught there in millions, as also in the Jordan and the Jabbock; but the Arabs, less accustomed to systematic work than the Jews of old, follow easier plans—the simplest and most disgusting of which is throwing poisoned bits of meal-cake into the water, and then wading in to make a collection; "a custom which sure no other nation is like to rob them of!"

Another way of going to work is by pelting the fish with stones, which can be done very profitably where the shoals of yellow *musht* congregate. Some of the Bedawîn, probably taking example by travellers, fire charges of small shot among them, and so get a bag; so thick are these shoals that it is even said that a revolver bullet has been known to kill three fish. Hook and line may be found very occasionally, but, as a rule, where the practices mentioned above are not resorted to, the fishing is done by small dip-nets or large hand-nets; in the former case, the fishers, standing on the rocks, lower a kind of bird-net which can be closed by the pulling of a rope, from rocks or wooden platforms, and haul up at intervals of an hour or so. Where the hand-net is in use—it is a kind of cross between a butterfly- and shrimp-net—the fisherman wades in up to his waist with a bag on his shoulder, and is content to catch the fish one or two at a time. The fish of the Syrian waters are of many different species, but few are peculiar to the country.

Going farther afield to the more distant islands—and probably meeting *en route* the sea-serpent, which is one of the ribbon-fish tribe frequenting very deep water and measuring from fifteen feet—we come across other flying-fish than those mentioned in an earlier chapter. The flying gurnard, for instance, which, in addition to possessing the power to take long leaps, can support itself in

A SPIDER'S WEB AS A FISHING-NET: A STRANGE NEW GUINEA DEVICE

A very huge and strong spider's web, common to New Guinea, is used by the natives as a fishing-net. They set up in the forest a bamboo, bent as in the picture, and leave it until the spiders have covered it with a web in the manner shown.

mid-air for a minute or so by means of its long breast-fins. This the inhabitants of the South Seas shoot with arrows and eat. Another delicacy among these islanders is the *palolo*, a slender marine animal three inches long, whose body is divided into joints, each of which is supplied with a pair of gills; the natives gather these in great numbers from the coral reefs, and bake them wrapped in the leaves of the bread-fruit tree.

One of the most extraordinary nets to be found in the whole world is that used on the New Guinea coast; a net of Nature's own providing. A local spider is in the habit of weaving a web about six feet in diameter, the meshes of which are so tough that they will not only resist considerable water-pressure, but will easily stand the weight of a one-pound fish. The canny natives cut long bamboo poles, bend the ends into a loop, and leave them all day in the forest where the spiders are most plentiful; when they return they find that the industrious creature has converted each bamboo into a sort of gigantic tennis-racquet or lacrosse-bat, and with this the fisherman retires to the nearest stream or back-water and whips out the fish singly as they rise.

The Sandwich islanders and the people of the Ladrones are exceptional as savage fishermen, having no fear of fairly deep water. The latter think nothing of going fishing in thirteen fathoms in canoes which British fishermen would laugh or shudder at; light-built *proas*, but rigged with one sail, in the construction of which their ancestors most likely copied the Malay pirates. The boat which the Hawaiians use for fishing and porpoise-hunting is very long and very narrow, pointed, and curved upwards at either end, and capable of holding five or six men. By an ingenious system of "outrigger" the terrific surf is rendered almost powerless to upset this craft; for standing out from one side of the boat are two light poles, across the ends of which is lashed a beam similar in shape and length to the boat's keel, so that at a distance, you might think you saw two boats fixed parallel to each other. The outrigger forms a stay to the boat on the side whereon it is fixed, and the other side is equally supported because only a very great strain could possibly weigh up such a contrivance. The paddling is done from the stern, and fishing begins as soon as the little vessel is clear of the reefs; and in a very few hours she has as many fish as she can hold. The catch is taken ashore alive in pots and skin buckets, and disposed of at the public market, many of the islanders consuming it not only uncooked but still living.

The Australian fisheries have developed remarkably during the last half-century, apart even from the whaling and pearl-fishing, huge fleets being engaged in turtle-, dugong- and oyster-fishing; more than a hundred species of edible fish are trawled for off the coast of New South Wales alone. The few remaining coast aborigines live on the coarse-fleshed sting-rays which are thrown up living and dead by the tide; and on such other fish as they can catch on the barbed bone points of their spears. The Kanakas of the Melanesian Islands are skilful in the building of canoes, but, as with the Fuegians, the women do the fishing, while the men eat each other.

ESKIMOS SPEARING FISH

They wait patiently at a hole in the ice until a fish comes near the surface, and then strike.

AND STRANGE FISHERMEN

It is necessary to add a few lines concerning other Arctic fisheries than those which we shall presently touch upon. There is not much to be said. The Eskimos would be willing enough to catch the fish, but there are so few to be caught; the *cottus*, a spiny-headed creature which British fishermen call the "Father Lasher," with a small kind of cod, the Arctic shark, the salmon, and the *mysis* or opossum-shrimp, are almost the only fish that will venture so far north. In winter time the Eskimo makes a hole in the ice when possible and, with his bone-headed spear or barbed fork, patiently sticks such fish as come near the surface; in summer he goes in his canoe or *kayak* —which he has cleverly made from what odd bits of wood he can scrape together, and covered with skin—and, with a line made of sinew and a fish-bone hook, angles for whatever he may be lucky enough to catch.

CHAPTER XVIII

PEARLS AND PEARL-DIVING

How pearls grow—Loose and fixed pearls—The fish that contain them—The Ceylon Banks—Native divers—The pearl fleet—Scene in the Gulf of Manaar—A noisy crew—The "shifts"—Method of lowering—Sharks—A curious superstition—Landing and piling the oysters—How they open—Varieties of pearls—Other grounds—Dredging for pearl-shells—The *argentine*.

WHAT is pearl? Put briefly, it is the result of layer upon layer of carbonate of lime being wrapped round a tiny nucleus that lies hidden within some shell-bearing mollusc.

Most shell-fish are provided with a secretion wherewith to line their homes, making the otherwise harsh shell a smooth and comfortable refuge for the tender body that lies within it; and this secretion, which, in its hardened form, we know as nacre or mother-of-pearl, is spread by the fish in very thin translucent films, the outer one of which consequently acquires an opaline or iridescent surface. When the shell is thus lined, its tenant has still good store of the secretion left, and this it devotes to covering any small particle that has no business within the valves; for shell-fish, though their nervous system be, in most respects, very elementary, are exceedingly sensitive to tickling or scratching.

A grain of sand will sometimes work its way between the body and one of the valves, thereby causing an irritation which the mollusc at once proceeds to check by gradually covering the intruder with carbonate of lime films, one upon another like the coats of an onion, till it is as smooth and polished as the inside of the shell itself. Again, when a dog-whelk or other boring animal that preys on oysters has succeeded in drilling a hole through the shell from the outside, the little creature within will sometimes plug up the aperture with its secretion and laboriously spread layers over the nucleus thus formed. The result in either of these cases is that a pearl will be found adhering to one of the shells.

The more valuable pearls, however, are found loose inside the mantle of the mollusc, or at least slightly connected with it; and these have a somewhat different origin. It often happens that one of the ova is lifeless, and, not being thrown out with the rest at spawning time, gradually increases in size, because, though infertile, it is still supplied with blood-vessels from the parent body; then hardens and becomes an even greater source of irritation than any foreign object would be—till it has been "insulated" with nacre and made a pearl of. These will be the globular and pear-shaped pearls—pear-shaped, because at times the connecting link or pedicle between the egg and the body is also covered with the films. One of the latter sort has been taken weighing 3¾ oz. troy, 2in. long and 4 in circumference. I believe it is still to be seen at the South Kensington Museum.

Any shell-bearing mollusc may contain pearls, though

they are most often found in certain species of oysters. Very fine ones have been discovered in the ordinary British fresh-water mussel, notably from the Welsh and Scotch rivers; the best known of these being one that was found at Conway in the seventeenth century and presented by the Lord of the Manor to Catherine of Braganza, wife of Charles II; it is still preserved among the Crown jewels. The sea mussels found at the mouth of the Conway are still crushed for the sake of any pearls they may contain.

About a year ago a large spherical pearl was taken from a Whitstable oyster; and pearl-bearers, both mussel and oyster, are so continually found off the coast of Scotland that a local fishery has more than once been seriously mooted even in our own time. In the seventeenth and eighteenth centuries such an industry was carried on there, over a hundred thousand pounds' worth of pearls being shipped to France between the years 1760 and 1800 alone. The Chinese oyster, too, often contains a very small pearl.

In a general way, however, we can only expect to find the genuine article in really warm seas and at a considerable distance from the shore, as in the case of Ceylon, the East and West Indies, Central America, and the Persian Gulf. The pearl-oyster proper (*Meleagrina margaritiferus*) has a shell that is almost semicircular and of a greenish colour outside, the inside being lined throughout with an unusually thick and hard nacreous coat; the two valves are joined together by a very long straight hinge. Such fish are found either singly or in huge clusters, clinging

Boats Waiting near the Guardship at the Ceylon Pearl Fisheries

Whilst bags of oysters are sealed to prevent theft.

to rocks that are covered with seventy feet and more of water; or lying huddled together on "banks" such as the celebrated ones in the Gulf of Manaar on the west coast of Ceylon.

It is often asked why pearl-oysters are not dredged for, like others. In Australia and elsewhere the fishermen have tried this method, and there is no special reason why it might not become universal, beyond the fact that the depth (nine to thirteen fathoms) is somewhat against it. There is this to be said, also; three divers working for ten hours can bring up three or four thousand oysters between them; while, working with dredges, by the time they had sorted the desirable from the undesirable, they would not have caught much more than half that number; further—the fisherman, whether Asiatic or European, *will* do as his fathers did.

Pearl-divers—Hindoos, Sinhalese, Coolies, Negroes, and Arabs—have been trained to their work from childhood; trained to hold their breath under water, to stand the pressure that must be expected in such a depth, and to gather a bag-full of oysters in rather less than a minute. Partly to realise what that pressure means, you have only to lie at the bottom of a six-foot swimming bath while you count sixty, and then reflect that a pearl-diver stays the same length of time, and more, under twelve or thirteen times that depth, busily working with his hands the whole while.

Short as the Ceylon pearl season is—it lasts but from the middle of March to the end of April—the divers, as they are now paid, can earn enough during that time, if they are lucky, to satisfy their humble wants for the remainder of the year. Some employers have a fixed rate of payment; others go on the profit-sharing principle, each boat taking a fourth of the proceeds of its catch, and the divers sharing that amount equally.

Long before daylight the boats, hundreds of them, put out, each of them rigged with a gigantic sort of lug-sail and carrying a crew of from five-and-twenty to sixty, including ten or more divers. Navigation in these waters is a tolerably simple matter. There are no tides to speak of, and the powerful coast currents which to a stranger might be dangerous are known, every inch of them, to the Sinhalese.

Unfortunately for those interested in the pearl-fisheries, this happy condition of the sea only exists from the last week of February till the second of April, possibly the end of April. By that time the hot season is over, and the island, lying as it does in the course of the two monsoons (the south-west till September and then the north-east till January and February), is henceforth subject to heavy seas such as no diver could descend in. Hence the six weeks' season.

On reaching the banks a signal-gun is fired and then soundings are taken, though many of the fishermen know the ground so well that this may often be a superfluous measure; still, as within the same half square mile, depths of five and of a hundred fathoms can exist here, the precaution is not to be wondered at.

By daylight, the whole scene on the pearl ground is the very antipodes of what is to be witnessed among a British fishing fleet. For the most part the sea is dead calm and oily-looking; the sky is a brilliant, cloudless blue, and the sun is already scorching the naked shoulders of the fishermen, for the boat has cast anchor at but nine degrees above the equator. Instead of the muttered word or two and the silent obedience to orders that would characterise an English or American crew, there is a frantic babble of tongues, often in four different languages; violent gesticulating, arguing, and squabbling, and an occasional free fight, till we might well wonder how these men ever get through any work at all. But the overseer, sometimes a Portuguese or an Englishman, restores order at last, and the first "shift" of divers bestir themselves and make ready for the task. Where ten divers go to a boat, they work in shifts of five, turn and turn about.

When once the ropes are run over the blocks or the gunwale, all signs of laziness disappear; the shouting and bustle certainly do not diminish, on the contrary, they are part of the business, as will presently appear, and they rather increase three-fold. Everyone now seems to move as if fixed on springs, and so swiftly is the work carried out that it is not until you have watched half a dozen descents that you realise what is being done. The shift of divers stand in a row along one side of the boat and beside each of them is a sort of projection something like a ship's davit, with a block at the end of it, through which the rope will be hauled. From it depends a short length of the rope, to the end of which is fastened a large, smooth stone weighing about forty pounds. Some boats dispense with the davit-like contrivance, in which case the rope is hauled over the gunwale like the tow-line of a net. Others have merely a high horizontal rail over which the rope is hauled.

On the upper side of the stone a loop like a stirrup is left in the rope, large enough to hold the naked foot of the diver, so that you may say he stands on the stone with one foot and maintains his perpendicular by clinging with one hand to the lowering line. At a signal from the first diver, his rope is let go and, weighted by the stone, he sinks rapidly, the line-holders continuing to pay out rope till the sudden slacking announces that the bottom is reached. Instantly one of the crew springs to the gunwale and hauls back till the line is taut again, and then, still keeping his hand on it, waits for the jerk that may come at any moment from below, giving the signal to draw up.

On many boats the divers work in pairs, one lowering and hauling the other once or twice and then changing about. If we could follow one of these black bodies to its destination we should see the diver tearing off the oysters in bundles from the rocks or shingle-bank, almost squatting on his hams, or hanging to a reef by his toes, one arm hooked round the rope while, with the disengaged hand, he swiftly packs his shells into the net bag that hangs over his shoulder. At last he can stand the strain no longer; he pulls the rope and is hoisted up as fast as the windlass handles can be turned, or, if the boat should not possess such a contrivance, as fast as one or two men, hauling hand over hand, can pull in the warp. When he rises above water there are hands ready to help him into the boat, often a very necessary measure on account of the strain he has undergone.

As to the length of time that an "undressed" diver can remain under water, there is remarkable divergence; the shape of the man's chest and shoulders and the condition of his heart and lungs are the things that decide that matter, together, of course, with the amount of pressure to be sustained. Eighty seconds would perhaps be a reasonable average, though Mediterranean sponge divers have been known to stay down three and a half minutes.

But does not a sensible diver keep one eye on the oysters and the other on the sharks? it may well be asked. Possibly; but some of them are constitutionally unable to keep their eyes open at all, relying instead on their sense of touch; their lids drop when they enter the water, and cannot be raised until the diver comes up again, as many swimmers are aware from their own experience.

As to the sharks which, more's the pity, certainly do abound in the Gulf of Manaar, it is but rarely that they pursue, let alone attack, a pearl-diver, and we may regard ninety-nine per cent of the ghastly tales about these monsters as fables. Sir E. Tennent, who may be taken as an authority on all matters relating to Ceylon, writing over forty years ago, says that not more than one well-authenticated instance of a pearl-fisher's meeting his death in this manner could be quoted within a space of fifty years. In the first place the shark has almost invariably a dread of human beings and, at any time, may be scared away by sustained noise. The presence of such a number of boats and the splash of the stone weights are enough to frighten him away from the scene; indeed, the shouting and bustle of the crews is to be regarded largely as a special entertainment got up by the Sinhalese with the avowed intention of keeping him at a safe distance. The dark skins of the divers, too, are generally believed to constitute in themselves a sort of scare-shark, so much so that the Arabs and the more light-skinned of the Ceylonese are in the habit of smearing their bodies with a semi-permanent black dye. A few of them take a further precaution, though they themselves would admit that in most cases it is a needless one; carry in their girdles two or three short spikes made of iron-wood which, if need arise, they are prepared to poke into the eyes of the monster.

One rather interesting superstition still lingers among a few of the older divers in connection with the shark. I mean the resorting at the beginning of the season to the hereditary shark-charmer, a being who is endowed, they maintain, with power to exorcise the voracious creature, and turn him back from any person thus charmed; the ceremony connected with the exorcism is a very ancient one, presumably rather magical than religious. By some of the natives an annual visit to this personage is thought insufficient, so it occasionally happens that a boat's crew will not sail unless the charmer or some individual deputed by him accompanies them to the pearl ground.

If not too exhausted by his efforts, the diver on coming to the surface will merely hand in his catch and hang for a minute to the boat's side while he takes breath and then go down again; but, after a few such descents, he will be very willing to be lifted aboard and let another man take his place. Working thus alternately, diving scarcely stops for an instant till the midday signal gun is fired, or till the boat is full, when she at once makes for the shore as fast as she can, anxious to be as near first in the field as possible in order to get a good price for her cargo. Sometimes a boatload means as many as from twenty to forty thousand fish, and these, packed in baskets or sacks, are taken ashore, after having been sealed by an emissary from a watch-boat, and carried to a large enclosure some distance up the beach, checked, packed in heaps of a thousand, and promptly offered for sale by the auctioneers. Buyers from all the ends of the earth, and of all classes, are waiting to bid, and each boatload is gradually disposed of.

Thus heaped up out of their natural element, the fish are dead in a couple of hours, and then the heat of the sun begins the work of putrefying them. The smell—but let us change the subject. Artificial means of opening the oysters have been tried frequently in different parts of the world, as, for instance, in South and Central America by the sixteenth-century Spaniards, who were wont to force the valves by exposure to a fierce fire; but such methods have generally resulted in serious damage to the contents by discoloration and breakage. In Ceylon also, impatient buyers, imitating the example of the auctioneers, who are forced to open a few on the spot as samples of what the heap for sale is likely to contain, will wrench open the valves with their knives. In the hands of an experienced man this is a risky operation, and when performed by a neophyte it is largely a case of fools stepping in where dredgers fear to tread. How many laymen can open a "common or garden" oyster for eating without cutting a hole in their hands, and hacking the fish into a nasty, dirty mess?

When the few days of putrefaction have done their work, "washing" begins, an occupation which calls for consummate care and patience—and plugged nostrils. Taking the shells a couple of hundred at a time, the washers throw them into a tub of water, keeping careful look-out as they do so for the loose pearls—the most valuable of any—which have a tendency to roll away and get lost. More often than not these lie near the mouth of the shell; but they may also be concealed within the body, or near the hinge. The fish, of course, sink, while the dust, mites, and other dross rise to the surface. The dirty water is gently poured off and replaced by fresh, and so on till nothing remains but shells, rotten oysters, and possible pearls.

Next, the shells are handed out and closely examined. Strangely enough, those pearls found adhering to the upper or rounded valve are generally pronounced worthless, though, naturally, there are exceptions; those on the flat valve are nipped off with delicate tools, and finally the empty shells are set aside for the value of the nacre lining.

Then the malodorous mass that is left in the tub has to be felt and examined inch by inch; work that can only be

A GROUP OF CEYLON PEARL DIVERS

Pearl divers—Hindoos, Sinhalese, Coolies, Negroes, and Arabs—have been trained to their work from childhood.

done by people endowed with delicacy of touch. The men engaged in this are watched as closely as diamond-field negroes. Many employers will not even allow them to remove their hands from the tub except to give up a "find." When every perceptible pearl has been extracted, the putrid fish is laid out to dry, and then sorted all over again for the sake of any treasures that may have been allowed to pass unnoticed.

The sorting or sifting of the pearls is the next process; and this is done by means of a large brass colander. The pear-shaped and the larger spherical pearls are set aside for subsequent drilling, the smaller sifted and re-sifted and classed according to their size; the smallest of all are packed away for export to China, where a far greater trade in "seed-pearls" is done than the local fisheries can possibly keep supplied. Among other ways of utilising them, the Chinese physicians calcine them and employ them in their medicines.

The Ceylon pearl-fisheries are probably the least reliable of any, and one year's returns are in no way a guarantee for those of another. This, no doubt, is largely accounted for by the fact that the varying depths make only a great number of small oyster-beds instead of a few large ones; so that, even without taking into account the cod and other ground-fish that feast on shell and oyster whenever occasion arises, the number of "brood" must necessarily fluctuate when at any time the spat as it is cast is liable to float away to depths beyond reach of even a "dressed" diver.

On the other hand, the Arabian fisheries, that are

carried on near the coast of the island of Bahrein in the Persian Gulf, seem to vary very little from one year to another, their average annual worth being reckoned at about three hundred thousand pounds.

Those of Western Australia, too, are proving both regular and remunerative. The native Polynesian divers who are employed often prefer to go down unweighted, first smearing their bodies with grease. Among these folk the women are unquestionably the better divers.

Some allusion should be made here to a comparatively new industry—pearl-shell fishing, which is greatly on the increase owing to the manufacture of artificial pearls and to the steady demand for mother-of-pearl. Nearly all round the coast of Australia as well as in the Dutch East Indies, mussels, oysters, and kindred fish are continually being dived or dredged for, solely for the sake of the nacre which they contain. West Australia alone sends away about a hundred thousand pounds' worth of such shells every year—just four times the value of that colony's pearl-fisheries. At this work also, the Polynesian divers are in great request.

Apropos of artificial pearls, there is a considerable industry among the Mediterranean fishermen in netting the *argentine*, a very brilliant, silver-coloured fish of the salmon order. When caught it is opened, and its sound or air-bladder removed and specially treated for the sake of the coat of nacre with which that part of its anatomy is covered.

CHAPTER XIX

WHALES AND WHALING

A profitable if risky industry—One or two historical details—The home of the whale—Old and new methods of catching him—Harpoons—"Blowing"—The whale's trail—Throwing the harpoon—A nerve-destroying trade—The tow-line—Other shots at the monster—A cut at the tail—The death—Cutting up—The whale's enemies—Rorquals and cachalots—A modern whaler and its equipment—The harpoon-gun and the bomb-lance—A disappointing whale—Various uses to which the carcass is devoted—Sperm oil and ambergris.

THE Cetacea, the order to which the whale, as well as the porpoise and the dolphin belong, are marine mammals, more or less fish-like in form, warm-blooded, breathing by means of lungs, and inhaling air while on the surface of the water. You may seek throughout the animal kingdom and not find a creature more valuable after it is dead; not an ounce of it need be—or, nowadays, is—wasted; blood, bones, skin, entrails, all are of some use; and the man who gave two hundred pounds for a carcass might look to make cent per cent profit on his investment.

The body is more or less spindle-shaped, ending in a tail which, unlike that of the fish, is transversal or horizontal. It is this member that is mainly instrumental in moving the enormous body, for its flippers are relatively weak and are used principally to balance its movements. The nostrils are usually placed on the upper part of the head, by which arrangement the whale can breathe without raising the head far above water; the skin is hairless. Whales proper are generally classified as toothless and toothed; the first group including the Rorqual and the Arctic or Right whale; the second the Cachalot or Sperm whale.

The whale-fishery dates back to very ancient times. The tales of whaling, as prosecuted by the early American Indians, are not perhaps to be taken seriously; the tale, for instance, of the intelligent Florida savages, who were wont to spring on the back of the creature, plug up one of his nostrils with a wooden peg, go down to the bottom with him and up again; hammer another plug into the second nostril and then leave him to suffocate. But of the antiquity of *harpooning* there can be no doubt. It is said of Leviathian, in the Book of Job, "Canst thou fill his skin with barbed irons, or his head with fish-spears?"

And there is certainly no room for doubt as to the ancient Eskimo method, for many of these strange little people still follow the plan with which they are credited in very early chronicles of travel. A flotilla of kayaks surrounds one of these monsters, and the hunters throw harpoons, to which huge bladders made of sealskin are attached. With a few of such spears sticking into it, the poor whale cannot possibly dive (or "sound"), for he is very effectually buoyed to the surface by the bladders, and the Eskimos can slaughter him at their leisure.

Otherus, a ninth-century German navigator, saw more than two hundred whales taken in two days by Biscayan fishermen in the White Sea; in fact, the Biscayans had practically the whole of the whaling industry in their hands up till the seventeenth century; for most nations (the Japanese and the Eskimos excepted) regarded the pursuit of the monster rather as a sport than as a business.

The Spaniards and the Dutch forcibly took the trade away from the Biscayans, who fell into the secondary position of guides and teachers, and even English mariners were glad to learn of them. In the seventeenth century the Dutch applied their proverbial business capacity to the work; pursued the whales to Spitzbergen, and founded the village of Smeerenbourg ("Grease Town") on Amsterdam Island; and, when the animals were gradually chased from that neighbourhood, instituted the Greenland fishery.

For a long while the British met with but poor success at the business; but, in 1732, Government offered large subsidies (which were doubled in 1749), and so, bit by bit, England and her colonies rose to the front rank as whalers.

Up to the earlier part of the nineteenth century, a favourite ground for the fishery was round about Disko Island; but now many of the Arctic whales have sought refuge still further north in Baffin Bay, etc. In the eighteenth century, explorers from the United States resolved to try whaling off the Falkland Islands and Patagonia, and pushed their researches to the Antarctic regions; and now America and England rely largely on the produce of these fishing grounds. But it is not necessarily the cold latitudes in which we must look for whaling; the African, Australian, and New Zealand coasts; Japan, Corea, and Norway offer ample scope; for the whale will go wherever he can find food, whether the latter be the molluscs of the French and Scotch coasts, or the opossum shrimps of the Arctic regions. When a whale is thrown ashore or caught near the coast in the British Isles, it is, like the sturgeon, a Fish Royal, the head being the property of the king, and the tail, of the queen.

Steam and gunpowder have robbed whaling of its sporting and romantic features to a very great extent, but not altogether; you cannot go into deep water, whatever may be your boat and equipment, in pursuit of a giant considerably longer than a cricket-pitch, that may elect to smash all the small boats—and some of the large ones—within reach of his ponderous tail, without feeling a little bit like a mighty hunter. The Norwegian and American fishermen laugh at the notion of harpooning a whale in the old-fashioned style; and use only the harpoon-gun—which we shall presently consider. But first let us watch the traditional method, which we can do very well from a Dutch or Shetland whaler.

The ship will probably be a three-master, with fore- and main-mast square-rigged, having a crew of five-and-thirty; and with her will be half a dozen four or five-oared boats. When a likely ground is reached a look-out man is posted aloft, and, at his signal, the small boats are lowered. At the helm of each boat is an old hand with whom most of the responsibility rests; in the bows is the harpooner, waiting to throw as soon as the word of command is given.

The harpoon calls for some description. It is about three and a half feet long and has two parts—the iron, and the handle or shank, which carries a quarter of a mile of rope. The iron tapers from the shank to the neck above the barbs, then spreads out into a broad-barbed spear-head, the outer edges of which are very keen, while the shoulders are thick and blunt; so that when once the barbs are fleshed there is no pulling them out.

Suddenly the coxswain sees a sort of broad whirlpool or eddy spreading near the boat, and, at the same time, there is a rumbling and an upheaving in the same vicinity; then a black muzzle and blow-holes appear on the surface; the whale has come up to breathe. Then up shoots a double column of vapour from the blow-holes, each column curving outwards and rising several yards in the air; then the head and tail—perhaps the whole body—become visible, only to sink again before a harpoon could possibly be made to reach him. The whale does not do things on a small scale; when he breathes he makes himself heard several hundred yards away, and, if he is agitated, the sound is audible for a mile or two. The "columns" are composed of the warm air from the lungs of the animal, mingled with some amount of watery vapour and particles of fatty matter, hence they are only visible when the surrounding temperature is low, just as we can only "see our own breath" on a cold day. The vapour quickly dissolves, but the greasy particles are left lying on the surface of the water, and so afford an indisputable "trail," which the whalers are not slow to take advantage of.

The coxswain has carefully noted the angle at which the creature's tail was inclined, for that is an indication of the direction it will have followed; also the quantity of the grease spots, from which he will be able to tell whether the whale has taken a long or a short breath, for upon this depends the length of time it will remain under water, and according to his deductions he gives his commands to the crew.

Presently comes a repetition of the rumbling and eddying; the helmsman has not been far out in his reckoning; the whale is coming to the surface only thirty yards away from his boat; the other crews see it and start rowing with all their strength. But the coxswain of the nearest boat takes things gently; certainly he wants to get within half a dozen yards of the whale, but he does *not* want his boat to come in contact with the animal's tail, or to get a knock with a huge flipper that will swamp her or smash her to splinters.

Holding his spear with both hands, and supporting himself against the curves of the bow, the harpooner awaits the signal.

"Let go!" or "Strike!" shouts the cox suddenly, and all the men hold their breath in their excitement and suspense, for so much depends on the shot. If the harpoon should be thrown awkwardly or with insufficient force, it may merely prick the skin, and fall out again by its own

HARPOONING A SPERM WHALE

As the coxswain shouts, the harpoon whizzes through the air, and the barbs, cleaving their way through skin and blubber, fix themselves in one of the hard elastic muscles of the whale.

weight; or, having taken up a temporary position half in and half out of the flesh, it may easily be expelled by a special muscular action on the part of the whale. In either of these cases the loss that would be sustained by the crews is incalculable, for the wounded creature, having escaped, will gather together its friends and its neighbours, and the whole "school" will dash away out of further reach. Judge, then, whether the harpooner should not be a man of unshakable nerve. Yet some are not; some turn livid and tremulous the moment the harpoon has left their hands, and, if the shot should fail, probably could not make a second, even if the lives of the crew depended on it. Seasoned whalers will tell you that the work is more nerve-destroying than all the other fisheries put together. The risk is so awful, death so certain, if a false step be made; the stake at issue such a huge one (for so great are the rewards that a poor man may become rich in no time), that everything combines to make whaling infinitely worse than pearl-diving, and as bad as the gambling-tables, as far as nerves are concerned.

As the cox shouts, the heavy dart whistles across the few yards of space, and the barbs cleave their way through skin and blubber and tissue, fixing themselves in the fibres of one of the tough elastic muscles which close over them with a spring, and from which they can never be torn while the animal remains alive.

"Good shot; look out for the line!" says the man at the helm.

The harpooned whale has this in common with the hooked salmon—you never know what he will do next.

It goes without saying that a great deal depends on where he is hit; if a motor nerve or important muscle is badly injured he may try to make a hurried escape, and yet be deterred from doing so by the pain which his first instinctive motion causes. Thus there may be time for a second harpoon, either from the same man or the cox, or even from another boat; for, badly hurt or not, the animal generally hesitates for a few moments before deciding on a course of action.

Suddenly it plunges under—keep clear of the rope if you value your life. A trawl tow-warp is bad enough to get entangled in; but if you should be caught in the coil of a harpoon-line you are in for a journey of a couple of hundred yards or more—in the direction of the bottom. The line, which is probably coiled in a couple of tubs, runs out at terrific speed till you begin to think that this part of the sea is bottomless. But after a time the rate is reduced till the coil scarcely seems to move; the rope hangs slack, and so far perpendicular that you find yourself wondering whether the whale intends coming up immediately under you. Another move of the line; no more runs out, but the part that hangs over the bow is taking a horizontal direction, and, a hundred yards or so to leeward, a similar whirlpool to that which you noticed before is forming; a bluish patch rises above water and moves forward at a moderate pace till the line is taut again; the whale has come to the top, still conscious that something is sticking into it and cannot be got rid of, but not yet prepared to find a boat-load of men hitched to that something.

Meanwhile other boats are rowing "full tilt," to get in a shot at the prize, the more so that, now the animal has appeared above water, it is seen that the harpoon has fallen too low—too near the belly—to cause a really serious wound. The only hope is to get up with him again, or else to be content to let him tire himself out, a proceeding which may last all day and possibly all night. One boat ahead of the rest seeks a convenient spot from which to throw, for a whale is not an animal to be "headed off in front" at pleasure. Guided by the lie of the tail, the cox steers for where he can be moderately sure of safety when the whale starts forward, and then shouts to his harpooner. The spear flashes through the air and seems as though it would catch the monster above the fin-joint.

But before the point can reach him, the whale, having now drawn the first line taut enough to have found that there is resistance at the end of it, rolls forward without sinking, and the second harpoon is lodged considerably nearer the tail than the fin. The tortured animal wanted but this fresh spur to goad him into a headlong rush forward; there is a yell from the first boat as it is dragged almost out of the water for an instant, and then, at the full length of its cable, is towed along at break-neck speed.

"Chuck us a line, sharp!" cries the cox to the boat nearest to him as his own flies past her. The harpooner in this boat is prepared for the emergency and throws his painter deftly into the hands of the other cox, who thus joins up the two little vessels. If there should be a possible chance, a third will seek to join herself on in like manner, for every extra weight will tend to shorten the whale's journey.

Groaning and roaring so that it can be heard three miles away, the wounded creature dashes on till it has exhausted the length of line that hangs to the second harpoon, then pauses for a moment, for it finds the weight behind increased by a third boat. Now it is the turn of the helmsmen to feel nervous; each one of them has but two eyes—one for his boat, and one for the whale; and just now he would give a considerable sum to possess a third, to keep on the other two boats. The two that are tied together are in little danger from each other, but a collision between them and the third depends largely on the whale's pleasure. He has enough rope to keep him from "rounding on" the crews, for unless anything unforeseen should happen, they can dodge him before he can get to them.

The remaining boats, meanwhile, are watching for an opportunity of giving chase whenever possible, or are lying in wait in case the whale should turn their way. One sharper or luckier than the rest has been able to pull round to the whale's far side as he stops, doubtful whether to dive again or not, and the men in the towed boats breathe a little more freely as they catch a glimpse of her sharp bows near the monster's tail; for they know that with a little luck a fatal blow is about to be struck.

The harpooner in this boat is leaning so far forward that every moment it seems as if he must overbalance; holding not the ordinary harpoon, but a broad-bladed lance

Severing a Whale's Vertebral Column.

Instead of a harpoon a broad-bladed lance or a tethered axe is used. In the scene depicted the ormer is being used.

or a tethered axe. His crew are resting on their oars, or gently backwatering if the current is with them, while he and his cox stand with their eyes fixed upon the enormous tail. The beast is going to dive again and, the moment the tail is raised, the harpooner is going to try for a cut at the backbone.

The tail rises, and before it can fall or the head disappear, the harpooner, at the risk of his own life and those of the crew, throws his lance under it. There is another fearful roar from the whale which almost drowns the cox's shout to the rowers to backwater, and the tail drops inert as the four oar-blades lift the little craft out of harm's way.

A triumphant shout from the crew informs the other boats that the blood is streaming from the new wound, and they know that the lower part of the whale's vertebral column has been severed. Meanwhile these others are not idle, for they have pulled nearer again, and their tow-ropes are once more hanging slack as the unfortunate animal makes another dive. This time he scarcely seems to be down a moment, then up again, and, distracted with pain and with rage at not being able to shake off his tormentors, makes a feeble turn to the right, presenting a broadside to the three boats that are fast coming up with him. He will never get away now, for his principal means of locomotion is useless.

Another harpoon whizzes from the foremost boat; the point cleaves its way through an artery and the blood spurts out in spasmodic jets. Again he dives, but for less than a minute, and when he comes up to blow there is something else ejected from the blow-holes besides vapour —two streams of blood, which the fishermen know is a sign that all is over with him. He may live another hour, making frantic little plunges that avail him nothing, but he will never swim another mile. As a fresh harpoon strikes him he sounds once more, this time almost without a roar; is down for a couple of minutes, then comes up slowly and lying on his back. Poor whale! his days are ended; let him bleed—the more the better; the less likely he is to sink.

And now the body must be towed, perhaps a couple of miles, back to the ship; heavy work for even four or five boats' crews; but at last the enormous carcass is pulled alongside the larger vessel and moored to her; and then, unless they are going off after another catch, the work of cutting up begins. At one time this used to be done by the men standing on the body with spiked boots and cutting off the rolls of blubber as far as they could. A more recent method consisted in cutting away the flesh under the mouth with spade-shaped axes; removing the tongue, and then slicing off the blubber in almost spiral strips from mouth to tail, and hauling it aboard. The blubber was then split into thicknesses of about half an inch and boiled on deck over a furnace that was kept fierce by the unmelted pieces of fatty tissue skimmed from the top of the cauldron. To prevent danger from fire, there was a space between the grate and the deck, through which cold water constantly flowed.

The average amount of blubber taken from a whale would be about twenty-five tons. The blubber-coat lies immediately under the skin, and is six inches thick, except that on the under-lip, which generally has a depth of two or three feet.

The toothless whales are compensated for their want of teeth by the presence of baleen, or "whalebone," which is arranged in their mouths in a rather peculiar manner, plates of this valuable substance lying along the palate, their inner edges terminating in fringes of filaments which fall like a curtain over the interior of the mouth, and serve as a strainer to the animal's food; for, as is well known, the swallowing apparatus of this species is relatively small, the largest fish it can take being a herring.

Mankind is not the whale's only enemy. As near home as the Hebrides a battle may not infrequently be seen between a whale and a group of "threshers" or fox-sharks. The thresher is about thirteen feet long, and has a very effective weapon in its upper tail-fin, which is as long as its whole body, and with which it can deal a blow of terrific power. Sometimes springing several yards in the air (these creatures can jump as high as a mast-head) it will deal bang after bang on the luckless leviathan, the reports of the blows echoing like rifle-shots. The fishermen say that there is a secret understanding between this amiable fish and the narwhal, and that while the fox-shark thrashes above, his ally thrusts and stabs below, till between them the whale bleeds to death and affords them a meal or two.

Another variety of the toothless or baleen whales is the Rorqual, which has a soft back fin and curious puckers along its upper side, and sometimes reaches a length of more than a hundred feet. Round the Maldive and Seychelle Islands, in the Indian Ocean, are the favourite hunting-grounds for them, and the American and Scandinavian whalers have almost a monopoly there.

The typical toothed whale is the Sperm or Cachalot, eighty feet long, and frequenting both the northern and southern seas. It is easily to be distinguished from any other of its tribe, if only by its enormous square head; the back is black, the belly white, the skin soft and silky. It is gregarious, and travels in shoals of a couple of hundred. More pugnacious than most other species, it will turn to bay when attacked, and will deliberately charge or butt the pursuing ship. It is hunted principally for the sake of the oil secreted in its head and in a tube running along its back (spermaceti); its teeth yield an inferior sort of ivory; its body is used up like those of other kinds, and ambergris is taken from its entrails.

It has become proverbial on account of the love and care bestowed by the mother on her young; and no wonder. Over and over again fishermen have seen the mother sacrifice her life for the sake of her little one. Indeed, when a whale-boat encounters a suckling mother, it invariably attacks the young one, knowing that, in her anxiety to save the offspring, the older animal will not only interpose her body between it and the boat, but will be so taken up with shielding it that she will become an easy prey to the harpoons. She will even put her fin under the little thing's body to help it to swim the faster when pursued.

The modern whaler is very different from anything we have yet considered. First, there is the stout three to five hundred ton vessel, with her crew of about fifty hands, her six or eight double-pointed rowing boats, thirty feet long, and manned by six; her seventy-five horse-power engine, with her armoury of windlasses, boilers, oil-tank (built to hold nearly three hundred tons of oil), and her general workmanlike turn-out. And secondly, there is the boat beloved of the Norwegian and American whalers—a still more business-like craft; a fast hundred-ton twin screw, as obedient as a steam yacht, with an elaborate look-out forward, and one of the most deadly inventions of our day—the harpoon-gun—rigged up in her bows.

The first may be seen setting off from Dundee for a two-year cruise in the Antarctic regions; and a very gambling prospect she has before her. In 1895 a Dundee boat, the *Arctic*, came home from a short trip with ten whales, which meant five tons of whalebone, at that time worth ten thousand pounds, as well as twenty thousand gallons of oil. Recent scarcity of Antarctic whales has, of course, tremendously increased the value of the catches—to such an extent, in fact, that whalebone, which fifty years ago sold at the rate of a shilling a pound, is now worth about thirty times that amount.

The second kind of boat, which in a few years is destined to drive most other whalers out of the field, may be seen to the best advantage south of Greenland. Watch her as she routs out a cachalot or a fin-back. As before, the whale heralds his appearance by roars and grumbles and eddies, and the boat, travelling her twelve or thirteen knots an hour, is quickly in a position to launch her deadly shaft. The gun, seventy-five pounds in weight, four and a half feet long, including three feet of barrel, is fixed on a swivel; it has a range of from thirty to forty yards, and an ordinary pistol-handle. From this is fired the "bomb-lance," an American invention, a sort of improvement on Devisme's *balle foudroyante.* It is a cast-iron tube containing a small quantity of gunpowder; is pointed at one end, and at the other, which is tethered, has a match or fuse which, when the ball has penetrated into the whale's body, explodes the powder. If by any chance this explosion should take place in one of the lungs, the whale is dead instantly.

Many improvements have been tried—some carried into effect—on this deadly contrivance. A great many years ago, when it was first used, a celebrated French scientist, Dr. Thiercelin, tried the addition of various chemicals to the powder in the bomb, and ten Newfoundland whales shot in this manner died within spaces varying from four to eighteen minutes.

The still newer Norwegian improvement is a bomb with a shank fitted to it; the bomb enters the whale's body, carrying with it this shank, explodes, inflicting dangerous if not mortal injuries, and, as the animal moves forward, the pull on the line to which the weapon is fastened sets free two or four grips, or pins hinged at one end, which embed themselves barb-like in the flesh, thereby fixing the shank so that it cannot possibly move.

As the boat comes within a few fathoms of the whale,

the gun is fired, its explosion being echoed by a second as the bomb bursts, and the whale gives an agonised bellow and disappears, dragging the tow-line after it at electric speed. It should be mentioned that the cachalot can comfortably remain under water for nearly an hour. When he comes up again perhaps he is a quarter of a mile away, blowing and roaring so that we suspect he has not been injured in the vital part. Steam is put on, but not too much; at any moment the formidable giant is capable of turning and making a dash at its pursuers, and while one half of the skipper's energies are expended in trying to get within range again, the other half are given up to preparing to dodge any sudden turn the whale may be pleased to make.

But instead of charging he sounds again, perhaps several times; the boat hesitates and slows down. On his reappearance there are signs that he is weaker; true, he now begins to try the full length of his tether; he even starts to tow the boat along at a good rate, but his speed very soon flags.

"Don't spend another charge on him; let him tire down," is the skipper's order to the men in the bow; and, even as he speaks, the rope slacks again, and very slowly the mighty body begins to roll over on to its back. A chorus of cheering rises from the boat, but is speedily changed into a chorus of something else as the whale suddenly disappears from view. The crew look gloomy, and with good reason; they can cut away that cable as soon as they like, for the whale has sunk and will shortly be the sole property of a colony of fifteen-foot Greenland sharks that are lying in wait with an eye to such a contingency.

Naturally everyone has a reason to offer for the disaster; one fellow swears that the whale was wounded in the abdomen; another that it never once spouted blood; either may be right; for half a dozen reasons a dead whale is liable to sink; invariably if the water have rushed into its windpipe.

Such accidents, however, are comparatively rare; it is more likely that the whale will float, and that the sharks will be cheated by his being towed ashore; or, if the boat has a busy day before it, by his being buoyed up and left for a time. Boats of this sort, that go no great distance from home, carry no gear for quartering the whale; they merely tow the carcass as near to the shore as possible, whence it is drawn in chains up the beach, by steam-power, to the butchering sheds. On some boats they have a practice, before mooring the body, of inflating it with air pumped in by the engines, very much as boys blow out a frog; it can then be hitched to a buoy without fear of its sinking, unless one of its enemies comes along and makes a hole in it—a danger which is warded off by a man and a gun being left in charge, in a small boat.

I said further back that not an ounce of the whale need be wasted; its flesh is as sweet and wholesome as beef; the oil, and the whalebone from the toothless whales, are of course of great value; the skeleton is made up into all sorts of "earthenware" vessels; and now some sages have arisen to show that the skin can be tanned for leather and the milk of the females converted into condensed milk.

The spermaceti from the head of the cachalot is freed from the *phocenine* or rank oil which it contains by treating it with chloride of lime, oak-bark, and sulphuric acid; is clarified, and henceforth known as sperm oil, a crystalline solid fat from which wax candles are made.

One more word about the other valuable whale-product —ambergris, which is simply incompletely digested food taken from the intestines, generally in hard lumps, four or five from each cachalot. It is of the consistency of beeswax, so much so that it adheres to the knife when it is scraped and a moderate heat suffices to make it soft and oily. Its peculiarly sweet scent is increased by heat or friction. Immense quantities are imported into Southern Europe for the manufacture of perfumery, and among the Easterns it is still used as a flavouring in cooking.

CHAPTER XX

HOW SPONGES ARE PROCURED

What sponge is—Where it grows—Sponge-diving—The undressed diver—A "dressed" diver at work—His dress—The diver on the bottom—Signals—Coming up—Dredging for sponges—Awkward gear—Sponge-harpooning—The spy-glass—The Adriatic trade—Sponge-culture—Florida Keys—Sponge-hooking in the Bahamas.

A SPONGE is a skeleton, not of one animal but of countless thousands, and it represents, as Professor Huxley has expressed it, "a kind of sub-aqueous city, where the people are arranged about the streets and roads in such a manner that each can easily appropriate his food from the water as it passes along."

This skeleton may be flexible and elastic and horny, as in the case of the ordinary washing sponge; or it may be calcareous, chalky, and therefore useless for the purposes to which we ordinarily devote this substance. The animals which inhabit it, and which are almost at the bottom of the zoological ladder (for they come under the head of protozoa), take the form of a jelly-like mass, not unlike the uncooked white of an egg; and this separates itself from its shell or skeleton when the sponge is lifted out of the water and squeezed.

Sponges are not by any means confined to salt water, although those of commerce are invariably marine; nor are they necessarily a rarity in any warm or temperate part of the sea, but they develop better and reproduce more freely in some beds than in others. They were regarded by the old naturalists as peculiar to the Mediterranean, but we all know that small varieties are found round the British coasts; the beautiful "mermaid's glove" or five-fingered sponge is not seldom found in the oyster-dredge, or, for that matter, on the fish-hook. Moreover, in the year 1840, a European sponge-merchant discovered that the valuable substance was as common as mussels on the reef between Florida and the Bahamas, and since then the West Indian industry has in some respects promised to rival that of the Mediterranean.

The spongy skeleton adheres very firmly to the sea-bottom or the rocks on which it grows, and how to obtain it uninjured is a very serious problem, which the fishermen have endeavoured to solve in various ways: by diving, by dredging, and by harpooning or hooking.

The first method is the oldest and, from the merchant's point of view, the safest and most profitable, and it has been practised round about the Greek Islands, Sicily, the Levant, and the north of Africa for ages. Six thousand men are now employed in the Levant sponge-fishery alone, and about the same number in other parts of the Mediterranean. These Greek divers, like those of Ceylon, are trained to their task almost from infancy, and become gradually accustomed to working under water and to enduring a pressure so great that less than half of it would mean death to the untrained man.

But sponge sometimes chooses a depth of from one to

two hundred fathoms for its habitation, and we have seen, in the case of the pearl-divers, that thirteen fathoms is a depth that taxes an undressed diver's powers to almost their full extent. Some of the Sicilians and Greeks will venture to fifteen, but the brief time which they are able to remain under water at that depth is of little use for such hard and lengthy work, and the effort seems almost to rob them of the power to wrench the larger sponges free from their natural moorings. Therefore, the boat-owners have of late years been glad to engage professional divers of another sort from England and France, or from among their own people, who, when "dressed," can remain down a very considerable length of time. Such men boast that they could stay for ever in five-fathom water, and any one of them who knows his business can do sponge-work in fifteen fathoms for at least an hour, and can remain in from twenty to fifty fathoms for longer than an undressed diver could stay in ten; all the same, even an exceptionally strong British diver would refuse to work for any length of time in more than twenty-eight. Hence the need for dredging, or other mechanical means, when the sponge-ground is covered with more than fifty fathoms of water.

Let us watch the undressed divers first. Their way of going to work differs in some respects from that of the pearl-fishers. When the depth has been taken, and the position of the sponges ascertained by means of a spy-glass, a rope, equivalent to the depth, is made fast by one end to the boat; to the other end is tied a large white stone, triangular or oblong, which has a hole drilled through one corner. The man, instead of putting his foot in a loop, gives the weighted end of the line a turn or two round his breast and then springs into the water like an ordinary swimmer; some prefer merely to hold the rope by one hand. Sharks, we know, are plentiful hereabout, and there are no shark-charmers. Still one seldom hears of a diver being attacked; there is always a gun or two on board, and there is the same amount of bustle and splashing and shouting as in the Gulf of Manaar.

Arrived at the bottom, the diver—if he be in the habit of keeping his eyes open—uses the white stones as a landmark, for there is no reason to suppose that he will be lucky enough to drop in the middle of a sponge-bed. If the water be clear he will then leave go of the rope and wander round, always able to find his way back as long as he can see the stone. But, as often as not, there is trouble going on at the bottom; a fight among the ground-fish, or a dolphin poking about after molluscs, and the water is as thick as a London fog—even the man's own movements, in some grounds, are sufficient to cloud everything. In such a case the diver dare not let go of the rope, but must carry the stone about with him. Hurriedly tearing off all the sponges that lie to his hand, he stuffs them into his net-bag (some men carry no bag, but tuck their gatherings under the left arm), gives a couple of jerks to the rope, and he and the bag and the stone are swiftly hoisted up.

It may be asked, How is the man at the top to tell the difference between the signal for hauling and the natural tugs on the rope caused by the diver in moving from point to point? But the man at the top, it must be remembered, is a fisherman, and the sense of touch of a man who has to do with lines acquires a subtilty that might almost be compared to a musician's "ear." Unconsciously he follows every one of the diver's movements hither and thither, and, in ninety-nine cases out of a hundred, could be relied upon to haul up at the right moment without any signal at all.

The diver is now lifted into the boat and gets his breath while the next man goes down. I have seen it stated that whenever these fellows come to the surface, blood flows from their mouths, ears, and noses. How many gallons of blood do the authors of such a statement suppose a man can afford to lose in the course of a day? As a rule, once and once only does a Mediterranean diver expect to bleed in this manner, and that is when he goes down for the first time after being away from such work some months—as, for instance, on the first day of the season. What is more, the divers regard this as not only a healthy sign, but as a sign that they are fit for their work. Indeed, if any man should find that bleeding does not then occur he will not attempt another descent that day, nor will he start regular work till he has bled.

The dressed diver's performance is a far more pretentious affair, for, as the reader is aware, he must be supplied with air all the time he is down; also, the lowering and hauling of a man to whose natural weight a dress weighing a hundred and forty-seven pounds (ten stone seven!) is added, is a very different matter from dealing with a naked man. A successful diver must be both born and made, and any member of the trade could tell, almost at a glance, whether or no a stranger would ever be of any use for such work. The ideal diver is the short or medium-height man, with markedly sloping shoulders and very deep chest, such a build being the best calculated to resist the terrible water-pressure.

The dressing of the man is rapidly performed by one or two members of the crew; and here a brief description of a diver's "rig" may be of interest to the reader. The "dress" goes on first, and consists of coat, trousers, and socks all in one piece; this fits very loosely to the figure, is made of mackintosh and lined with india-rubber, and round the cuffs of this strange garment rubber rings are fastened to keep it water-tight at the wrists. Then comes the heavy breast-plate which is of copper, and serves to relieve the chest of undue pressure; and to this is screwed a band of brass which goes round the chest to the back. The heavily-weighted boots are then laced on, and the cord or "life-line" knotted loosely round the waist. Lastly there is the somewhat gruesome-looking helmet, with whose shape all are familiar; the "eyes" are window-panes on a small scale, protected by wire gauze. The life-line is then carried up the left side of the body, passes through a clip on the helmet, then is brought down again over the chest where it meets a short cord which has also been tied round the waist.

Now the breathing apparatus. The nozzle of a wire-lined rubber tube, like a garden-hose, is screwed into a hole on the side of the helmet; the tube is carried under one arm, and looped up once more to the helmet; the other end of the tube communicates with a two- or three-cylinder air pump. It can, of course, be joined up to any length, and is made as long as the life-line.

Thus habited, our diver is lifted over the side of the vessel on to a ladder which runs some little distance under water, and when he is certain that all his gear is quite safe, he lets himself go. One man watches the life-line, another pays out the tube, and one or two more turn the handle of the air-pump. As soon as he reaches the bottom, the diver takes from his shoulders a coil of thin cord which he has brought down with him—the "track-line." Perhaps one end is weighted; if not he ties it to whatever fixture he can find and then sets off on his travels to the end of his tether, which is a fairly long one, letting the track-line run from his hand as he goes; stopping every now and then to gather the finest and largest sponges he can see, and packing them as closely as possible in the net-bag that hangs over his shoulders.

If the trawler feels some excitement when the first opportunity arrives of peeping into a net that has come up from the bottom, what must be the diver's first feeling on finding himself free to roam about for an hour on one of the world's oldest if not richest submarine treasure-grounds? What would not most antiquarians give to spend an hour in such a spot, off Sicily, or Cyprus, or Greece?

Men can gather sponges and yet keep a watchful eye on possible submerged treasure, and in this way very valuable

HAULING UP A SPONGE-DIVER

Nowadays much of the sponge-fishing off the Greek Islands is done by "dressed" divers.

articles have often been fished up. Sometimes the diver brings up a "surprise packet" on speculation. I knew one Mediterranean diver who, with great trouble and at some risk, succeeded in taking on board a mysterious iron box, that suggested at least deeds, if not banknotes, jewels, and bonds. When he came to open it in the presence of an admiring and expectant crew, he found nothing but a ruined silk hat and a dozen collars that—insult added to injury—were a size or two too small for every man on board.

Meanwhile, how has our man been managing about his breathing? The question is not so idle as might seem, for all men do not respire alike, and inhaling air that has been pumped down from a height of about sixty yards, is not quite the same thing as breathing in the ordinary way. Perhaps too much air is being sent down; perhaps not enough; perhaps air that has already been used is being forced back by the fresh draught. Certainly the latter should not occur with a diver who knows his work; for the helmet contains two valves through which all foul air can be ejected. To regulate the supply from above, one of the crew keeps his hand continually on the life-line, and calls out the signals as they come up from the bottom to the men who are working the pump. If the diver wants more air he gives three sharp jerks at the rope; if he already has too much, two jerks. From time to time he also gives a special "all right" signal—a very necessary precaution when he may not be expected above water for nearly an hour; for in that time there is no telling what might happen. Apart from sharks, saw-fish, and sword-fish which may at least discommode the diver or interfere with the gear, there is always the possibility of something going wrong with a man's heart when he is at work in great depths; the air-valves, too, cannot be guaranteed never to get out of order; therefore this signal is resorted to, unless there are several divers working together on the same spot.

When he can remain down no longer, the sponge-fisher very carefully fastens his bag and even ropes it to his body; then gives the "pull up" signal—one long sustained pull till the hauling begins. The care that he has expended in making his catch quite safe is explained now. To come up in the natural position, head foremost, requires a certain amount of effort on his own part; an awkward or half-exhausted diver may come up feet first, or lying on his back or face; for there is no certainty that the weights will "trim" properly when the dress is inflated; and that being the case, what would become of a loosely fastened bag?

The hauling up of a diver is not greatly different from the hauling up of a net or a dredge, as regards the rope and the weight; it is hard work for two men; often impossible for one. But there is also the tube to be seen to, and this is where the difficulty comes in; for on the one hand, the hauling of it should keep pace with that of the life-line; on the other, no undue strain must be allowed to come on it. At last the weird, black figure appears, totters up the ladder and waits while the men lift him on board; then off comes the helmet, and then—

but we all know what the first breath of unimpeded air is after we have been confined in a close atmosphere; multiply the pleasure of that by a hundred. But use is everything; in a few moments our diver will be off to the bottom again.

Dredging for sponges is probably a less-known branch of the trade; it forms the winter industry of the Greek fishermen of Asia Minor and North Africa,—winter, because then the equinoctial and autumn storms have had plenty of time to tear up the seaweed which would otherwise fill up the dredge, or hamper the movement of the gear.

The dredge is worked from a large sailing-boat, in most cases the tow-line being fastened to the bowsprit. Generally speaking it is only used in water that is too deep for the divers; but, in the island of Syme—one of the chief centres of the sponge industry—and on parts of the Syrian coast where the sponges sometimes lie close in to shore, it is shot from a large rowing-boat and hauled in from the beach. This dredge is a formidable-looking arrangement; imagine an immense packing-case three feet high, and about eighteen feet square; bigger round, that is to say, than a room of average size; open at the top, and having a large net-bag hanging from the bottom. The meshes of this net are four inches square, and are made of camel's-hair cord as thick as a man's finger.

This unwieldy apparatus is thrown overboard on a good sponge-ground and towed gently along as if it were a trawl, the boat drifting wherever she likes. Like a trawl, too, it is hauled up, two or four bridles connecting the tow-line with the frame. As the sponges are taken out, they are squeezed dry and thrown in the hold, and the dredge is dropped overboard again.

It will easily be understood that such an awkward method of working would not be much favoured by fishermen who are lucky enough to find sponge in moderately shallow water. For those who object to the dredge and who do not care to dive, there is still the harpoon; and this is the favourite tackle with many of the Greek fishermen on both sides of the Mediterranean (for the sponge trade of North Africa is mainly in Greek hands).

The large sailing vessels thus engaged take with them several small boats from which the harpooning is done; two or three men to a boat. The harpoon is simply a fork with a very long handle, to which an additional handle can, if necessary, be screwed. Each boat carries the spy-glass of which mention has already been made—a very crude yet satisfactory means of seeing to the bottom and discovering the lie of the ground. It is sometimes unkindly described as a bucket with a glass bottom, and indeed it is not much else, being a zinc cylinder about eighteen inches high and big enough to admit a man's head; with a circular sheet of glass let in to the bottom of it. When such an instrument is pushed a foot or so below the surface a man can see through as much as thirty fathoms of moderately clear water.

As soon as the sponge is sighted, the digging and poking and stabbing begin, and it is surprising what very large catches skilled men can make in this manner.

HOW SPONGES ARE PROCURED

Whatever may be the means chosen for obtaining the sponge, its treatment when taken ashore is pretty much the same. It is first rinsed and squeezed till every particle of gelatinous animal matter has been got rid of; then it is exposed to the air for a day or two, after which it is taken back to the water and thrown into an enclosure made of planks and stakes, and left to clean itself. Then it is taken out again, trodden vigorously by bare-footed men till it is once more squeezed as dry as possible, and finally is hung up to dry before being sent on to the picking and sorting warehouse. These sponges, it should be remarked, are the finer ones, used for bath and toilet; the cheap, coarser articles used for horse and carriage-washing come from the American grounds; but, before we discuss those, there is another European ground which calls for mention.

Along the east side of the Adriatic Sea sponges are found at almost all depths, and the fishery, which is carried on by the Dalmatians and Croats, is in a very flourishing condition. It is done from small boats and by means of harpoons. These men employ a similar spy-glass to that of the Greeks, and they facilitate its use in a very ingenious, if simple, manner. Every boat carries a small supply of pebbles, and, when the look-out man wishes to inspect the ground, he dips four or five of these in oil and tosses them one by one in a curved line in front of the boat. Each pebble, as it sinks, scatters tiny drops all the way down, which help to clear the water, thus affording a more unobstructed view to the spy-glass.

The Dalmatians and others have latterly taken to

breeding sponge on scientific lines, which merely means that they avail themselves of the natural reproductive instinct of the animals which it contains. In the autumn the seeds or gemmules which occur in the interior of the sponge body begin to form themselves, and gradually every seed develops into a sponge particle, which during the following summer becomes an ovum; and this, on becoming fertilised, as often as not separates from the main body of the sponge, attaches itself to some rock or other object, and, little by little, grows into a separate colony of animals. By experiments, scientists have proved that a small bit of sponge torn from the main bulk will, if circumstances are favourable and if there are sufficient gemmules contained in it, quickly increase in size through the breeding of its occupants; and now the rearing of sponges is as much a recognised industry as oyster culture is.

From the coast of Florida to the Bahamas there stretches a long and—from a seaman's point of view—very dangerous chain of islands, mostly of coral formation, and known as the Florida Keys. Some of the islands are just below sea-level, others just above; others have been slowly worn down by the action of the water and remain at varying heights below the surface. On and about these reefs it was accidentally discovered that sponge had been breeding very freely, probably for many centuries; and so, during the last sixty years the horse-sponge trade has grown up—mainly on the Bahamas side of the reef; and so profitable has it become that the islanders are now exporting sponge to the annual value of nearly a hundred and twenty thousand pounds. The beds extend over several thousand square miles, and are, in all reasonable probability, inexhaustible.

Here sponge-diving is almost unknown; what need, when in many cases the sponges grow so close to the surface that it looks as if you could gather them with your hand? Instead, the fishermen use the harpoon, or a hooked form of it; a three-pronged rake, we might better term it. Every week a fleet of schooner-rigged boats, of any size up to twenty-five tons, sets off from the shores of a few of the islands, each carrying several two-men dinghies or dories, like those used by the Newfoundland cod-fishers, and manned largely by negroes. While the ships lie at anchor the little boats pull about over the reefs, the sponge-hooker lying over either stern or bows, and snatching at everything that looks promising.

Hooking here requires far greater care and skill than in the Mediterranean, for everybody knows how soft horse-sponge is, and how easily torn. The aim is to slide the rake immediately between the rock and the root of the sponge, and so wrench it bodily off.

At the end of the day the dinghies pull back to their schooner, and the sponges are stowed away on board. After a week of good catches the fleet is able to return and land the cargo, if "land" may be allowed to mean bringing the sponges in to shore by the boat-load and throwing them straight into the "crawl," as the West Indians call the staked enclosure such as has been described. Here the sponges lie a few feet under water, and for a week or two are periodically squeezed and rinsed; then they are thrown on the beach to dry, and are packed for sending away.

The people of Queensland too are now developing a not inconsiderable trade in sponges.

CHAPTER XXI

DOLPHINS, PORPOISES, AND MANATEES

The dolphin—Misconceptions about it—Dolphin-catching among the Faroe islanders—Fresh-water dolphins: the Inia and the Soosoo—The grampus—Porpoises—Fishermen's hatred of them—The narwhal—Its tusk—An Iceland narwhal-hunt—The Greenlanders' method—The Caaing whale and the beluga—Trapping and seining belugas—The dugong and the manatee—A manatee-hunt.

THE cetacean family includes many water monsters that, though scarcely classifiable under the head of whales, are hunted or "fished" for in much the same manner, and generally for similar reasons; such are the dolphin, the porpoise, and the like. These have in common with the whale a fish-like form and a horizontal tail, and like them belong to the mammalia. Let us take the dolphin first.

One very interesting point in connection with this animal is that in appearance it is very unlike the popular conception of it; and for this there is a good reason. Classical mythology practically raised it to an object of worship. Neptune, said the Greeks, turned himself into a dolphin on a certain occasion; so did Apollo; therefore temples that were dedicated to either deity were more often than not ornamented with representations of the sacred sea-beast. Many of these images were at first very roughly executed; sculpture had not yet reached the high perfection which it subsequently attained, and probably none of the artists had ever seen a dolphin very near. The later sculptors were too loyal to the work of their predecessors as well as too much bound by tradition to attempt to alter or improve on the generally accepted idea of what a dolphin ought to be, and so century after century went by, still leaving the people under the impression that it was a sort of dog-headed fish.

So far from its head being round, it has a much longer and sharper muzzle than the porpoise, and has been known from time immemorial among the French fishermen as the *bec d'oie* or goose-bill. Its average length is a little over seven feet. It has a most shark-like appetite, and will not only gorge itself on fish, but will make a meal of an elderly, or wounded, or dying brother; and, as its mouth is furnished with about a hundred and eighty long, pointed teeth, it is well equipped for such a repast. The home of the common dolphin is the Mediterranean and the North Atlantic; but varieties are found all over the world, the largest known species being the grampus, which may be seen anywhere north of our own shores.

The dolphin has blow-holes or spiracles; but, unlike those of the whale, they are joined together so as to make but one opening, which is placed a little above the eyes. In colour it is black, gradually shading off to white under the belly; in addition to its flippers it has a long pointed back-fin, and so swift are its movements that it is sometimes called the Sea Arrow.

In days gone by, sailors and fishermen credited the animal with all the ferocity and voracity of the shark, and told weird tales of shoals of them pursuing a boat for the sake of a meal of human flesh, making wild dashes and jumps to seize the crew, even leaping on board after their prey, and being deprived of it only after a battle in which axes and guns figured.

This belief has died hard, for the reason, I suppose, that "a lie that is half a truth" is harder to fight than "a lie that is all a lie." For the dolphin *does* swim after ships and boats, and he does jump aboard sometimes, though not with the intention of attacking the crew. He is an exceedingly astute being, and has discovered that from time to time a good deal of waste food and rubbish is thrown overboard, and that this attracts the fish in great quantities; fish that under ordinary circumstances would elude him by their swift dodging or by diving into the mud; therefore, because a boat generally means a meal, he will follow it for miles. As to his jumping on board, he may do that out of sheer playfulness, or by accident, when springing up in pursuit of a fish that has leapt into the air in order to escape him.

His extreme fondness for the flesh of the various flying-fish is well known. In the warmer parts of the Atlantic he will spend his entire day in hunting them; leaping up after them and sometimes snapping them in mid-air; lying in wait just below the surface at a spot where one is likely to fall, or dogging one particular fish till he has thoroughly tired it out. In leaping or springing he closely resembles the salmon, curving his tail round as far as he can, and then "letting himself go."

The special hunting-ground for these creatures is on the east coast of Stromö, one of the Faroe Islands. Here, from July to December, the dolphins come into shallow water; you may almost say that they lie about on the shore. Usually they come in detachments of from three to four hundred, under the guidance of a few old males. The islanders are strangely lethargic over their fishing, considering that they are of Norwegian descent; they sadly neglect their opportunities with the cod and other fish, and few of them will pursue the dolphin except when the work is thus made easy for them. Then bands of men armed with clubs, spears, or axes go down to the beach before daylight, and lie in wait behind the rocks till dawn, when the animals begin to come in to shore.

At a signal whistle, every one springs out and lays about him vigorously. It is tame work, for the poor creatures are far too much surprised and terrified to offer resistance, and those that cannot flee are soon killed. Then the women and children come down and, with the men, haul the carcasses on to the higher ground where they cut them up. The "train-oil" from them is taken away by the steamers that call periodically at Thorshavn.

It may not be generally known that there are two or three species of fresh-water dolphins, by which I do not, of course, mean such as may sometimes swim up the rivers from the sea in search of food, or for other reason,

DOLPHIN HUNTING

A avourite hunting-ground or dolphins is on Stromö, one ot the Faroe Islands. Here, from July to December, they come into shallow water or lie about on the shore, and bands of men armed with axes and spears lie in wait for them behind the rocks.

but those which live wholly in fresh water. One of them, the Inia, inhabits the upper waters of the Amazon and some of the lakes round about; its length varies from seven to twelve feet, and it differs little from the common dolphin except in having a longer and more pointed snout. The Indians and Bolivians pursue it for the sake of its flesh and its valuable oil. Before daybreak a small fleet of canoes will set off up the river and, hiding under the gloomy, overhanging trees, wait for the inia to come up to feed. As soón as one of them appears, two or three harpoons are launched at it, for only by swift killing can the men hope to make a fairly good catch. The animals do not come in shoals; seldom will there be more than a dozen in one place, and at the least noise these will dive, reappearing nobody knows where; so the fishermen dare not use guns. All the harpoons thrown at one animal must come from the same boat, for he is not averse to doing a little towing, and though if he found three boat-loads moored to him he could not do them much harm, the noise he would make would alarm the other animals, and spoil the chances of the remaining boats. When a boat has killed her catch she paddles silently and rapidly away, towing the inia close behind, a man being stationed in the stern with a long lance to keep off the alligators that might try for a mouthful of the carcass.

A very similar cetacean of the same size, called the Soosoo, is found in the Ganges, where it affords amusement to British sportsmen, and profit to such of the Hindus as take the trouble to hunt it.

DOLPHINS, PORPOISES

The giant of the delphinidæ, the grampus or gladiator dolphin, reaches a length of twenty and even five-and-twenty feet; is one of the most voracious of the tribe, and is found in various of the northern seas, travelling in quite small herds. Such a herd will collect round a whale, and between them kill and eat it. Sometimes they vary their tactics; surround the whale, hustle and bully it, drive it backwards and forwards for a whole day or more till it is dead beat, and then, between them, tear out and devour its tongue. The strength of the grampus is proverbial, and when a harpoon is fixed in it, it will make no difficulty of towing a boat-load of men for several miles before it is tired out. Many years ago a small grampus was seen in the Thames near Blackwall. Four men rowed after it and pierced it with three harpoons, and just when they thought their capture safe and their task finished, the powerful young beast started off full-speed up the river against a tide that was running eight miles an hour. After a couple of miles it dived, and then came to a dead stop, seemingly exhausted, and the oarsmen pulled triumphantly towards it, expecting to find it dead; but, as they came within about a fathom of it, the grampus suddenly shot away again, scarcely seeming to notice the pull of the boat when the rope had run taut again, and swam beyond Deptford—another three miles—before it would own itself conquered. A full-grown grampus would probably have towed thrice the number of men to Twickenham, and then been prepared to run them back again to Tilbury or Southend.

Probably most readers have seen porpoises, if only at a

distance, for big shoals of them frequently put in an appearance close to the shore: Hunstanton and the neighbourhood is a good place to see them. These animals bring out, as strongly as anything, the fisherman's rooted belief in the Infernal Powers as a creative force. "The Almighty never *could* ha' made sich varmints as them," observed a really saintly old salmon-fisher who was giving me an account of their depredations among the Norwegian salmon. And indeed the porpoise's appetite for these fish is so insatiable that it will pursue them up the rivers. For a small shoal to take a trip up the Seine as far as Rouen is a mere nothing; it is a matter of history that they have been seen even beyond Paris. Nor is it only the salmon that appeals to their greed. Ask the herring and mackerel fleets their opinion anent the porpoise. It breaks up the shoals, rushes like a bull at a gate against a fleet of herring-nets, with disastrous results to the owners, and harries the mackerel literally to death.

It is the smallest of the cetacean tribe; one of them that measured five feet from tip to tail would be of average size. It has a dolphin-like body, though with rounder muzzle and head. A shoal of porpoises is like an immense black shiny patch on the water; so closely do they crowd together and in such vast numbers, that it is difficult to understand how they can move at all. They exhibit all the love of playing and gambolling that is seen among the dolphins, and as much curiosity as a fish or an Arab; hence perhaps some of the gruesome nursemaid tales about the "sea-horses" that swim after and devour the unwary bather.

Though the animal is so valuable, there is little systematic porpoise-hunting nowadays except among the Lapps and Greenlanders. If a whaleboat should happen to fall in with a shoal, it will harpoon as many of them as it can without going out of its way, and the Norwegian fishermen will shoot or spear them in the same spirit in which a gamekeeper sends a charge of shot after a stray dog or a weasel. But in the Middle Ages porpoise-hunting was a fashionable sport in England and France: the meat was highly esteemed, and in Henry VIII's time it was even a royal dish. The Greenlanders still eat and enjoy it; they hunt it with light harpoons, and the catches are towed ashore in great quantities.

The oil, which the Greenland fishers export to Central Europe, is obtained from the boiling down of the blubber, which, as in the whale, lies immediately below the skin. It is firmer than that of the whale, and usually about an inch deep, and the oil from it requires less treatment in the clarifying of it than any other form of cetacean fat. The hide when tanned is exceedingly tough, and is used largely in making hoods for carriages.

The narwhal, or sea-unicorn as it is often called, has a dolphin's body, but its head is shaped more like that of a seal; the blow-holes, as in the dolphin, have but one outlet. The chief feature which distinguishes it from all the other cetacea is its wonderful sword-like tusk, which in reality is an elongated tooth, sometimes more than half as long as its body (the tusk of the female is seldom more than ten inches long). Sea-unicorn, by the way, is rather a misleading nickname, for very frequently the animal has two of these ivory prolongations, the incisor tooth of the lower jaw being lengthened out so as to rival that of the upper. The animal may be found anywhere between the shores of Iceland and Greenland.

The terrific power of the formidable weapon with which it is provided may be gauged from the fact that the narwhal on seeing a ship will make a dash at it, thinking it to be some species of whale, and, if the vessel be of wood, will drive its tusk right through her side or stern. The result to the narwhal is not pleasant; if it should succeed in piercing the *side* of the ship, the tusk will be snapped off by the force of her motion; if the stern, the animal will become as much a fixture as a nail driven into a fence, and will be towed along and starved to death. From this it may be imagined how much chance a whale stands against a shoal of sea-unicorns. Yet, in spite of their fierceness, they play together as merrily as dolphins.

The Icelanders use large, heavy rowing-boats in pursuing the narwhal. "Pursuing" is scarcely the right word in this case, because a boat might chase a narwhal till doomsday and never come up with it, for when the animal is alone its pace is something like that of a salmon. If, however, he should meet a friend, though fifty boats were after him he would still want to stop and fence with his tusk and play about for a while.

But as a rule they swim in enormous shoals, making but little progress, fishing or playing in long irregular lines about the Iceland fjörds. The fleet of boats—each with a crew of about five—lie in hiding among the rocks, waiting for a shoal to come within reasonable distance of the shore; and as soon as the long straggling lines are close enough, the boats dash from their hiding-place and glide swiftly and silently between the rows.

Then all in a moment there is confusion and panic among the shoal; for narwhals are only courageous against a passive foe, or one of their own kind; and as the long oar-blades are whisked sharply out of the water and everything is made clear for action, they fall back one upon another, make one futile attempt at flight, and then content themselves with huddling together and spouting or groaning. In this position they are powerless to defend themselves, even if they would, for the long tusks have become hopelessly mixed; sometimes half a dozen will be thrust together like so much trellis-work, and not one of the owners can stir. Perhaps one of the more daring of the males will make a feeble dash at the boat, but there is always a fisherman ready to receive him.

The fishing tackle is a pole, eight or ten feet long, with either an ordinary whale-harpoon head fitted to it or else a three-tined fork with barbed points. These the sturdy boatmen work untiringly, stabbing on all sides as far as they can reach, pitchforking the smaller carcasses on board bodily, and leaving the others to take care of themselves till they can be roped up together and towed ashore.

Although they see their brethren being butchered on all sides of them, the narwhals still make no attempt at escape; some few perhaps will dive, but when they want breath they generally seem to come up again in the midst of one of the lines of struggling animals.

The work is often lucrative enough; but, as is always the case with the more profitable forms of fishing, very risky and uncertain. Sometimes, in the very heat of the slaughter, one of the men will discover that the boat is leaking; it has been punctured by one of the ivory swords round it, which, driven accidentally and with but little force against the timbers, has succeeded in making a hole but not in staying there to stop it up. Hastily the few carcasses taken on board are pushed out of the way and attempts made at checking the leak. This however is idle, for, by the time the men have discovered and stopped one hole, they have realised that the water is still coming in from other holes and that the boat must now surely sink. With their heavy nailed boots, and their already sodden woollen leggings, swimming will be impossible; and unless another boat can get at the sinking crew, there is not much hope for them. And a boat may be ever so near, yet powerless to help; for the very thickness of the shoal, which under ordinary circumstances would mean wealth to the fishermen, is now a horrible obstacle, effectually preventing the progress of another boat towards the unfortunates. Cases have been known of a crew being drowned or gored to death by the terrified narwhals while another boat was within a few fathoms of them.

The modern Icelanders have ceased to regard the tusks as merely useful as arrows, tent-poles, and charms; instead they export them, and get a very high price for them; for narwhal ivory is harder, and will bear a higher polish, than even that obtained from the elephant. All kinds of superstitions circled round this tooth or tusk in ancient and mediæval days, the chief among them being that it was an antidote against all poisons. Even as far down as the sixteenth century we find Charles IX of France believing that a fragment of the tooth put into his wine-cup would counteract the effect of any poison that an enemy might have placed there. Later all sorts of squabbles arose among naturalists as to the use that the tusk is to the animal; some still maintain that it is employed solely in burrowing for molluscs which, with skate, cod, and squid, are its food; and that its having been found in a dead whale or a ship's timbers is pure accident.

The Icelanders strip off the hide and employ it in various ways, and export the oil from the fat; this is said to be of better quality than that from whale-blubber. But they do not eat the flesh. The word "nar" in Icelandic signifies a corpse; and the natives argue that an animal does not get called "corpse-whale" for nothing; and they abstain. In that respect they are a good deal more particular than some more civilised folk who will enjoy crabs and eels which undoubtedly have a partiality for the form of diet which the narwhal is unjustly accused of relishing.

As the weather gets warmer the shoals swim northwards to the Greenland coast, sometimes in the straggling files already described, sometimes "shoulder to shoulder," in one line a couple of miles long. They stay here till driven southwards by scarcity of food, but often a small shoal will be cut off by the sudden winter and frozen up.

Then a special use of the long tusk is made apparent; as the animals cannot remain under water altogether, they charge upwards at the ice, and gradually succeed in breaking open a breathing-hole, which they keep free from the continually re-forming ice. It is at these holes that the Greenlanders find their narwhal fishing-grounds; sometimes they are numerous, sometimes there will be only one in a space of several square miles.

The fishermen collect in great numbers round the hole, every one armed with either a gun or a three-pronged fork, and before they have been waiting long the suffocating animals appear in hundreds. The "catching" is a wholesale massacre; the men with the guns fire as fast as they can, while the harpooners drive their weapons into the dead or dying bodies and pitchfork them into heaps on the ice.

The Greenland men have none of the Icelanders' scruples about eating the narwhal; in fact, they regard the flesh as a great delicacy. They cut up the carcass into joints, which they smoke as we should smoke bacon.

Before we proceed to the vegetable-eating delphinidæ, there are two other animals we must notice—the Caaing Whale and the Beluga, or white whale, both of them ardently pursued by the northern fishermen. The caaing, which the Scotch fishers call the black whale, used invariably to be classed by naturalists with the dolphins, but it is now generally regarded as a separate cetacean species. Sailors often call it the howling-whale and the pilot-fish, though why the latter it is difficult to say, unless on account of its collecting, dolphin fashion, and swimming in shoals after the ships. In shape it is more like a very long and very fat porpoise than anything else; it is about the same length as the grampus, but the thickest part of its body sometimes measures eleven feet through, so that the animal would touch the ends, sides, ceiling, and floor of a fairly long corridor. Its colour is glossy black, with a white streak running the whole length of its under side.

The Orkney whalers make good profit of this animal, for it is easily taken, and relatively almost as valuable as the whale itself. It is no friend to the Scotch cod-fishers, for it eats the catch and sometimes runs off with the tackle. The pursuit and destruction of it must usually be regarded more as a branch of other sea trades than as a separate fishery.

This is not so with the "Greenlander's Whale," as the beluga is sometimes styled. This animal seems to be a sort of link between the caaing and the narwhal, and its home is nearly the same as that of the former; that is to say it belongs to the Greenland coast, but travels as far south as the Faroe Islands, and in America is found as low down as Newfoundland. Very occasionally it comes down to our own coasts; about sixty years ago one of them was captured some distance up the Medway, and one was killed on the Scotch coast in 1815.

In length it is seldom more than fifteen feet; it has a broad, blunt head and no tusk, though it has about seventeen front teeth, which generally fall out as the beluga passes middle life. Its skin is quite white, and so soft that only a well-embedded harpoon will retain its position. Yet, strangely enough, this skin, so soft while fresh, makes the toughest of leather when tanned.

The Greenlanders kill thousands of belugas every summer, and in winter the animals are caught in the narwhal ice-holes, at least half a dozen of them finding their way to every hole. They are either very stupid or else very timid and gentle, for they flee at lightning speed if they know themselves to be pursued; they seldom offer any resistance to the harpooners, and are rarely seen attempting to attack any other animal, although, like the caaing, they have no objection to snapping up a hooked cod-fish or ling. Shoals of them are seldom seen near the coast, generally they remain in deep water or hang about the entries of the fjörds in wait for the salmon. The little ones and the females are, as a rule, placed in the middle of the shoal. The young are born black, then become pink and eventually white. The name Sea-canaries has often been given to them because when they are under water their bellowing is deadened to a peculiar bird-like whistle.

The beluga enjoys the distinction of being the only cetacean for which nets are set. At the mouths of the fjörds a kind of salmon-trap on a large scale is moored, and a day seldom passes without several being caught. The Danish Greenlanders go farther than this and make some very respectable catches with the seine. Its meshes are made of fine rope, each opening five or six inches square, and the net is shot either from a couple of cutters or from lugger-rigged rowing boats. The oil is sent south by Danish steamers, and the flesh is smoked for eating, like that of the narwhal.

Some of the cetacea do not live in the sea altogether, and some are vegetarians. There is a class which spends much of its time in the rivers and is known by the generic name *manatidæ*, the two best-known specimens of which are the dugong and the manatee; one or two species of this class have become extinct during the last couple of hundred years—notably the *Rhytina*, on which Behring's shipwrecked crew lived for eleven months in their island solitude, a hundred and fifty years ago.

The dugong fishery is, among civilised people, quite a modern industry, that has arisen on account of the animal's oil, which, it was discovered some years ago, contains all the strengthening medicinal properties of cod-liver oil. Its home is round Polynesia, the East Indies, and Ceylon, and boat-loads of harpooned carcasses are taken ashore by Dutch and Australian fishermen. Many are killed in the river mouths and even on the sea-shore, for the flippers of the manatidæ enable the animals to drag themselves along the ground.

All these creatures are singularly mild and gentle in their disposition, and maternal affection is even more strongly shown by them than by other cetaceans. Therefore the young ones are always aimed at by the harpooners, and the mothers, instantly interposing themselves between the young and the enemy, are easily speared. A brutal practice obtains among the Malay fishermen of harpooning a couple of baby dugongs and towing them along as a decoy; the mothers follow and become easy game. This may be good business but it "isn't cricket."

The manatees, or sea-cows, or *femmes poissons*, show just the same tenderness and, in addition, a peculiar clannishness. In great herds they often leave the sea and enter the rivers of Central and South America; a few old males go first, then the bulk of the herd, wives and children in the middle. If a harpoon should suddenly dart out on them, the males try to cover the retreat of the females, and if one of either sex be harpooned the rest will gather round the wounded animal and try to set it free.

But the greater part of the manatee-hunting is done higher up the rivers. Here the animals may be seen lying about on the weedy, muddy banks, feeding as peacefully as cows; yet the Indian fishermen know that this is no place to take them, for at the first unnatural sound or unusual sight they disappear. The harpooner must therefore decide upon one of three courses; either hiding in the weeds on the bank, at the risk of being eaten by alligators, and waiting for the chance of the manatee's coming up to breathe; or walking boldly along the bank and launching a spear at the "cow" when it is sleeping; or thirdly, setting off before daylight in a canoe and catching the animals off their guard when they come up unsuspectingly to feed at dawn. The second method is more satisfactory and less precarious than it sounds; for the manatee must sleep sometimes, and does not necessarily choose the night for the purpose. When sleeping he always floats along with the current, his muzzle above water, and so is an easy target for the skilled harpoon-thrower. But by such means these valuable creatures are only caught one at a time, and the aim of the hunters is to make a "bag"; therefore they prefer to surprise a whole herd.

Manatee-hunting is just the reverse of inia-harpooning; the latter, we have seen, must be done suddenly and swiftly, before the capture of one of the animals has frightened the rest away; whereas if one manatee of a herd be struck, the rest appear in a moment. As soon as the blood of one of them begins to flow, the others take it as a signal that one of their kinsfolk is in trouble, and flock round him, affording one of the most pathetic sights in nature; all the herd moaning and crying, some trying to drag out the harpoon, others seizing the line in their teeth and endeavouring to bite it through. On such an occasion the whole herd is entirely at the mercy of the hunters, for the unwounded animals may be relied upon not to leave their brothers to their fate.

The flesh is rich and tasty; some people say it resembles beef, others that they would not know it from pork. An important characteristic is that it will keep firm and sweet for a long while; no small advantage when we bear in mind that the manatee's favourite home is round about the equator. The leather of the tanned hide is exceedingly durable, and is now becoming costly in Europe.

The Indian harpooners still believe many of the quaint

stories about this creature, which their fathers told to the early sixteenth-century European explorers; especially the superstition that if it finds a corpse it piously watches over it till someone comes to bury it, or till it sinks in the water.

CHAPTER XXII

TURTLES AND TURTLE-CATCHING

Turtles and tortoises—The terrapin or snapper—Catching turtles with fish—The *remora*—Shooting with tethered arrows—Turtle-diving—Tortoise-shell—A horrible method of obtaining it—The hawk's-bill—Its shell—Seining for turtles in South America—The Galapagos tortoise—The green turtle—Methods of taking him.

ALTHOUGH turtles and tortoises cannot be called fish, some account of the catching of them must find a place in a book on fisheries, unless the word is taken in its narrowest sense.

We have seen that when men go fishing it is either to provide food for themselves and others, or else to procure some substance which, though not eatable, is valuable as an article of commerce. Sometimes the prey they seek fulfils both purposes, as in the case of the sturgeon; and just as from that fish the fisherman gets food plus isinglass, so from the turtle he gets food plus tortoise-shell. Of the tortoise proper we shall not have much to say, except in the case of a larger variety; for, in addition to its generally being a land animal, its shell is seldom of great value, and only the flesh of special kinds is eaten. It was one of the "unclean" animals which Moses forbade the Israelites to eat, and judging by the smaller species, one can conceive that they were seldom tempted to break the levitical law in this respect; for where the meat of these creatures is concerned, there is no medium between excellent and disgusting.

It is not easy to draw a sharp dividing line between turtles and tortoises, for their charactertistics frequently overlap; one cannot say that the tortoise belongs to the land, and the turtle to the water, for there are land turtles and water tortoises, just as there are inedible turtles and edible tortoises. A generally accepted method of classification is to divide the genus *testudinata*, to which both belong, into four species: marine, land, river, and marsh; but for the present purpose it will be sufficient to say that turtles have their limbs lengthened and curved backwards so as to serve as fins or flippers which they can use when swimming, whereas tortoises have not this feature, and though some can live in the water they are generally stationary while there, making little pretence at doing anything but drinking.

The characteristics which are common to both are the short, puffy body encased in a shell which is made up of two shields, an upper and a lower, cemented together at their margins. The shell is really an orderly arrangement of hard plates covering everything but the head, tail, and legs which usually are encased in a tough, scaly skin. Both animals breathe by means of lungs. Those that pass their lives on land live entirely on vegetable diet, while the others frequently make the smaller molluscs an article of their food. It is said that both can go for months without nourishment of any sort.

The marine turtles are to be found anywhere in the

tropical and sub-tropical regions, and sometimes even in colder latitudes. Their weight and size are very variable; some of them turn the scale at seven hundredweight. The age which they reach is still a much-disputed point; but satisfactory proof has been given that some have lived for eighty years.

Generally speaking the turtle is quiet and inoffensive; too well protected by Nature for it to have many enemies, and too stupid and sluggish to offer violence. There is an exception where the alligator-terrapin is concerned; this, known also as the snapper, is a fresh-water turtle found in the pools east of the Rocky Mountains and in certain parts of South America. It has a tail like that of the crocodile, and is an implacable opponent of all other reptiles, spending half its time in slaughtering young alligators. More power to that turtle! Unluckily it is not only one of the eatable sort, but its flesh is more highly prized for the table than that of any other of its kind; and therefore it is hunted down without mercy, thus benefiting the few, when, if left alone, it would be an advantage to the many.

The smaller terrapins, too, the red-bellied and the yellow-bellied, caught respectively in Virginia and Florida, are also much valued as delicacies, as is also the salt-water terrapin of Florida and the Gulf of Mexico. Large fresh-water turtles, three feet long, are taken from the Ganges, Yang-tse-Kiang, Nile, and other great rivers, and are largely eaten by the natives.

How to catch and kill animals so well shielded naturally, is a problem which both savage and civilised hunters have tried every means of solving. A bullet is effective, if of the right sort and fired at the right spot; and many Englishmen who have tried turtle-shooting in the Indian Ocean or the Gulf of Mexico speak highly of the sport. But men killed turtles long before guns were heard of. How?

In his progress towards civilisation man adapts quite as often as he invents; and just as the fisherman made use of the wind as a means of propulsion for his boat, centuries before engine-building was ever thought of, so he pressed the cormorant or the gull or other animals into his service, often before more artificial means had occurred to him. Some of these "adaptations," as we know, survive to this day, and among them the using of a fish as a turtle-catcher. There is a curious little creature called the *remora* or sucking-fish, found in the Mediterranean, the tropics, and sometimes as far north as our own coast. Its special characteristic is an elongated disc which covers its head and extends over part of its body, and by means of this it can fix itself firmly to any object by suction. From the remora's habit of clinging to other fish or to the bottoms of boats, it soon suggested itself as an excellent turtle-catcher, for only very great force or careful leverage can dislodge it when it has once fastened itself on to anything; and to this use it is still put in certain parts of the Mediterranean.

When such fish happen to be netted they are at once placed in pots of water and carefully fed and looked after by the fishermen; a tight-fitting ring is fixed round the slender part of the body just above the tail, to which a cord can be tied at need, and then the turtle-catcher is ready for action.

When a hunt is about to take place the men carry a few of the fish on board the boat in their pots, and row off in pursuit of the first turtle they see. If the turtle should happen to be asleep, as often happens in deep water, a noose is slipped over his neck and he is killed by a few blows on the head. If he be awake and swimming with his back to the boat he will still be easy game, for if he be not actually deaf as most fishermen assert, he is at best very dull and slow-witted, and will often allow the men to come within hitting distance before he attempts to escape.

He may happen, however, to turn suddenly, catch sight of the boat and swim calmly off in another direction. Now is the remora's chance, and everything depends on how it will behave itself. As soon as the boat is within a few fathoms one of the men throws a tethered fish; all things being favourable it lights on some part of the turtle's anatomy, clings with forty-leech power, and is only to be removed with a slip of wood or metal when the turtle has been comfortably hauled in and made fast alongside.

But often things do not go so well; the man misses his aim, perhaps, or the turtle happens to dive just as the fish is thrown. Then the remora is not so teachable as the cormorant, and it may absolutely refuse to stick at all; and the exasperated fishermen may see the turtle swim blissfully off while the fish goes the opposite way. Perhaps it will be drawn up clinging tightly to a bit of sodden drift-wood; or it may choose to dive under the boat and take up a position on the keel whence nothing can dislodge it, and where it will probably be crushed when the boat is beached.

The South American Indians, in hunting the fresh-water turtle, still use sometimes the tethered arrow, which is supplied with a movable point; some account of a similar weapon has been given in Chapter XVII, and a brief description of it will suffice. The harpoon or arrow, which is shot from a short but powerful bow, has an iron head, the base of which fits into a wooden peg, the other end of which is inserted in a hollow at the tip of the shaft. A long coil of stout twine is wound round the arrow, one of its ends fastened to the shaft, the other to the point. The immense strength of the bow causes the arrow-head to pierce the tough shell, and the shock of the concussion liberates the shaft; the string—forty yards of it—rapidly uncoils itself and, whether the turtle dives, sinks, or swims away, the shaft is left floating. Men are waiting in their canoes and, the moment a turtle is hit, one of them seizes the stick and proceeds to tow the animal ashore, where, if it is not already killed, a blow with a cudgel soon puts an end to it.

But since tortoise-shell has so greatly increased in value, methods injurious to the shell are seldom used except by sportsmen, and wherever we look nowadays we shall generally see the fishermen trying to take the creature alive, and this may be done in various ways. In the Indian Ocean and the Dutch East Indies, whence some of the finest tortoise-shell is exported, the islanders still follow a plan that is at least a couple of hundred years old. Putting out to sea in stout-built sailing canoes, the crews seek a favourable spot for their work (and such a spot is not easily decided upon, for some of the best turtles go sometimes hundreds of miles out to sea), and when this is found, slow down and watch for the first prize that appears.

On board each boat, in addition to the crew, are several expert swimmers or divers. One at a time these stand up in the bow, and at sight of a turtle one of them springs overboard after it, and then the sport begins. Sometimes a dozen men from the same boat will be occupied with a dozen turtles. On reaching one of the reptiles the diver swings himself on to its back and sits with his legs tucked under him, thus throwing out as little shark-bait as possible, and gripping with both hands the edge of the shell above the neck. The frightened turtle plunges forward or dives, the fisherman still acting the part of Old Man of the Sea, and, whenever it is possible, trying to guide the clumsy movements towards the boat. Everybody, unless prevented by total immersion, is shouting at the top of his voice in the hope that the noise may drive off any sharks that may be in the vicinity, and some of the crew stand by with guns to put an end to any such interloper.

At last the turtle is exhausted, the boat steers towards the diver, who, as soon as a rope is thrown to him, loops it round the neck of his capture, and when he has seen it towed safely alongside, dashes off towards the next turtle that shows itself.

Sometimes one of these fellows, in spite of all precau-

TURTLE-FISHING

On reaching the turtles the divers swing themselves on to their backs, and sit with legs tucked under them, throwing out as little shark-bait as possible.

tions, does get snapped up by a shark. In the case of the divers in some localities one does not hesitate to say, "Serve him right," for their abominable method of obtaining tortoise-shell from the hawk's-bill turtle is a disgrace to mankind. Some inhuman wretch once discovered that shell taken from the living animal is more easily treated, and may be a little more valuable than that from a dead one, and so devised a means of effecting this atrocious purpose, which is still in use in certain islands of the Indian Ocean.

The turtle is suspended over a slow fire, or, in some cases, is tied down and covered with smouldering charcoal, till the upper shell begins to curl outwards; then this is torn off the body with knives, so that while still hot it can be pressed flat between two boards. The wretched creature thus not only tortured needlessly but left for a time with no protection against possible enemies, is turned loose into the sea again. This is simply piling brutality on brutality, for though the shell gradually forms again, it is thin and of poor quality and practically valueless. The infliction of some pain is almost unavoidable in any form of fishing; but that there should be civilised buyers who are willing to profit by such loathsome acts towards a defenceless creature is a disgraceful fact. The turning loose of the turtle after this brutal operation is a comparatively modern practice. At one time it used to be killed when the shell had been removed, and eaten; but the march of civilisation has taught the islanders that the flesh of the hawk's-bill is flavourless and unpalatable.

The Javanese and the islanders of Keeling and the Celebes still eat this turtle, and are content to kill it before removing the shell. They most often hunt it in shallow water, either from canoes or by wading; the turtles are brought ashore, killed by blows, and then immersed in boiling water till the plates are loosened.

The hawk's-bill is scarcely one of the giants, for it rarely weighs more than about two hundred pounds. Although, as we have said, its flesh is hardly eatable, it produces the best tortoise-shell in the world; it may be found throughout the Indian Ocean and in the tropical parts of the Atlantic and Pacific, some of the finest coming from New Guinea. The head is of a curious bird-like shape, whence its name.

The carapace, or upper shell, of this turtle is made up of thirteen plates arranged in three longitudinal rows, five in the middle and four on either side, the largest of which would weigh about half a pound and measure thirteen inches by eight. These are the valuable portions of the shell. In addition the animal has twenty-four "hoofs" or small plates, which form the serrated margin round the carapace; but these, like the under shell, are of comparatively little value.

Another way of catching the turtle alive is by means of a kind of seine-net; this is the method that, among the Gauchos and South American Indians, has almost entirely superseded the old one of shooting or harpooning. Generally it is only employed for the capture of the fresh-water species, but it may sometimes be seen in use among the negroes of the Bahamas, who work it from the seashore.

TURTLES AND TURTLE-CATCHING

The South Americans employ a seine long enough to reach almost from one side of a narrow pool to the other. The bunt is unusually deep and often has a tow-rope to it, so that it may be used exactly like the tuck-seine of the pilchard-fishers; i.e. both perpendicularly and horizontally. It is corked above, and lightly weighted below.

With the exception of two, all the hunters stretch themselves round the pool as far as possible, getting as close to the water's edge as the marshy banks will allow; and with sticks or poles beat the tufts of grass and rushes in order to frighten any of the turtles that may be lurking there into open water. Meanwhile the two other men have each got into a canoe, carrying the seine between them to one end of the pool and there shooting it, the canoes gradually separating till the net is fully extended, the bunt-line — if used — being joined to a longer one which is thrown ashore. As soon as the net is in readiness the knocking and howling on the banks is increased, and goes on for perhaps two or three hours, the canoemen meanwhile paddling as gently as possible, a stroke now and a stroke then, towards the far end of the pool. As the net becomes nearly full they pull more sharply, and when at last they can no longer stir it they throw the tow-rope to their mates on the banks, leap to land, and all pull together, drawing the net into bag-form and pulling it high and dry. I have heard that oxen are sometimes used for the towing, but cannot say how far this is true.

Now everybody gathers round the opening of the net, which is disposed in such a manner that only one or two turtles at a time can escape, and these, as they come out, are clubbed on the head. Though the mesh is a very large one, valuable fish are not infrequently caught with the turtles; sometimes a good-sized alligator is also swept in, and extinguished with a bullet or cudgel before it can make itself in any ways objectionable.

The land tortoises of the Galapagos Archipelago, although they are not fished for, should have a passing mention. These spend the greater part of their time away from the water, but visit the streams and pools periodically, staying there about three days at a time. They are so large that it would take six or eight men to lift one of them, and anyone who likes can sit on the back of one and ride at a speed averaging six yards per minute, or a mile in five hours. On being approached they draw in head and limbs and drop with a loud clatter and a good deal of hissing; but all that the rider has to do is to take his seat and give a few light blows on the hinder end of the shell; then the legs come out again and the vehicle moves on.

These reptiles are of great value in more ways than one. The eggs, which are spherical, white, and rather larger than those of a hen, are laid in the sand and carefully covered, and the natives take them for food whenever they can. Some of the animals yield as much as two hundred pounds of solid meat, which is either eaten fresh or is salted and dried for export. The fat is rendered down into a thin oil which now commands a high price. Unless the tortoise is really fat the natives do not kill it. Its condition is ascertained by a small slit being made in the skin near the tail, and if the fat is not then found to be thick enough, the tortoise is set free again.

Strangers in the parts frequented by the Galapagos tortoise have, in days gone by, been very much surprised to find well-beaten, path-like tracks leading to and from the springs and streams; these have been made by the tortoises in their periodical pilgrimages in search of water. On reaching a pool or river they take in a "sea-stock" or camel's supply of water, which will last them till the next visit; and thirsty travellers on meeting the animal have often saved their lives by killing it, just as desert wanderers are sometimes reduced to slaughtering a camel.

The most popularly known of all the turtles is that from which the soup is made, the green turtle, whose home is all over the warm quarters of the world, though it is supposed to have been found originally off Ascension Island; it abounds in the West Indies and is often taken on the high seas, hundreds of miles away from anywhere. Its flesh is a very profitable article of commerce and its eggs are highly prized for their richness. It is the largest of its kind, often weighing six hundred pounds and reaching a length of six feet or more.

While it remains in the water the West Indian negroes dive after it in the manner already described; but it is often found on the beach strolling about in great numbers, and it then forms an easy if ponderous capture. The hunters surround a small group of them, cutting off all retreat to the water's edge, and then, with a batch of men to each turtle, turn them over on their backs. This is not as easy as it sounds; figures are deceptive, but if we bear in mind that a green turtle is somewhere about the size and weight of a grand piano, we shall not only appreciate the difficulty of the men's task, but shall hear without wonder that when it is once on its back the huge mass can never right itself again and is easily killed. This, however, is not an invariable rule among the *testudinata*, for the Galapagos tortoise, which sometimes weighs more than the green turtle, is more agile, and makes no trouble of getting back on its legs when it has been turned over.

CHAPTER XXIII

AFTER THE SEAL AND THE WALRUS

The pinnipeds—The seals and their young—Seal-hunting among the Eskimos—The seal as a fighter—The Eskimos' summer season—Varieties of seals—Sealing among civilised fleets—Methods—Dangers of the work—A seal-massacre—How the seal-colonies are founded—Sea-elephants, sea-lions, and sea-bears—The walrus—His enemies—A big catch—Modern methods of walrus-hunting.

THE pinnipeds or fin-footed animals, under which head are included seals, sea-lions and walruses, are even less like fish than are the cetacea, for they possess four legs—or members which serve as such; they are generally regarded as the link between the land and the water mammals; but as they spend a good part of their lives in the water, and are shot or clubbed or harpooned for the sake of their skin, fat, etc., we shall devote a chapter to these remarkable animals.

A whole book might easily be written about the characteristics and uses of the seal, for its many peculiarities seem to render it a thing apart from the rest of the animal kingdom. It is born on land, and is even obliged to learn to swim before it can trust itself in deep water. Its land movements are certainly neither swift nor graceful, for its funny little feet are hampered by their webs, and so its motions are carried on mainly by the muscles of the body, with the result that its "walking" is merely a series of awkward, shuffling hops; and practically the only use its limbs are to it when not in the water, is as a means of climbing rocks, ice, or a sloping beach. Once in the water, however, few fish could be more swift and untiring than they.

Over their little ones learning to swim, many curious stories—some of doubtful truth—have been told. Close observers say that the young are never driven into the water by their parents; they maintain that these have little or nothing to do with the swimming lessons, for the little ones teach themselves. Those that lie nearest the water's edge set the example to the rest by wriggling into the sea and splashing about in an astonished, half-frightened manner; when their heads go under they struggle upwards again, crawl on to the beach, and go to sleep. On waking, they return to their task; the same thing happens over and over again; dip, ducking, nap—always the nap—until the neophyte has become a proficient swimmer.

Among the seals we shall not see that touching affection of the mothers for the young that we witnessed with the cetaceans. The fathers, or bull-seals, do indeed protect the babies as long as they remain under their eye, but if a little one choose to wander away from its home, no effort will be made on the part of either parent to protect it or bring it back.

Seals are by no means confined to the northern regions, though they are perhaps more at home there than elsewhere. Both the seal and the whale are often erroneously supposed to cling entirely to the Arctic regions; but there are few non-tropical quarters where some pinniped or other may not be found. On the northern coasts of the British Isles they are plentiful enough; they have often been seen in numbers off the Norfolk coast even; and in inland seas like the Caspian or Lake Baikal, thousands of them are to be found. River estuaries and narrow channels are their favourite resorts, because here the fish on which they feed are less scattered about and more easily obtained. For their land residence, some choose sandy beaches, well sheltered from high winds; some go to the other extreme and prefer a rocky, unprotected shore. In fine weather they are content to lie about on the beach or rocks and doze; but when the weather is rough they will scamper about and play like children.

Among the Eskimos, sealing is almost as old as the people themselves; one can no more dissociate the Eskimo and the seal than one can think of the Irish peasant without his pig; there is scarcely an inch of the animal that these clever Arctic folk do not utilise. The flesh is tough and not sweet-smelling, yet they eat and enjoy it; they make soup of the blood, and drink such of the oil as they do not use for heating and lighting. The skin is, of course, made into clothes or used to cover their kayaks and tents; the tendons become bow-strings, sewing cotton and cord, and the tissues, dried and stretched, admit a certain amount of light when fastened over the opening of the hut.

The Eskimo has various methods of obtaining the

animal that, when dead, serves him in so many capacities. Often he harpoons it as he does the narwhal, in ice-holes; with this difference, that he, and not the hunted animal, makes the hole. In winter time many thousands of seals get "iced up," just as the dolphins do; but they must come up to breathe from time to time, although they close their nostrils when they plunge, and though there is a very long interval between any two respirations. Therefore the holes which the fishermen make in the ice are just so many seal-traps, and all that the men have to do is to stand round the hole and spear each luckless creature as it comes to the surface of the water, drag out the carcass, and take it home.

When the frost begins to break up, the seals struggle out of the water and begin to jump about on the ice or the rocks. Then the Eskimos vary their methods of hunting. A band of them, armed with clubs, spears, or axes, watch the movements of a flock of seals and gradually manage to cut it off from all return to the sea; then spread themselves round it and gradually close in. A seal looks such an innocent, gentle beast when you see it amusing itself at the Zoological Gardens or Brighton Aquarium; its merry, yet pathetic, eyes look as though they belonged to an animal that could offer no resistance to any persecutor, human or other; but sealers tell a different tale. True, it will not actually pursue a man beyond the limits of what it regards as its own ground; but in order to escape to the water when death is otherwise imminent, it will make as good a fight of it as any other animal. A bulldog is a small thing, but we do not care to be

AN ESKIMO METHOD OF SEAL-FISHING

The Eskimo has various methods of obtaining the seal; often he harpoons it through ice-holes.

bitten by one, and a seal's bite is rather worse than that of a bulldog, and a seal has the same affectionate way of clinging to anything that happens to come between its teeth. Its nails, too, are not to be lightly considered, seeing that with them it can tear a large cod piecemeal.

When the prisoners see that there is no escape, their first instinct is to huddle together as closely as possible; this is the hunter's safeguard, for if that instinct bade the animals open out and make a concerted attack, they could soon tear a small body of their would-be slayers to pieces.

Gradually the circle closes in, and the outer rank of seals, howling with rage and fear, spring up on their hind-quarters and prepare to do battle. The springing up is rather like the bending of the salmon or the dolphin, for it is done by means of the backbone, which is so flexible that the animals can bend themselves almost at a right-angle, the upper part of the body being kept perpendicular while the lower remains horizontal.

If you want to kill a seal quickly, hit him on the nose with a stout stick—if he will let you get near enough to him. One would naturally suppose that a long spear would be most effective; but the seal is far from being a fool; in nine cases out of ten he will be sharp enough to seize the shaft between his teeth, and even if he do not snap it, there is no getting it away from him; moreover, a spear-point would have to be driven very deeply to do him much harm. Often the Eskimos find that the best plan is to let the animal occupy himself with a pole or harpoon while they club him across the nose or head.

AFTER THE SEAL

In summer the hunters have a wider field, and pursue their game in a manner that more nearly approaches genuine fishing. In the deep bays and gulfs of the Greenland coast, hundreds and thousands of seals may then be seen disporting themselves. These are principally the kind known as the Atak, or Greenland seal, distinguishable by their short, wiry hair that has nothing of the semi-woolliness of the common seal about it; it is a great deal larger than most of its brethren, often measuring from six to eight feet in length.

The natives, seated in their kayaks, take up a position among the floating ice-blocks, to which the animals will sometimes flee on seeing the boats. If possible they will try to take the seals by surprise, drifting silently in pursuit of single individuals. Arrived within about twenty feet of one of them, the hunter sits holding an oar in his left hand and a harpoon in his right; to this harpoon is attached a bladdered line, the same thing on a smaller scale as that used by the Eskimos in whaling. Keeping the buoyed end of the line between his knees or feet, he throws the harpoon; and, if it finds a good mark, he tosses the bladder into the water. Generally the seal dives, taking the bladder with it, but only for a moment; weakened by pain and loss of blood, it is less able than usual to hold its breath, and soon comes to the surface again, when the nearest Eskimo gives it the *coup de grâce* with a stick or lance. After a while the sea becomes dotted all over with bladders, and fishing ceases for the day; the lines are collected and joined up in lots which are equally divided among the kayaks, and towed ashore.

Another large animal of this neighbourhood is the Capuchin or hooded seal, eight feet long, and possessed of a peculiar hood-like organ above its head which it can bring down at will over its nose. Its bite is as undesirable as that of a mastiff, and it barks remarkably like one; varying the bark by a long, wailing whine when attacked. It will come further south than the Greenland seal, and is pursued by the North American sealers as well as by the Eskimos. Most of the skins sold in England come from this animal. Another peculiarity that it has is the power of distending its nostrils when diving, till they look like two great bladders or pouches; and it can remain under water longer than the other varieties. The Capuchin must not be confused with the Monk-seal, or *pelagius;* this inhabits the coasts of Sardinia and the Adriatic, and is said to be the special *phocaena* whose skin the Romans regarded as a protection against a lightning-stroke; Augustus Cæsar is supposed to have carried such a skin with him wherever he went.

The Russians, though insignificant in a general way as fishermen, are clever and energetic sealers, but they cling for the most part to old-fashioned methods. In pursuing the Greenland seal they build high wooden towers, from which watchmen posted there can tell the numbers and movements of a body of seals; and the fishermen act "upon information received." Dragging small boats over the ice, they pursue the seals to the water; though many hunters prefer to dress themselves in long white smock-frocks which will prevent their being distinguished from the background of snow, and enable them to shoot or spear the animals almost at leisure. This practice is probably copied from the Eskimos, who even used to go the length of sewing themselves in sealskins and, at the risk of being torn to pieces, crawl among a herd and kill as many as possible with their bow and arrows.

Sealing among the British, American, Dutch, Scandinavian, and Japanese fleets is a most important industry, and is carried on as systematically—if not as profitably and with as much risk—as whaling. Good-sized ships of 300 tons and over are fitted out for the work, each carrying oil-tanks, boilers, etc. British Columbia alone owns several fleets of such ships. The means of catching depends on the neighbourhood, time of year, etc. For open-sea work, harpooning or shooting from small boats is the surest; and, where the fishermen are active and industrious, two men can often garner a boat-load in a few hours. In spring, this method is terribly dangerous in the northern regions, for the ice is breaking up, and huge hummocks of it are floating about; the sea is rough or choppy by reason of the melted snow torrents that are everywhere emptying themselves into it, and the weather is still bitterly cold.

The greatest peril is from the floating ice; an oarsman who knows his way about, can easily dodge a single block that is making for him; but let him get into a current among a couple of dozen—perhaps a couple of hundred—of such blocks, which are cheerfully jostling and clashing together! I am not quoting an isolated or out-of-the-way case; such a position exists only too frequently, and the annual list of casualties that arise in this manner is an alarming one. In avoiding one ice-lump the boat perhaps pulls between two others; if she is going with the current, well and good; she is through before the blocks can possibly meet; but often the current is awry and broken, and as she passes between the hummocks she finds herself penned right and left by ice, and in front by a force of water that she can ill battle against; the hummocks bear down upon her and she is cracked like a nut. If possible the crew will scramble on to one or other of the blocks and it may be well with them; but the hummock may float away, carrying them out of reach of their companions, to be eventually drowned or starved.

Round about the Baltic, and in parts of North America, and sometimes in Scotland, the breeding season among the animals is taken advantage of by the fishermen, for then the seals are on land and can, with care, be taken a whole colony at a time, and shot or clubbed. The seal, be it remembered, is one of the most intelligent beings in existence, and all its acts and movements are undertaken with method and system. In summer the males, or bulls, come ashore and seek out convenient homes for the females; these will not arrive till nearly a month later. The bulls which come first naturally are able to choose the best positions—in caves, if possible; if not, in well-sheltered spots among the rocks. Late comers must take their chance; they will *try* to take someone else's pitch, and a fight, sometimes to the death, will be the result. Even the fighting is done on systematic lines. Two bulls approach each other, each one pretending to be interested in something that is going on elsewhere; as they come together, one will make a feint with teeth or nails, dodge, and roll behind the enemy, hoping to take him from the rear. After a good deal of such fencing, one will fix the other by the "scruff" of the neck, driving his teeth through skin and blubber, and gripping so that only immense force can dislodge him; and when the teeth are wrenched away, they carry off a good deal of skin and fat with them.

When the females come ashore the fighting will have to begin all over again, for each bull means to possess as large a harem as possible. He goes down to the water-edge, courteously conducts the lady of his choice up the beach to his home, and leaves her there while he goes in search of more wives. While he is gone another bull will come, take the bewildered cow by the neck, and drag her gently to his own home; this, of course, means a subsequent fight. Meanwhile, the females at the water-line have become bones of contention, and each bull's strength and ingenuity must be exerted to the full before he can carry off and keep his various wives. The size of the harems depends on the fighting powers of the husbands; one will have five females, another thirty-five. Sometimes one cave will contain nearly a hundred families of ten, and in such caves the young are brought forth and suckled.

The sealers choose night time for a descent on one of these colonies, for by day the bulls are too wary; even at night they make some attempt at posting sentries, in imitation of the walruses. Putting off from their ship in small boats, the fishermen, each carrying a stout pole shod with iron, and an unlighted torch, creep silently to the nearest cave, and on entering, every man seeks out a place where he can press himself as close to the rock wall as possible. Suddenly someone strikes a match; this is a signal, and everyone lights his torch and starts shouting. The wretched animals, thus taken by surprise, huddle together or rush for the entrance; and now is seen the wisdom of each man having packed himself in as small a compass as possible, for the stampede is sometimes terrific, and anyone who attempted to stem it would be trodden down and crushed to death, if not torn in pieces by the infuriated bulls.

The first rush is allowed to pass unchecked, but when it is over, the massacre of those that have stayed behind commences; and in this way an enormous pile of carcasses is soon stacked up on the shore, ready to be taken aboard or to be cut up on the beach.

As a rule the skins are removed there and then, and with them the thick blubber-coat which adheres. The depth of this coat may be anything up to four inches; that taken from the young seal is the best and most plentiful, for a very interesting reason.

While the bulls have been settling about their future homes, watching them and their families night and day, what time have they had for obtaining food? Seals live on fish, and cannot, or will not, eat anything else; and for two or three months the whole colony, or "rookery," has been away from the chance of fishing. During all that time the adults have sustained life by absorbing the fat with which their bodies are so liberally supplied.

The skin and blubber thus obtained is made into

bundles and taken aboard, though many fleets set up their furnaces on the beach and boil the carcasses as well, for these yield a surprising quantity of oil.

When the ships reach their own ports the blubber is separated from the hides; the latter are dried and salted for export to England and the States, where they will be converted into leather, while the blubber is crushed by machinery, steamed, exposed in open tanks to the air and sun, and finally put into barrels.

Between Cape Horn and the Tropic of Capricorn are various other kinds of seals. One of them, the narrow-snout, more nearly approaches a fish form than any other, for its claws are small and drawn together, so that they look like the serrated edge of a fin. The roaring noise made by this variety during the night has often deluded sailors into the belief that it proceeded from the bellowing of cattle on shore.

To the fishermen there are but two classes of seals, haired and furred. Under the first head come all those that are pursued for the sake of their fat and their hide; under the second, those whose thick growth of velvety under-hair makes the animals one of the most valuable captures that the sea has to offer. True, the fur seal has plenty of oil of its own, but it is of so rank a nature that it is seldom thought worth while to go to the expense of clarifying and cleansing it.

The best fur-yielders are the seals from round Cape Horn and those found in the Behring Sea; several millions of the latter haunt the Alaska coast during the season. Yet, in spite of such apparent abundance, the fishermen observe the greatest care as to what animals they destroy. The invariable rule nowadays is, kill no females. There need be no difficulty in keeping to this regulation, for size is the predominant distinguishing feature between the sexes; whereas a well-grown bull-seal will be seven or eight feet long, the cows rarely reach more than four feet.

The skin is at its best when the young male has reached nearly the age of three years. As soon as the animals are killed the skin is removed, separated from the fat and well coated with salt. A sealskin that has been newly removed would be almost unrecognisable to those who have only seen the article when worked up into a lady's jacket. Apparently it is a mere rough mat of coarse, long hair. If, however, the coat be closely examined it will be seen that the hair is simply an outer covering to a thick mat of soft fur.

To get rid of the long hairs is easier than would appear, for the roots penetrate far more deeply than those of the under hair. Therefore it suffices to peel or scrape the inside of the skin with sharp knives till the roots are cut free and the long hairs come away like separate threads.

The skins thus prepared are shipped to London or New York for final treatment. Their value varies according to size and fineness; some are worth a sovereign, others as much as five pounds. Recently South Africa has gone in largely for sealing, and several thousands of skins taken in the Indian Ocean are sent from Cape Town to London every year.

Three other important members of the family are the

sea-elephant, the sea-lion, and the sea-bear, all pursued whenever it is possible, for the sake of their skin and fat. These have an external ear and are otherwise distinguished from the true seals by the formation of their limbs and teeth. The sea-elephant—or elephant-seal, as the fishermen call it—reaches a length of twenty-five feet and more, and the males have a prolongation of the muzzle which has some resemblance to a trunk. It is to be found principally off the southern shores of South America, but it has no objection to fresh water, and large specimens have been shot in the rivers or on the marshy banks or pools some distance inland. The people of the Argentine regard the tongue of the animal, dried and salted, as a very great delicacy, though the rest of the flesh is uneatable. A great many elephant-seals are harpooned by the Antarctic whalers in the outward or homeward course of the ship; the oil is more valuable than that from the whale, and the skin, though useless as "sealskin," is tanned for carriage-covers, etc.

The sea-lion is less terrible than its name suggests, and like other seals, will only bite in self-defence. It gets its name on account of the thick mane which covers its head and shoulders, and perhaps by reason of its generally savage appearance and loud, lion-like bellow. Those of the south—Chili and Patagonia—are generally snapped up by the whalers for the sake of their oil; but the northern lions—those from Kamchatka, the Aleutian, and the Kurile Islands generally—become, with the seals of that neighbourhood, the property of the Japanese sealing-boats, large steam-craft built on European lines.

The sea-bear, a kind of fur-seal, is very valuable, and is rapidly becoming extinct; its fur is of a pale brown, almost yellowish tint, and this used to be exported from North China in great quantities. Some years ago, however, the Russians contrived to get the greater part of the trade away from the Chinese, and they have pursued the animals so ruthlessly that they have left none for anyone else.

The establishment of a close season for sealing has happily now put a stop to the wholesale destruction of such valuable animals. By agreement among the ship-owners, almost the whole of the seal-fishery is at present confined to the early spring.

The walrus, morse, sea-horse, or whale-horse, is easily distinguished from the other pinnipeds by its two upper canine teeth which, projecting downwards, form two powerful tusks; in length it is about thirteen feet; in shape very much like a seal; in colour from tawny to dark red. It is only found in the northern seas—round Kamchatka is a favourite locality—and it is hunted by the natives or by the big sealing-fleets for the sake of its somewhat scanty though exceedingly pure oil, and of its tusks, which are from fifteen to thirty inches long, and are of the finest and hardest ivory.

The use of the tusks is not primarily as a weapon, but as a means of progress. In climbing an ice-floe the walrus digs the points in the surface of the ice and easily drags himself from spot to spot.

The skin is tanned and used in various manufactures, or is cut up into thongs which are absolutely unbreakable;

the flesh is boiled down for oil, and the tusks come away uninjured when the head is immersed in boiling water.

On land the animal is far more awkward in its movements than the seal, though just as active in the water. It can remain a long while below the surface, having, like all the other pinnipeds, special reservoirs into which the overstrained veins can discharge the blood which would otherwise suffocate them when breathing was suspended for any length of time. A fisherman can distinguish a walrus from a seal at a great distance by its manner of diving; whereas a seal sinks as naturally as a whale, a walrus heaves up its back, rolls forward, and then disappears.

The walrus is almost a vegetarian; its throat is so small that it could not even swallow a herring, and it lives on seaweed, which it ekes out with molluscs scraped from the rocks or burrowed out of the sand with its tusks. It is of milder disposition than the seal, though a terrible enough opponent when forced to fight for its life. Its great enemy is the Polar bear, and in the fights between the two animals the bear does not always win; more often than not a bear that has been indiscreet enough to pick a quarrel with a walrus is soon glad to retire, gored and torn and bleeding. To guard against a surprise visit from its foe, the intelligent sea-horse places sentinels which give the alarm by loud signal roars, at the first sound of which the walruses all scuttle off to the water. While on the land or on the ice they are generally careful never to rest far from the water-line.

As a profitable occupation, walrus-catching is not what it used to be; two hundred years ago a few English sealers slaughtered eight hundred of them in six hours. Such a thing could scarcely happen nowadays, for past experience has given the animals a horror of ships and men, except when feelings of revenge are aroused in them; and they seem to be steadily migrating further and further north. Moreover, on landing, their instinct inclines them to rocks and ice-floes which are inaccessible to men and often to bears.

Nevertheless, the Japanese, American, and English fleets score a pretty good total among them in the course of a year, both land and water hunting. The procedure is much the same as in sealing, except that the vigilance and unity of the bands make the task more difficult and uncertain. The only very successful way of killing walruses on shore is for the crews to sneak in as quietly as possible, and shoot the sentries before they can give the alarm; then to spring ashore and line up between the water and the herd. On shore the animals are unable to harm any persecutor who can keep them at arm's length, and the whole colony soon fall victims to the axes and pikes of the fishermen.

In the water the case is altered, and the risk is so great that many seasoned whalers and sealers will have nothing to do with such work. The instinct of the herds tells them when the odds are against or in favour of them; if they are strong in numbers, and there is but one boat, the men will do well to content themselves with what they can kill by firing at long range. Even then a herd will often follow a boat for miles.

When several boats are attacking, the walruses swim

away, but they can often be "cornered" on account of their refusal to land when pursued. Then when they find themselves hemmed between boats and shore they make a united dash for the nearest boat, and the fight is generally a lively one. Some of the heavy tusks hook themselves over the gunwale, and the boat is held prisoner, while others of the herd puncture the timbers and try to tear the vessel in pieces or drag it under; and it is not till rifle and axe have been plied unceasingly that the men can regard their lives as their own.

This is but another example of the dangers and hardships which are part of the fisherman's lot. Whether he is in pursuit of walrus or whale, codfish or herring, his calling is a perilous one; and what he adds by his industry to the wealth of his country is too often won at the risk of his own life.

INDEX

INDEX

INDEX

INDEX

INDEX

INDEX